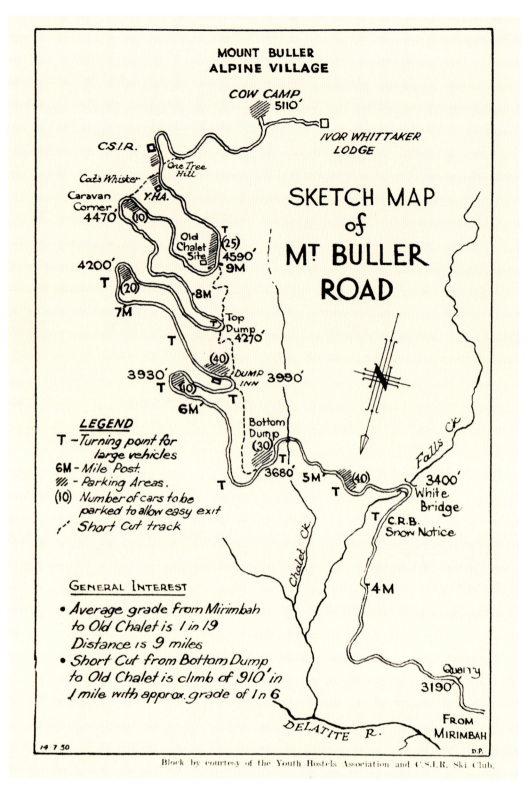

MOUNT BULLER
ALPINE VILLAGE

COW CAMP
5110'

IVOR WHITTAKER
LODGE

C.S.I.R.

One Tree
Hill

Cat's Whisker

Caravan
Corner
4470
(10)

Y.H.A.

SKETCH MAP
of
M⊤ BULLER
ROAD

Old
Chalet
Site
(25)
4590'
9M

4200'
T
(20)

8M

7M

T
Top
Dump
4270'

3930'
T
(10)

(40)

DUMP
INN
3990'

6M'
T

Bottom
Dump
(30)

Falls Ck

LEGEND

T – Turning point for
large vehicles
6M – Mile Post.
▨ – Parking Areas.
(10) Number of cars to be
parked to allow easy exit
⌐ Short Cut track

T
3680'
5M'
T
(40)
3400'
White
Bridge

T C.R.B.
Snow Notice

Chalet Ck

4M

GENERAL INTEREST

• Average grade from Mirimbah
to Old Chalet is 1 in 19
Distance is 9 miles
• Short Cut from Bottom Dump
to Old Chalet is climb of 910' in
1 mile with approx. grade of 1 in 6

Quarry
3190'

DELATITE R.
FROM
MIRIMBAH

14·7·50
D.P.

Block by courtesy of the Youth Hostels Association and C.S.I.R. Ski Club.

This map, prepared by two of the original ski clubs, CSIR and YHA, was published in
Schuss, the Ski Club of Victoria magazine in 1950. *SCHUSS*

The front cover shows the view along Mt Buller's West Ridge in winter 2003, with the village away to the right and Mt Stirling and the Victorian Alps in the background.
JEAN-MARC LAROQUE

The back cover is a view of the mountain from High Street in Mansfield. This photo, taken in 1924, was presented to the small band of skiers in Victoria at the time, as bait for them to make the trip to the mountain. They never looked back. NAMA

The aerial photograph over the Mt Buller village and resort area on the inside front cover was taken in February 2007, in the wake of the 2006-07 bushfires. The West Ridge photographed on the front cover in winter is to the top left of the summer photograph. THEODOR HESS/SKYFAST/BSL

The map spread across the inside back cover has a similar perspective to the inside front cover photograph.
BASE MAP © DEPARTMENT OF SUSTAINABILITY & ENVIRONMENT, 2008, REPRODUCED BY PERMISSION
MT BULLER DETAIL: BSL/ED MAHON/MARK ASHKANASY

At right is a view of the mountain across the Delatite River at Mirimbah, shot in 1950. ERIC BURT

Mt Buller

The story of a mountain

Indigenous Australians are respectfully advised that images of deceased people appear in this book.

Produced for the publisher, the National Alpine Museum of Australia, by tSm Publishing Pty Ltd, 2008

tSm Publishing
PO Box 631, Bright, Victoria, 3741, Australia
www.theskimag.com

Photo editing
Mark Ashkanasy, Alpine Images

Design and creative
Anthony Pearsall, Typographics

Text copyright © 2008, Jim Darby and the National Alpine Museum of Australia

Design and typography © 2008, the National Alpine Museum of Australia

National Alpine Museum of Australia
c/- Post Office
Mt Buller, Victoria, 3723, Australia
Tel: (03) 5777.7235
www.nama.org.au

National Library of Australia Cataloguing-in-Publication Data:
Darby, Jim, 1957-
Mt Buller: the story of a mountain.

Bibliography.
Includes index.
ISBN 9780646476605 (hbk.).

1. Mt Buller Alpine Resort (Vic.) - History. 2. Ski resorts - Victoria - Mount Buller - History. 3. Mountain resorts - Victoria - Mount Buller - History. 4. Mount Buller (Vic.) - History. I. Ashkanasy, Mark. II. Title.

919.455062

Designed, produced and printed in Australia.

Typeset in Garamond 10.5/13

Publisher's note: This is a historic work based on primary and secondary sources and, extensively, interviews or oral histories. Every effort has been made to ensure the accuracy of the information contained herein and acknowledge its source. Every effort has been made to trace copyright owners in pictorial and artistic works. The author and publisher would welcome any information to correct or expand the record; please contact NAMA at the address above.

Proceeds from the sale of this book go to the National Alpine Museum of Australia.

Sunrise over the village, 2007. MARK ASHKANASY

Mt Buller

The story of a mountain

Jim Darby

Photo editor: Mark Ashkanasy

Author's acknowledgement

IT IS A gift when a group of people trust you to tell their story and support you all the way through. That support and trust from the National Alpine Museum of Australia, in particular its chairman David Hume, the NAMA book committee and its chairman Michael Monester and NAMA's museum manager, Margaret Franke-Williams is greatly appreciated. The depth of their historic collection is unmatched, as is the quality in its organisation. That collection and the feedback and thoughts of the people involved with NAMA have enriched this content; they have watched it grow with care and interest. Any mistakes that may have, like a snowflake, drifted quietly past them, are mine, not theirs.

The Dyson Bequest and the Grollo Ruzzene Foundation and other supporters are acknowledged elsewhere, but it needs to be reinforced that a publication of this depth would be impossible without their contribution. I was also fortunate to be able to tap into some of the passion and enthusiasm Rino and Diana Grollo and Nick Whitby and Monica Grollo and other members of their family have for the mountain and the mountains. Their support, ideas and resources, and in the end patience, have meant everything. They had plenty to tell me, but they too gave me free rein to tell the tale as I saw it.

I also thank the book's production team – photo editor Mark Ashkanasy, copy editor Mary Kerley and creative director Anthony Pearsall for their exacting technical skills, their creativity and their endurance.

The skiers that went before us had some greetings that were salutations of camaraderie, not exclusivity. At Mt Buller, two stood out, two that said it all: some would say *ski heil!* and some would say *bon descente!* We all speak the same language.

I DEDICATE MY part in this book to my family, above all to Marnie Brennan for keeping the show on the road while I wandered off down this winding track of a book – for that alone, but more besides, anything I have done here is as much her work as it is mine – and to our inspiration, Olivia, Patrick, Cosmo and Joanna Darby, skiers all.

I also dedicate it to the memory of my parents, Geoff and Heather Darby, who gave life to every wonderful thing I've seen and experienced above the snow line.

Jim Darby, The Wordhouse, Mt Macedon, December 2007

Frozen Snow Gum, 2003 by Michelle Coppell, silver gelatin print,
100cm x 100cm. PRIVATE COLLECTION

Jane and Bruce Dyson. DYSON

The Dyson Bequest

BRUCE AND JANE DYSON shared a lifelong passion for alpine skiing, based on family traditions. Bruce, his brother Peter, members of their Sea Scout Group and friends established Yurredla Ski Club and constructed the ski club lodge at Mt Buller in the early 1950s.

Jane's mother Kit Tinsley (Moore) was a pioneering skier and ski racer during the 1920s and 1930s and Jane was a passionate member of the Australian Women's Ski Club at Mt Buller for many years.

Bruce and Jane enjoyed successful ski racing careers, both representing Australia. Bruce also held official positions with the Mt Buller Committee of Management, Victorian Ski Association and Australian Winter Olympic teams.

Their love of skiing and Mt Buller was a family affair; Bruce's father Jack Dyson was an outstanding bushman who spent many years hiking through the Victorian Alps and in 2006, Bruce's brother Peter enjoyed his sixtieth consecutive year of skiing at Mt Buller. Bruce's nieces (Anne, Sue and Kaye) and nephew (John) and their children are all active skiers and participants in Yurredla Ski Club. Jane's children, Kate (dec), Robert, Rose and Sarah all retained their interest in skiing.

The Dyson Bequest is pleased to be involved with the publication of this book. The bequest, a charitable foundation established by Bruce and Jane Dyson in 2000, was the main beneficiary of Bruce's estate in 2002 and Jane's estate in 2004.

The current trustees of the Dyson Bequest, John Dyson and Rose Gilder, believe Bruce and Jane would be delighted with *Mt Buller, The story of a mountain* as Mt Buller was such a special place to them and remains so to their families and their descendants.

The National Alpine Museum of Australia is grateful for the generous contribution of the Dyson family, through the Dyson Bequest, towards the publication of this book.

Sunset on the summit (above centre). JOHN NORRIS

Rino and Diana Grollo. CHARLIE BROWN

The Grollo Ruzzene Foundation

IN THE HISTORY and development of Mt Buller, Rino and Diana Grollo (Ruzzene) stand apart from other ski lift operators. Despite the commercial realities and risks of alpine investment, they sought to ensure that more people could share and enjoy the physical and visual magic of the Australian bush and its mountains.

The connection stretches back to Rino Grollo's teenage years, in the early 1960s, when he visited the mountain with his father Luigi and brother Bruno, who had the contract to build the dam that would become Mt Buller's water supply.

Rino and Diana continued those travels to Mt Buller and its surroundings, camping and on day trips, in summer and winter with friends and family.

This passion for the high country saw them buy a property at the base of the mountains near Merrijig. Later they bought a property on the mountain to facilitate easier winter sport participation with their own family.

Rino and Diana's involvement and investment in Mt Buller deepened. First they purchased the Abom, then the ski lift company and then built the Mt Buller Chalet Hotel and Apartment complex because they believed sustainable commercial accommodation was required. Rino and Diana have reshaped the mountain, the village and its community in many ways, supporting projects such as the university campus, the Olympic Winter Institute, the Mt Buller Chapel, the Clock Tower, the Village Square and the mountain's art and sculpture.

The couple were drawn to nurture and love Mt Buller with commitment and passion; this passion continues through their children and grandchildren.

Rino and Diana's desire to see Mt Buller's history recorded expresses their love for the mountain and their appreciation of the enriching memories and community spirit it has given them and so many others.

The National Alpine Museum of Australia is grateful for the generous contribution of the Grollo family, through the Grollo Ruzzene Foundation, towards the publication of this book.

But the man from Snowy River let the pony have his head,

And he swung the stockwhip round and gave a cheer,

And he raced him down the mountain like a torrent down its bed,

While the others stood and watched in very fear.

From *The Man From Snowy River* by AB 'Banjo' Paterson

CONTENTS

A 21st century take on a 19th century legend. Watkin McLennan riding Mt Buller's Summit Chutes, July 2007. KIT RUNDLE

FIRST TRACKS

Mt Buller's first skiing legend, the Austrian Helmut Kofler;
an artist on the snow, photographed in the late 1920s.
EDWIN ADAMSON

Edwin G Adamson
A.R.P.S.

1 Marnong

In the days before the years had numbers the view from the top was no less spectacular. There were no roads or cleared tracks to ascend the mountains, but there were no blackberries to bar the way either. The lyrebirds were in song, but they were stealing the calls of the forest, not the scream of the chainsaw they later came to imitate.

WHY GO TO the mountains? Why head for the hills? Food, of course, but there were other attractions that endure: exploration and social contact, and the sense of wonder that the mountains feed and inspire.

It was a spiritual replenishment and a spiritual homage, to sat-isfy a thirst for the adventure of life and to make contact with fellow adventurers.

Judy Monk is a respected elder of the Taungurung people. She said her ancestors used the 'low ground for food and the higher ground was also a food source, for the bogong moths, but they

also used the higher ground for traditional ceremony purposes.

'What we've found in the surveys that Taungurung have been doing after the 2006-07 fires is, up in the high country, Mt Stirling and Mt Buller and so on, there are a lot of scarred trees, which are shield trees.

'The coolamons or shields were used to carry food and babies and also for fighting shields.

'There are also a lot of artifact scatters, where Taungurung people sat down and worked the stone to make spearheads.

'We also found canoe trees; they weren't up as high as Stirling and Buller, but going up towards Mt Terrible we found canoe trees,' Judy Monk said.

AT THE TIME of contact with Europeans, in the 1820s and 1830s, and stretching back centuries before that, the Aboriginal people of central Victoria were part of the Kulin Nation language group.

The Kulin Nation comprised five tribes – the Woiworung, Boonwurrung, Wathaurung, Djaja Wurrung and Taungurung – and each tribe had its own clan groups.

Taungurung people occupied the land as far as the Ovens River, all the way down the Goulburn to what is now Yea and Alexandra and beyond that to the Coliban River, near Kyneton.

The southern boundary is the top of the Great Dividing Range north of Melbourne and the western boundary is where the towns of Heathcote and Kilmore are now.

The Taungurung tribe was made up of nine clan groups. The clan called the Yowung-illam-balluk (literally, stone-dwelling-people) inhabited the area along the Goulburn River as far as Alexandra, through to the Howqua, Delatite and Jamieson rivers and the mountains like Mt Stirling and Mt Buller that shed their waters into those rivers.

On the mountains, outside winter with its then-repellent blanket of snow, small marsupials, alpine plants such as yam daisies and the abundant bogong moths were substantial food sources.

'Ceremonies would take place when the bogong moths came in; there would be a lot of negotiations and corroboree and business taking place between the clans during those times of plentiful food,' Judy Monk said.

'Those were opportunities of bringing all the clans together, not just the Taungurung but there would be business done with the other tribes around Taungurung as well – like Djaja Wurrung and Wurrendjeri.'

Three axe heads and a sharpening stone found in the Cow Camp area in the 1950s and now held in the collection of the Australian National Museum. HT REEVES

The mountains were not neutral ground however, some country was shared between different tribes but you 'wouldn't go into [other tribes'] country unless you had permission to come in and they utilised the message stick to signify they had that permission.' Judy Monk believes the elder men of the tribe would take young men to the top of peaks such as Mt Buller as part of their initiation, 'where you've got a 360 degrees view, they would be up there to show the young men the creation stories and the dreaming tracks and what the country was all about, it was a way of explaining things.

'At ceremonial times, the tribes would settle down to talk business, not necessarily all together. This was when the elders would ensure that proper law and tradition would be carried out.

'Men would discuss men's business whether it be initiations or territory and women would discuss women's business, whether it be birthing or ensuring the young girls were being taught properly in relation to what sort of foods to gather and that sort of stuff.

Looking north from Mt Buller over the valleys of mist towards Mt Buffalo with Mt Cobbler to the right. BOB BATEUP

'Women would also have corroboree business just the same as men would have corroboree business, but they would also have a big joint corroboree where everyone came together.'

As summer ended, fire was used in a calculated way, 'to regenerate tucker,' Judy Monk said. 'It was a tool that was used to ensure that when they came through in the next season, there was plentiful food.'

IN THE EARLY years of white settlement, the Delatite was called the Devil's River, a name given it by the early settlers 'because they'd hear the Yowung-illam-balluk having a corroboree and they'd think it was the devil down there,' Judy Monk said.

Her grandmother – Elizabeth 'Lizzie' Edmonds – was born beside the Delatite River.

The first white settlers made some recordings of the Taungurung language, even if their interpretations were inconsistent.

The Mansfield Historical Society records the word Murrang, meaning hand, as the name for what is now called Mt Buller.

In his 1846 field sketch of the 40,000 acre (16,180 hectare) Broken River Creek Run, Robert Russell recorded the name Mt Buller and next to it the native name Maaraain.

'The word for hand in our language is "Marnong"; what we're finding with reclaiming our language is that there has been an issue with the way early settlers interpreted our language, there have been a lot of discrepancies,' Judy Monk said.

Interpretations for the word Taungurung are as distant in English as Daung wurrung and as close as Taungarung and Taungurong. The tribe's board of elders has settled on the spelling Taungurung. Semantics aside, the clash of civilisations devastated the Taungurung and most people of the Kulin Nation.

WITHIN TWO DECADES of contact, their land was taken and their numbers were slashed. This occurred through armed conflict, through subtler but just as sinister means such as the poisoning of food – one incident, according to local folklore, killed Taungurung in their hundreds near Barjarg, along the Broken River – and through disease contracted from the settlers, to which the Aborigines had no resistance.

The colonial government made some attempts to quell the violence and establish Aboriginal protectorates but Aboriginal people had few places to go for security and safety. Some of the Taungurung found sanctuary at Wappan Station, the head station of the Hunter and Watson run.

Bunjil and Waa

The two moiety (tribal) totems of the Taungurung people are Bunjil the eaglehawk and Waa the crow.

Bunjil is the creator spirit of the people of the Kulin Nation; he carved figures from bark and breathed life into them; Waa the crow was often seen as a trickster, in contrast to Bunjil.

'A Koori myth from Victoria tells how Crow stole fire from the seven women guardians. In the Dreamtime only these seven women knew the secret of fire and refused to divulge how it was made. Crow decided that he would get their secret. He made friends with the women and found out that they carried fire at the ends of their digging sticks. He also found out that the women were fond of termites, but afraid of snakes. He buried a number of snakes in a termite mound, and then told the women he had found a large nest of termites. They followed him to the spot and broke open the mound. The snakes attacked them and they defended themselves with their digging sticks. This caused fire to fall from the sticks. Quickly, Crow picked up the fire between two pieces of bark and ran away. Now Crow in his turn refused to share fire with anyone. Every time someone asked him, he mockingly called out, "Waa, waa." He caused so much strife that even he at last lost his temper and threw coals at some of the men who were pestering him for fire. The coals caused a bushfire in which he supposedly was burnt to death, but the eternal trickster came to life and the survivors heard his mocking "Waa, waa" echoing from a large tree.' (Mudrooroo)

Bunjil and Waa are represented in a totem sculpture (right) at the Mansfield Visitor Information Centre, a display created with the Taungurung people. KIT RUNDLE

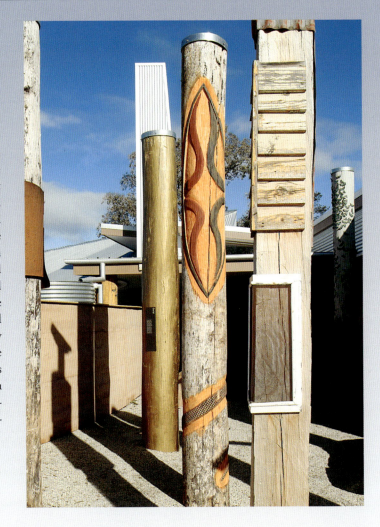

An undated photograph from Coranderrk entitled 'Last of the Victorian Aborigines.' SLV

John Bon, from Scotland, was the overseer of Wappan and took over the lease in the 1840s. At any one time hundreds of Taungurung camped on the banks of the Delatite River at Wappan. Some were employed by John Bon as station hands.

Anne Bon of Wappan Station was a Scot much younger than her husband; she continued running the property after his death and it was she in particular who befriended the Aborigines, and as a member of the Central Board for the Protection of Aborigines advocated on their behalf. (Tehan, p50)

The Chenery family at 'Delatite', Alfred and George, are also remembered as being sympathetic to the Taungurung people. (D'Arcy, p4)

Mohican Station, an Aboriginal Reserve of 16,000 acres (6500 hectares) at Acheron had been moved four miles (6.5 kilometres) up river by the local 'protectors' without consultation with the Aborigines. It was revoked in the early 1860s after a walkout by Aboriginal leaders due to continual settler interference. (Caldere, p10)

Despite this, Aboriginal reserves around the state and eventually most of the Acheron Aboriginal reserve was resumed for settlement, forcing the Aborigines to Coranderrk, initially created in 1860 of 4850 acres and occupied by a conflicted mix of Kulin and other Aborigines.

Coranderrk was gradually whittled away and finally revoked in 1950, to be sold for soldier settlement blocks with the small proportion retained in public ownership now the site of the Healesville Sanctuary. (Caldere, p14)

Ironically, the sanctuary, a wildlife park and research centre, hosts a project to preserve Mt Buller's mountain pygmy possum population.

Missions and reserves at least offered the hope of survival, but life was a pale alternative to the lives of Taungurung ancestors. The Taungurung became scattered around the state, as far afield as Framlingham near Warrnambool and Lake Tyers near Lakes Entrance. The use of their own language and the practice of their customs in traditional ways were banned or discouraged. As the decades wore on, they were further spread as part of the Stolen Generation.

'We have people now who are just finding out about their Aboriginal origins,' Judy Monk said. 'Some of us know where we've come from; we know our history, but we have Aboriginal people who were taken from their families and placed in foster care. They are just now coming back in and discovering their families.

'We have Taungurung people from as far away as Western Australia who are just now discovering their ancestors.'

The tribe's descendants are reclaiming their language and teaching it to their children and in projects such as the post-bushfire archaeological surveys, uncovering more Taungurung sites, particularly in the high country.

Once identified, the sites are recorded on a statewide register held by Parks Victoria and Aboriginal Affairs Victoria and protected under state legislation.

This means in the case of future fires on crown land, the firefighting agencies can identify the sites and ensure suppression lines do not go near them – in much the same way as habitat like that of the mountain pygmy possum is protected. (see chapter 18)

AT CAMP JUNGAI, alongside the Rubicon River near Alexandra, Taungurung hold camps to bring their people together and to have a better understanding of their language and traditional methods of tool making and arts and crafts.

At other times, the camp is leased to a group that conducts outdoor education programs for school groups, but part of each of those programs involves a cultural connection with the Taungurung people.

There is an Aboriginal cultural officer at the camp and the Taungurung's dance group also visits Camp Jungai and performs corroborees for school camps.

In 2003 all the clans from the high country, from across New South Wales into the Monaro region and the Australian Capital Territory, and from all the Victorian mountain country, had a historic meeting at Mt Hotham.

'It was the first time in 200 years that we'd all met. It was a very successful meeting where we reclaimed our right to have a meeting of first nations,' Judy Monk said.

The Taungurung hope to strengthen their ties with their traditional country: 'We want people to understand where we are coming from, that we are not there to do land grabs and any of that sort of stuff, but that there is recognition, understanding and acknowledgement of who we are and what our ancestry means to us.

'We'd like to see dual-language on the signs around these tourist areas, in English and in our Taungurung language. It is important to have our language acknowledged on signs as a recognition of connection to country.

'It would be deadly to have our language on the signs and have our moieties [tribal totems] Waa and Bunjil up there as well.'

Settlers

It had a noble and romantic edge, but the significance of exploration lay in the creation of pathways for new settlers and economic expansion in the growing colonies. However, it was almost 90 years between the first recorded European sighting of Mt Buller and the establishment of clear access up the mountain, beyond the tracks of its indigenous inhabitants.

HAMILTON HUME MUST have had the kind of curiosity and perseverance that make a good mountaineer or ski tourer. His first expedition was from his family farm at Appin, south-west of Sydney in 1814, when he was only 17.

He reached out into the district, to locations that would become known as Goulburn, Braidwood and Jervis Bay, but his best known journey was south to Port Phillip.

Hume joined Captain William Hovell in 1824-25 on a remarkable 16-week adventure that included discoveries such as the Murray River, its tributaries including the Mitta Mitta, Kiewa and Ovens rivers and land suitable for grazing between Gunning, near Yass, and Corio Bay. (Stuart H Hume, *ADB*)

They recorded a sighting of the peak the Aborigines knew as Murrang (*Mansfield Valley*/MHS, p50) and although they gave a majestic plateau the name Buffalo, they did not give Murrang a European name. That came in 1836 when an ambitious surveyor,

Thomas Livingstone Mitchell, made his journey through Victoria. Mitchell emigrated from Scotland in 1827, arriving in Sydney with his family to take up an appointment as assistant surveyor-general of New South Wales, becoming surveyor-general the following year. It was an important position in the colonies, not least for its role in their exploration and, related to that, their economic development.

Mitchell led expeditions into NSW, 'looking for a large river flowing to the north west.' (WDH Baker, *ADB*)

In the 1830s, with the number of free settlers growing and squatters demanding land, Mitchell led an expedition to trace the Darling River to the Murray. It was cut short by conflict with Aborigines along the Darling, meaning Mitchell failed to reach the junction of the two rivers.

'His third expedition was intended to fill this gap,' and eventually took him 'along the Murray to the junction of the Loddon

Hume and Hovell cross the Murray River in 1825.
FA SLEAP/SLV

where the country seemed so promising that he turned south-west into what is now Victoria and was so enchanted by the area that he called it Australia Felix [Latin for Fortunate Australia].

'As on all his expeditions, Mitchell systematically surveyed as he travelled. After seven months his error, so he claimed, was only a mile and three-quarters [2.8 kilometres]. As a controversialist and thirster after glory, Mitchell was sometimes strangely blind to the truth; but he was a painstaking and competent surveyor, and his claim may be believed.' (Baker, *ADB*)

It was on this remarkable journey of discovery through Victoria in 1836 that Mitchell saw the peak first identified by Hume and Hovell in 1824, the peak known as Marnong (meaning hand) by the Taungurung people.

Mitchell, perhaps with a knighthood in mind – an honour he lobbied for after this trip – named the peak after Charles Buller, an official in the Colonial Office in London.

The significance of exploration was in creating economic path-ways within the growing colonies. A notice from the Australian Journal Office, dated March 1, 1847 headlined 'Sir TL Mitchell's Expedition' announced for sale 'at this office and of the principal booksellers in the city, a map of the explo-rations of the above expedition combined with the travels of Dr Leichhardt.'

With the descriptive matter, the price was 3s, 6d or the map alone was 2s, 6d. 'This map is of the highest importance to the squat-ting interests,' the notice stated. (Clark, p274)

The squatters, selectors, gold miners, timber harvesters and millers, even the bushrangers, would follow these paths to pursue their interests and that in turn led to the demise of the indigenous population.

THE ABORIGINES HAD climbed the mountains now known as Stirling and Buller for thousands of years, but history has no formal record of their individual accomplishments.

It does record the first European to scale the mountains in the quest of science, the brilliant botanist Sir Ferdinand Jakob Henrik von Mueller (or Baron von Mueller).

He was born in Rostock and trained as a pharmacist at the University of Kiel, but was awarded a doctorate for his thesis on flora.

Von Mueller migrated from his native Germany to Adelaide in 1847 and in 1853 was appointed Victorian government botanist. In that year, he joined another botanist, John Dallachy, in an expedition to the Ovens Valley, where he reported indications of gold. (Deirdre Morris, *ADB*)

They climbed Mt Buffalo and, although enchanted by the plateau and excited at the discovery of new plants, von Mueller found it a dis-appointment in terms of alpine flora – 'Mount Aberdeen [the peak on the southern edge of the Buffalo plateau, so-named by Mitchell and now known as The Horn] offered hardly any plants of a true alpine character.' (from von Mueller's report, quoted in Lloyd, p8)

Dallachy and von Mueller separated and in early March 1853, von Mueller 'resolved to ascend Mount Buller, whose summits, at an elevation of more than 5000 feet are covered throughout the greater part of the year with snow. Travelling quite alone since leaving the Buffalo Ranges, the ascent was not accomplished without considerable danger. But I was delighted to observe here, for the first time, this continent's alpine vegetation … Mount Buller had never before been scientifically explored.' (Lloyd, p8)

Whether von Mueller's ascent on March 22, 1853, made him the first European to admire the view from Mt Buller's summit is unknown – squatters and their workers were in the area by this time and may have scaled the mountain, but von Mueller's writ-ten record is the earliest known.

Looking from the west over Mt Timbertop towards Mt Buller. An 1868 wood engraving by Robert Bruce. SLV

Baron von Mueller, Mt Buller's first botanist. MJ DANIEL/SLV

The journeys of von Mueller (right), complete with an unusually shaped Great Dividing Range (based on a map in Home et al). JENNY LAIDLAW

EUROPEAN DISCOVERY OF the Mansfield district came as a result of a search for straying stock. The story goes that in 1839, Andrew Ewan, who was working for squatters on a run called Ballowra at Seven Creeks, near Euroa, crossed the Strathbogie Ranges searching for straying horses and came across a lush valley with good water.

'He returned with the news and immediately John Howqua Hunter and Campbell Hunter from Ballowra came to investigate. 'As Ballowra was already overstocked, the Hunters moved cattle and horses to this new run which they called Wappan (after the Aboriginal name for the Delatite River, Wappang).

'Although it was always referred to as Head Station, shortly afterwards James Watson moved the main camp further up the river to the site now known as Delatite Station.' (*Mansfield Valley*, pp6-9, MHS)

In the 1840s through agriculture and the 1850s following the discovery of gold, Victoria's population boomed. Mansfield township was established to service the growing needs of agriculture and mining.

Further east, towards the mountains, 'Merrijig was proclaimed a village on the 18th of August 1868. This was only seven years after the first land was selected in this newly opened up area following the introduction of the 1860 Land Selection Act.' (McCormack, p15) There was an Irish influence in the area, which Adele McCormack traces to Tipperary. 'The Murphys, for instance were a big family who made several land selections … three of the Murphy sisters were pioneers in their own right as Mrs William Lovick, Mrs Richard Purcell and Mrs Sam Christopher.

'William and Catherine Lovick … first set up a hotel on the gold fields in Howqua … the next venture was establishing the Hunt Club Hotel, this building was of better construction and doubled as their home.' (McCormack, p15)

Gold discoveries in the area in the 1860s included Lankey's Creek, Stockyard Creek, Lickhole Creek, Cameron's Creek near Mt Buller, the Howqua Hills and a major field at Royaltown at Maindample. (MHS, p17)

Cattlemen herd their stock in the shadow of Mt Buller in a late 19th-century lithograph by Charles Turner. WALCH/TURNER

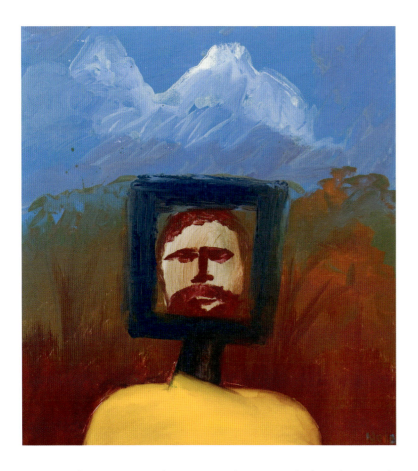

A 1979 Kelly painting from Sidney Nolan's series, this one with the bushranger in front of a mountain shaped something like Mt Buller.
PRIVATE COLLECTION

The exploits of the miners and bushrangers were the headlines, but it was grazing opportunities that drew people up Mt Buller. Frank and Robert Klingsporn obtained a licence to run stock on the mountain and took the first cattle up in 1873. By the end of the next year, the Lovick family obtained a licence and followed the tracks up for summer grazing. (MHS, p50)

It was Frank Klingsporn who beat the first serious path for tourism up the mountain. In 1913, he sought the assistance of the Mansfield Council to widen the track he used to climb Mt Buller. This route ran from the junction of Buller Creek and the Delatite River up to Boggy Creek and Burnt Hut Spur and is known today as the Klingsporn Bridle Track.

Widening it would have been in Klingsporn's own interests, to simplify the movement of his cattle, but it was also seen as an opportunity to promote tourism.

The railway connection from Melbourne to Mansfield had been made in 1891 and tourism was showing potential.

Frank Klingsporn 'donated £10 towards the cost, the Council gave £25 and a grant of £40 was sought from the state. Bushwalkers and riders made some use of this track, hiring pack and riding horses from the Klingsporns, but the winter snows remained unvisited for some years to come.' (Stephenson, p201)

Bushrangers were also active in the area, including the exceedingly nasty Daniel 'Mad Dog' Morgan who roamed the Strathbogies, the more courteous Harry Power whose 'lookout' takes in a magnificent view of the King Valley, and Ned Kelly and his gang who killed three policemen in a gun battle at Stringybark Creek, near Mansfield, in 1878.

Charles Buller

MT BULLER'S NAMESAKE was born on August 6, 1806 and well educated by English standards, attending Harrow school and later Trinity College at Cambridge University.

On his father's retirement in 1830, Charles Buller was elected a member of Britain's House of Commons, retaining a seat in that Parliament until his death on November 29, 1848.

In addition to his duties to politics and his constituents, Buller practised as a barrister and judge, but it was his association with colonial affairs that stood out.

'A popular Radical, he supported many reform measures. In 1836 he proposed and chaired the select committee on the state of government records and later he headed a committee inquiring into the election law in Ireland. Increasingly he demonstrated an interest in colonial questions.

Although sometimes criticised for his levity in parliament, he could be earnest and dignified.' (Heather Lyons-Balcon, *Dictionary of Canadian Biography Online*)

In 1838, as private secretary to Lord Durham, the governor-in-chief of British North America, Buller travelled to Quebec. Durham was charged with inquiring into the government of Upper and Lower Canada after a rebellion in 1837.

'Unlike Durham, who, he thought, "had too strong a feeling against the French Canadians on account of their recent insurrection," Buller was sympathetic, believing that the Canadians had been driven to rebellion by "long injustice" and "the deplorable imbecility of our Colonial Policy".' (Lyons-Balcon, *DCBO*)

A bust of Charles Buller in Westminster Abbey.
WESTMINSTER ABBEY/NAMA

Pioneers

The pieces fell into place for Mt Buller in the early 1920s when tourism was on a roll in Victoria. The state government was promoting Mt Buffalo, its chalet and its railway connections. Alpine recreation offered health and harmony in any season. The appeal of winter sports was growing alongside.

MANSFIELD HAD A spectacular mountain within view, one with an obvious blanket of snow through winter and one which might generate the same kind of tourist activity that Mt Buffalo appeared to be enjoying. The town also had a railway connection with the Melbourne-Sydney line. What more did it need?

Bert Walker, a Mansfield businessman, was making his way home after a meeting of the Mansfield Progress Association in 1923 and, talking to Harry Amor of the *Mansfield Courier* newspaper, was decrying the apathy in the district.

Walker knew Mt Buller, having first climbed it in 1907, aged 18, and on this evening he suggested to Amor the idea of 'building a hut at Buller Creek and opening up Mt Buller as a tourist resort.' (quoted in Dillon, p323)

That summer, they sought to build their hut at the base of the mountain. The road only went as far as Klingsporn's farm, about nine kilometres downriver from the junction of the Delatite River and Buller Creek, where Mirimbah now is.

Access was a barrier and so was the weather; 'The summer of

1923-24 was a very wet one, causing numerous delays to the project and plans to continue the work over Easter were also washed away.' (Dillon, p324)

The Buller Creek hut was never built, but around this time a vital piece of communication was published, one that was picked up by some influential people in Melbourne. It was a promotional brochure including a photograph of a snow-capped Mt Buller, seemingly as close to Mansfield as a peak in the European Alps might be to a mountain village in its shadow.

The brochure was presented at the inaugural meeting of the Ski Club of Victoria (SCV) on June 2, 1924.

Over the years which have gone all too quickly, my thoughts go back to the first inaugural meeting of the Ski Club of Victoria … at which were present about 20 enthusiasts who became foundation members of the club. One of these, the late Gordon Langridge, and our first president, produced a brochure issued by the Mansfield Progress

Association on the cover of which was reproduced a startling picture of Mansfield with the snow-capped peak of Buller seemingly arising from the outskirts of the town. Of course there was no mention of a telephoto lens on the caption of the photo. So the meeting there and then decided that a weekend exploratory trip would be made with an attempt to reach this alluring snowfield … I do not think that anyone had been farther afield than Mt Buffalo which was a 24-hour trip in those days. So the enthusiasm was contagious when here presented to us was an alpine peak within weekend distance of Melbourne – so we thought.
(Herbert Goldby, *Schuss*, May 1957)

Members of the first SCV party to scale Mt Buller's winter summit, in July 1924, and their guides; Percy Goldby (left), Clarrie Lambert, Jack Lovick, Bert Walker, Gerald Rush, A Dyer and Frank Lovick near Mt Buller's summit. FROM STEPHENSON, p207

George (left) and Jack Lovick outside their Mt Buller log hut in 1922. FROM STEPHENSON, p204

The SCV was on the way; its first trip to Mt Buller set out from Mansfield on the morning of Sunday June 8, 1924, less than a week after that inaugural meeting.

Bert Walker from Mansfield was joined by SCV members Gerald Rush, Gordon Langridge, Clive Morrish and Harry Tregellas. Gerald Rush recorded the trip:

> Left Klingsporn's at 8am; reached the foot of the Pimple [Mirimbah] at 9.20 and end of cut track at 12 noon. We then walked along the spur towards the summit for about a quarter of an hour. Carrying skis made the going very tiresome. About seven or eight inches of snow at end of track. For a few minutes the mist (which had been very heavy) lifted a little and we had a glorious view of the snowy summit. (Lloyd, p60)

Although the vast majority of their time was spent making the journey, rather than enjoying the destination, the SCV party returned full of enthusiasm. The next SCV trip was on July 5, 1924, and they returned better prepared, hiring the Lovick brothers, Frank and Jack, and their packhorses to carry some of the load and speed up the journey.

'Bert Walker recalls that on this occasion the snow was very hard, enabling them to get the horses right to Lovick's Hut [located on what is now known as Burnt Hut Spur].' (Stephenson, p202)

The party spent the night at Lovick's Hut and explored the mountain, skiing its open and treed terrain. On their way home to Melbourne they were entertained in Mansfield by the Progress Association. 'Bert Walker proposed the health of the Ski Club of Victoria … and hoped that it would be successful in establishing a good skiing ground on Mt Buller.' (Lloyd, p61)

These first two trips were teasers for Gerald Rush, back-

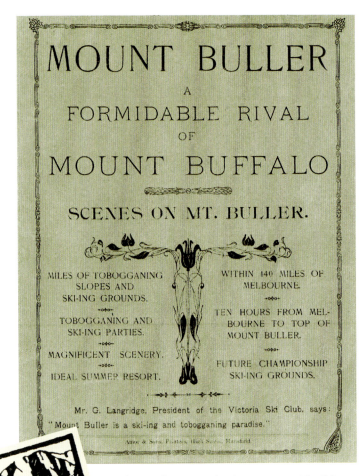

The supplement to the August 23, 1924 edition of the *Mansfield Courier*; the first shot in the marketing war between Victoria's mountains. NAMA

ground for a week-long adventure in August 1924.

His party of five met at Melbourne's Spencer Street station at 7.30am on August 15 to board the Albury-bound service. They changed trains at Tallarook, eventually arriving in Mansfield at 2pm. They spent the night in Mansfield and left before dawn to meet the Lovick brothers.

'After some tea and biscuits, provided by the ever hospitable Mrs Klingsporn … we were off again at nine o'clock in a merry cavalcade, with our skis across our shoulders, looking like a troop of lancers,' Rush wrote in a report for the *Xaverian*, the magazine of his former school.

He was complimenting the hospitality of Annie Klingsporn, who was married to Frank's son Bob or Robert. They owned Happy Valley which included all the land where Alpine Ridge and Pinnacle Valley resort are now situated, as well as across the Delatite River to the north. The Klingsporns and the Lovicks offered packhorses and other services to tourists at the time.

Rush's party encountered deeper and softer snow than their previous trip in July, making the going slow and difficult, bringing the packhorses to a halt and forcing the party to carry and drag most of their load to the Lovicks' hut. Gerald Rush:

Percy Goldby (left), Gerald Rush, A Dyer, Clarrie Lambert and Harry Tregellas below Mt Buller's summit in July 1924. FROM STEPHENSON, p202

A group on the mountain in 1932 (right) for the SCV championships walks down from the summit towards Boggy Creek. BROCKHOFF

After two miles of this dogs' work, we eventually arrived at the chalet, which is a log hut with an interior about 10 feet by seven [three metres by two] with a fireplace at one end. Every summer it is used for a few days by cattlemen who go up to muster the herds that have been left to fatten on the snow-grass. But in the winter, it rests undisturbed. It is lined inside with a tent but the floor is missing and there was black mother earth to be seen five feet below the level of the snow outside. It was woefully small, but it sheltered us in warmth for a week, and rough as it was, we soon learned to regard it as a kindly home.

Wonderful days followed our arrival. We simply lived on our skis, exploring every nook of the upper part of the mountain. A hundred yards or so above the hut, the tree line ends abruptly and a skier's paradise of clear, smooth, snowy slopes is presented ... [we skied] at a hair raising speed, racing in friendly rivalry; or as the fancy took us, down into the timber belt, rushing down through narrow lanes of trees; or on the practice slopes nearer home, experimenting with the innumerable subtle movements that lie at the disposal of the expert. In short we experienced all the joys of this wonderful sport, which within the last few years has caught on in a remarkable boom throughout the whole world in every country where snow is to be found. (quoted in Stephenson, pp204-207)

The 1924 Mansfield Progress Association photograph that featured in the brochure sent to lure the SCV. NAMA

RUSH'S PARTY ATE out for the entire week, not in restaurants as a guest of the Mt Buller village might now do, but outside in the snow on a makeshift snow bench, simply because the tiny hut was entirely taken up as a bedroom.

Rush was captivated by the mountain and the scenery, which, 'as might be expected from a mountain rising in lordly supremacy high above its neighbours is magnificent. At sunrise and sunset it is unforgettably majestic.' (Stephenson, p206)

An insert in the *Mansfield Courier* in September 1924 continued the promotion of Mt Buller over Mt Buffalo.

'On account of its accessibility and handiness to Melbourne, being many miles nearer than any other mountain with the same possibilities, it [Mt Buller] should rapidly become a very popular mountain for winter sports.'

The *Courier* supplement modestly declared that Mt Buller's peaks were 'snow clad for six months of the year, and in some seasons still longer periods.'

They were right about accessibility, but they might have been overplaying their hand on snow cover.

No matter, after 1924, the snowball was rolling and the skiers were on their way. The idea of building accommodation at the foot of the mountain had been discarded in favour of chalets in the snow.

Adventurers

The skiing population was still small in the second half of the 1920s, but it was growing. The skiers' enthusiasm for mountain sports was to guarantee the development of mountain villages.

CLIMB AND RUN skiing is unique. Step, after step, after step, crunched into spring snow or slugged out in a winter drift. The climb demanded experience and intelligence, to find the best path and ascend with the most efficiency. The run was all the more exhilarating for the effort of the climb. And the run could go as far as you wanted; there were no lift lines to limit you. The boundary was the snowline and you could glide all the way there; streaming along the open slopes with the wind in your hair and mountain views all around, dodging down through the snow gums and then, legs screaming from the effort of the climb and the burns of the turns, slipping quietly through the woolly butts, to climb again and run once more and breathe hard and boast and smile all the way back to the top. Ski waxing was crucial, as was the choice of the right wax for the weather and snow conditions you had and those that you were going to have. The discussion would be had with as much care and gossip and deliberation as a wine judging. Wax didn't just help the skis glide on the run, it had the potential to help them grip on the climb, although those with the resources might have tied seal skins to their ski bases when they weren't boot packing up the hill. The entire skiing adventure and the camaraderie and the mountains were the magnets.

Freeheeling on the summit in the 1930s. COURT

Marjorie Good (Leviny) skis the summit (above) in 1934.
MOORE/TINSLEY

Paul Cesnik (below) makes fresh tracks on the northern face of the summit, with Mansfield covered in a sea of cloud.
HAROLD GIBBS/COURT

NOT LONG AFTER that 1924 winter of first adventures, the Lovicks' hut burnt down, but the Mansfield Progress Association (MPA) stepped in and, persevering with its plans for a hut, built one at the top of Klingsporn's Bridle Path, less than a kilometre from the summit.

It was no easy task; packhorses carried the iron for the hut's roof and cladding from Klingsporn's farm and the timber frame was created from wood nearby and lower down the mountain.

'It was a commodious structure, its most comfortable capacity being 12, but on one memorable King's Birthday weekend in June, 29 enthusiastic skiers taxed its capacity to the limit.' (SCV *Year Book,* 1934)

Around the same time, a company with five shareholders – Alec Russell, Denis Sargood, Laurence Stokes, Hugh Trumble and Mansfield's Bert Walker – was formed with the intention of backing the building of a chalet at Mt Buller.

Rather than locate the chalet near the MPA Hut, they built it on land at Horse Hill, milling the woolly butt trees nearby for the frame and cutting a new track to reach the hut.

The mill was driven by engines 'packed up to the site by Jack Lovick and Tim Bullock on horses … the walls of the chalet were built of Cellotex board manufactured from sugar cane. It was light but tough and the chalet was completed in 1929. It had accommodation for 30 people and was reached by a bridle track eight miles [13 kilometres] in length, which the present road closely follows.

'For many years White Bridge had been as far as the skiers could go by car. From that point, they'd hike and haul their gear up the mountain or hire a packhorse to help with the load.' (Stephenson, p209)

There were gradual improvements in service; in 1932 the news came through that:

'Visitors to Mount Buller will be glad to learn a lock-up garage has been erected at the end of the road. The keys are available at Mr Lovick's Hotel, Merrijig; fee 1/- per day. The riding track to the chalet has also been improved so that river crossings are now avoided.' (SCV *Year Book*, 1932)

An SCV party set to scale the mountain for the 1932 championships. BROCKHOFF

Helmut Kofler jumping in the nordic style on the summit, 1932. BROCKHOFF

The access track to the chalet became a vehicle track in 1939, thanks in no small part to teams of workers who cut and widened much of it during the Great Depression of 1929-38.

ALTHOUGH ITS MEMBERS were also exploring the opportunities on the Bogong High Plains and around Mt Hotham, the SCV was still active at Mt Buller. The club held its championships on the mountain in 1926, using the MPA hut as its base.

Provisions had to be carried in from Mansfield, for which 'undertaking, too great praise cannot be given to the Mansfield [SCV] branch and to Mr Jack Lovick who had charge of the transport.' (Percy Goldby, SCV *Year Book*, 1926-27)

A good snow cover and sunny weather at the outset enabled Goldby and party to make a 'rough survey of the mountain … with the object of selecting the best slopes and directions for the various events … a good takeoff, large enough to accommodate 20 runners was found at the summit … in all the course so chosen would give a run of approximately one mile [1.6 kilometres] and under the conditions then prevailing, in the mornings could be covered at rare speed.'

OVERLEAF: A cross-country ski racer believed to be Cleve Cole, who died in tragic circumstances near Mt Bogong in 1936. In this 1935 photograph, the skier is described as the 'Victorian champion' and is on a cross-country course across the top of Federation with Corn Hill and the Crosscut Saw in the distance. The 'V' on the headband symbolises the state. EDWIN ADAMSON

Edwin G Adamson
A.R.P.S.

Alas, the conditions did not prevail; some races were run but the championship was cut short by rain, hail and snow – wild mountain weather. However, in his report, Percy Goldby was full of praise for the mountain's potential.

He wrote that the event served 'to bring the excellence of this mountain as a ski runner's paradise before both competitor and public, in so far as it has convinced the authorities that we must have a road to the top of Mt Buller. With the patronage of the club and the untiring energy of the Mansfield people, to this end, who knows what the next year or two will bring?'

SOME OF THE changes those years did bring came as a result of the arrival of Helmut Kofler, a formidable athlete who came to Australia in 1927 with his Austrian wife.

Swimming was the initial lure and he instructed it at Portsea in the summer. The connection with the snow was possibly made through the established overlap between people who holidayed at that seaside resort and Victoria's snowfields.

Mt Hotham was the first mountain Kofler visited, in 1927, and in 1928 he went into partnership there with Bill Spargo to manage the Hotham Heights Chalet.

By all accounts the relationship with Spargo didn't work and some time during 1928 Kofler and his wife made their way to Mt Buller. He became manager of the Mt Buller Chalet and in 1938 became its owner. Andrew Grimwade, who first skied Mt Buller with his parents Erick and Gwen as Kofler's guests in 1937, recalled him as 'very charismatic and very protective of his firewood, very mean putting it on, I remember him saying "one day somebody will put too much on and it will all burn down" which, of course, after his death is exactly what happened.'

Kofler had astonishing energy; he led the clearing of the Shaky Knees run and another between the chalet at Horse Hill and Cow Camp.

The 'Horse Hill Bark Hut' in 1929. This hut and a tent were used as shelter by the builders of the Mt Buller Chalet. The two people at left are unknown, second from right is Helmut Kofler and next to him the photographer Edwin Adamson. EDWIN ADAMSON

The Mt Buller Chalet at Horse Hill in its extended form, before it was consumed by fire in 1942. COURT

A small hut was built at Cow Camp in 1930 – on the current Kooroora site – and used as a day refuge for skiers. Water in the area made it a popular point for grazing cattle to gather in summer, hence the name.

Kofler and the SCV established snow pole lines to help guide skiers around the mountain – from the chalet to Cow Camp and the summit, with a branch down to Burnt Hut Spur. Kofler also installed a telephone line between the chalet and Mansfield. Skiing was his performance art however, and he appeared to have a taste for time in the air, building an enormous ski jump and using it to display his talents, although pride sometimes led to a fall.

Tom Mitchell: 'It had a 19 foot [six metre] platform and we'd all turn out and help old Helmut pack it with snow and then he'd

A stand of frosted woolly butt trees near Horse Hill in 1929.
EDWIN ADAMSON

Bill Tyrwhitt-Drake (left), Peggy and Helmut Kofler and an unknown
person kneeling. TYRWHITT-DRAKE/NAMA

go away just about to the top of Horse Hill and come screaming
down through the boles of mountain ash and we'd close our eyes
and some religious folk would cross themselves when Kofler shot
into outer space. The finale would invariably be an almighty
prang into the creek accompanied by a terrific burst of snow;
Austrian profanity and the sound of shattering timber.'
(Stephenson, p217)

Mitchell, a farmer, a gun skier and later a parliamentarian would
have a major impact on the Victorian mountains. He recalled that
after the 1939 fires destroyed key accommodation facilities in the
Mt Hotham area, Kofler saw an opportunity to expand the Mt
Buller Chalet and fill it with the skiers who would otherwise have
been staying at Mt Hotham.

At some point during the 1930s, the first Mrs Kofler returned to
Austria and Helmut Kofler began a relationship with a
Melbourne architect, Peggy Wilks, who designed the chalet
extensions.

Tom Mitchell was of the view that Kofler over-committed and
under-delivered on his chalet extensions and a ski tow he'd also
promised, so it 'ended in a lot of us having to dob in and form a
small company to save Buller from being taken over by the suppli-
ers.' (Stephenson, p218)

Mitchell had other recollections.

> Mrs (de facto) Kofler (Mark 2) was making a unique and
> most helpful contribution to everyone's comfort by paint-
> ing tin flowers and nailing them to the window sills. Mrs
> (de jure) Kofler (Mark 1) had by this time gone ta-ta back
> to Austria (where in 1965, she was still alive in the province
> of Carinthia) and Mrs (de facto) Kofler had taken her place.
> The Junior Ski Club of Australia took a dim view of this
> and after a few pungent words to Kofler, the drill was that
> the JSCA riding up the mountain on their horses would
> pass Mrs (de facto) Kofler (Mark 2) riding down with her
> nose in the air. This order of proceedings being reversed
> two weeks later at the end of the JSCA's season [in other
> words, Peggy Wilks had to vacate the chalet during the
> JSCA's stay]. (Dillon, p356)

Peggy (Muriel Margaret) Wilks and Helmut Kofler married in
1940. They must have been an adventurous couple. On
September 25, 1940, they, along with Ken Jones and Bill
Christensen were riding a timber trolley at Christensen's
Delatite Sawmills, on the lower slopes of Mt Buller, possibly
with a view to using some similar means of transport to move
skiers or chalet guests.

A newspaper article datelined 'Mansfield, Wednesday,' reported
that 'In sensational circumstances, Mr Helmut Kofler, proprietor
of the Mount Buller Chalet and his wife, Muriel Margaret Kofler,
were killed instantly when the truck in which they were riding at
the Delatite Sawmills jumped the gears and crashed down the
mountain side.

'Kenneth Jones and William Christensen who were also in the
truck were injured.

A bushwalker has a summer slumber on Little Buller in 1947.
KIESSLING

The trolley worked on a cable system with the car coming down providing momentum for the one going up. The system relied on a braking mechanism to slow the momentum of the downward car, loaded with timber. It failed and the two cars collided.' (NAMA)

They had been married five months and according to Tom Mitchell, 'Helmut urged his wife to jump with him but she hung back and split seconds later, Helmut and Mrs Kofler died horrifyingly. Mrs Kofler was pregnant.' (Dillon, p356)

Part of their physical legacy to Mt Buller went when in midwinter 1942, the chalet was destroyed by fire, although Kofler is remembered in the name of a lift and a restaurant on the mountain.

WHILE THE CHALET had absorbed some of the growing commercial demand with its development in the Horse Hill area, the SCV retained its focus on the Mansfield Progress Association hut at the head of Klingsporn's Bridle Path in the Burnt Hut Spur/Boggy Creek area.

However, after the setback of the Lovicks' hut going up in flames in 1925, the MPA hut also disappeared in smoke in the summer of 1933.

The SCV responded by replacing it with a hut of its own in the Boggy Creek Bowl. Robert Klingpsorn carted the materials up the mountain 'and the hut was usable on the scheduled long weekend in June (1933) … and accommodated 12 people on shelf bunks although the known record was 28 people.' (Lloyd, p98)

The SCV tried to launch a construction project in the late 1930s to get some better accommodation for its members at Mt Buller but this attempt failed and then World War II intervened.

The project was restarted with some funds from the will of Major Ivor Whittaker, a keen skier and enthusiastic SCV member who was killed in the Middle East during the war.

Numerous sites were considered, including Horse Hill or the Skating Rink, Cow Camp, the base of the Shaky Knees run and the top of Shaky Knees. The latter prevailed.

Water supply was a governing factor and the SCV's selection committee found that a '(running stream 150 metres up hill of the site) on the treeline at the top of Shaky Knees proved that flow to be an adequate supply from which lodge water could be piped.' (Lloyd, p112)

This is the site the Whitt still occupies, in behind the Ski Patrol base. It had considerable promise for skiers and some glorious

The final haul, bringing building materials up the mountain in 1947 for the construction of the SCV's Ivor Whittaker Memorial Lodge.
KIESSLING

mountain views, but access was a critical barrier as the road still stopped at the site of the old chalet.

Harold Doughty, an SCV member who operated a timber mill in Mirimbah had a solution. 'Over Easter 1946, Harold, his bulldozer and two of his employees carved out a rough road from the old chalet site, past the CSIR, round Hell Corner and over the Cow Camp saddle to the Ivor Whitt site.' (Lloyd, p116) The Hell Corner stretch had to be re-graded but Doughty's road alignment is largely intact now.

Building the Whitt was a major project. Construction continued through to May 1947 when Robert Whittaker unveiled the plaque commemorating his son Ivor and thus opened the 36-bed lodge.

In the relative simplicity of a 21st-century trip to the snow, it's difficult to comprehend the efforts of the SCV members in creating their accommodation, to build the road, find and then haul the materials and eventually build the lodge.

There is no doubting the lure of the sport and the mountains, and even if the chalet had shown that commercial success above the snowline was precarious but possible, it was the enthusiasm of ski clubs and their members that laid Mt Buller's foundations.

TOM MITCHELL PLAYED an increasingly significant role in the development of Victoria's ski fields. He and his wife Elyne, the author, were farmers at Towong Hill, near Corryong and made numerous skiing adventures into the Snowy Mountains, which are in view of their Towong Hill homestead.

Mitchell was elected to Parliament as the member for Benambra in

Outside the Whitt on King's Birthday weekend, 1947. The lodge was open, but the scaffolding remained in place for its completion over the 1947-48 summer. LLOYD, p125

The SCV's Boggy Creek Hut in the 1940s. Helen Schuster is holding the horse's reins. KIESSLING/NAMA

Don Richards (above left) and Walter Kiessling camping on King's Birthday Weekend in 1948 beside the ruins of the original Mt Buller Chalet which serve as a stand for shaving and ski preparation. KIESSLING

Ray and Denny Evans (right) in 1950, outside the almost-buried caravan they called Ullr, presumably at the site of the original Ullr Ski Club lodge near Cow Camp. COURT

1947, a seat he held until 1976. He was famous for knitting during parliamentary sittings, supposedly to return some form of productivity for the time spent in those sessions. He was an accomplished skier, skills he enhanced during travels in Europe, and was well connected within the small Victorian skiing community and an enthusiastic supporter of it.

Mitchell had the uninhibited ways of a country visitor when in Melbourne. Mick Hull recalled his greeting: 'On a sunny day walking up the quiet "Paris end" of Collins Street near the Melbourne Club, under the leafy peace of the great plane trees, the air would suddenly be rent by a ringing shout of "Ski Heil, Mick Hull," delivered at a volume more in keeping with a man in the saddle than the sedate atmosphere of Collins Street.' (Hull, p242) Mitchell pushed for the establishment of alpine villages in Victoria. At the time of his 1947 entry to State Parliament, the sport was growing in popularity and 'Victoria's snowfields, although barely accessible, were desperately short of accommodation. Early in 1947, the Victorian skiing population of 3000 to 5000 had only 200 beds, including those in the primitive cattlemen's huts at their disposal.' (Lloyd, p93)

Tom Mitchell recalled it this way:

Immediately after World War II things were grim at Buller. The old chalet had gone and except for about three hopelessly inadequate corrugated iron huts there was no accommodation at all on the mountain. To make things worse and more tantalising, the road was in a reasonably good state right to the old chalet site … At about 4pm on a Saturday afternoon at Buller you would suddenly notice a diminution of the skiers on the snow. They just seemed to be melting away. They melted away all right, dodging around clumps of gums, jumping from rock to rock, wobbling along one log and then wobbling along another until they came to all kinds of primitive "squats" under camouflage nets and other forms of disguise where they proceeded to cook their evening meal and camp the night. Caravans were ever whisked off into the bush and hidden.

Relaxing at the Cow Camp lunch hut in the 1940s, with the skier at centre managing a smile despite what seems to be some boot discomfort. NAMA

The Forests Commission who controlled the area (God bless them) fortunately at first took a benign and sympathetic view but eventually got justifiably worried as the number of these unsanitary fire traps grew in an important forest and catchment area. In 1947 or 1948 Dr Frank Moulds [of the FCV] and I discussed the whole question together in his office in the Forests Commission. There were various possibilities but the one we selected was the one adopted and that is why the area remains under the overall control of the Forests Commission, the village running its own local affairs under a Committee of Management. Thus at Buller, Australia's first Alpine Village was started. (Stephenson, p219)

The first meeting of the Mt Buller Recreational Reserve Committee was held at Mansfield Shire Office on December 17, 1948.
The chairman, Andrew Benallack, welcomed the committee and remarked that 'Mt Buller would become one of the most popular snowfields in Victoria and the initial planning must be basically sound if our efforts are to be worthy of the locality.'
Vern Corr who represented the Federation of Victorian Ski Clubs on the committee, agreed that sound planning was important but he spoke of the 'necessity for urgent action to enable clubs to commence building this summer and also of the suitability of Cow Camp site as being selected by a consensus of opinion over the past years.' (minutes, December 1948)
Mt Buller's time had arrived.

Go jump

'Before the recent war a few skiers such as Kofler, Romuld and Eric Johnson brought the standard of ski jumping in Victoria up to a high level. Distances of about 40 metres were attained on Kofler's Hill at Mt Buller. Due to the war and the untimely death of Helmut Kofler, this hill has become overgrown and the take-off platform fell into a state of disrepair ... Kofler's jump, the profile of which is still good, will probably be put into order for the 1949 season, so that jumps of up to 25 metres can be attempted.' (*Schuss,* March 1949, p 94)

The artists always attract a crowd, be it a 2007 rail slide or a 1930s jump. These frames are from a film of Helmut Kofler and his Chalet Creek ski jump in the 1930s and another jumper (bottom left) also near Horse Hill in 1952. SCV/BILL DARBY

THE MOUNTAIN

A view along Mt Buller's West Ridge
towards the summit in winter 2003.
MARK ASHKANASY

5
Lifts

Mountains and mountain sports appeal to all sorts of people, but the mix invariably includes some with engineering and entrepreneurial talents. At Mt Buller, these people built a lift system to match many in the world in quality and capacity, but it was created through a minefield of competition and red tape.

'THIS IS THE moment that changed the mountain,' said Merrick Summers, referring to a photograph of the Bourke Street rope tow's first day of operation, July 3, 1949.

It certainly was. At Mt Buller, it was almost as though they had eaten the forbidden fruit.

At every stage of their implementation and technological development, ski lifts have transformed the sport, but Mt Buller was blessed and cursed with numerous lift operators, virtually from the outset.

More than 25 years of willing sparring between the two that eventually emerged strongest – Blue and Orange or Bull Run Enterprises and Ski Lifts Mt Buller/Mt Buller Ski Lifts – saw Mt Buller's lift systems develop at a pace far greater than anywhere else in Australia, but divided the mountain, with skiers scattered one way or the other according to the colour of their ticket.

It began innocently enough when Merrick's father, Rob Summers, an active member of the Ski Club of Victoria (SCV), stood up at the club's general meeting in 1948 and wanted to know if members would be interested in a tow at Mt Buller.

Merrick Summers: 'I was at that meeting and it went into a fervor. After some discussion, the president asked who was going to run the project and the meeting fell to silence. He said to my dad, "Why don't you do it?" and my dad said "I will" adding with some irony, "It's just the thing for a research chemist".'

On the morning of July 3, 1949, the tow was tested and the skiers were then allowed on to the rope. The SCV's Bob Reece is on the left of the rope giving instructions. Dick Thompson is the rider gripping the rope. HAROLD GIBBS/SUMMERS

Rob Summers was appointed to run the SCV's ski-tow sub-committee. 'But it never actually met, not once,' Merrick Summers said. 'Dad just appointed people to do things and they did them.' His group mainly comprised SCV members who were also members of the Brighton Mountain Wanderers (BMW) Ski Club.

Their enthusiasm for the project was underpinned by a sketchy understanding of lift construction from local and northern hemisphere experience and sources like two Canadian ski instructors working at Mt Buffalo at the time – Herb Hall and Paul Heikkila. Australia's first motorised tow had opened at Mt Buffalo in August 1937. (Lloyd, p398)

In 1948, post-war rationing was still in force across Australia meaning that Rob Summers and his team needed to be as innovative as farmers and as resourceful as commandos.

When they eventually found an engine to run the tow – a truck engine – they couldn't obtain petrol, so Merrick Summers modified it to run on power kerosene, which was in abundant supply for agricultural and other uses.

Rope was another hurdle, Merrick said. 'We couldn't import the rope for it, so we went on bended knee to Kinnears [rope factory] and asked if they had a rope that could do the job, which they eventually supplied us with.'

The site selected was Bourke Street, an established ski run, but Rob Summers saw the wisdom in separating the tow from the skiers, so he sought and received permission from the Forests Commission (FCV) to cut a trail for the tow south of the ski run with a starting point at what is now known as Helicopter Flat.

'Dad went up for 23 consecutive weekends and I went for 16,' Merrick Summers said. 'We started work in 1948 and had the thing up and running on July 3,1949.'

Once constructed, the rope tow was not always a smooth operation. Overheating, failed bearings, rope-tension and rope-splicing problems plagued it during its first season.

Travel is an education. Some SCV members observed the rope tows in use at the Whakapapa ski field on Mt Ruapehu in New Zealand. 'We realised the New Zealanders had conquered the supported rope principle, so we followed that up and put in three support towers,' Merrick Summers said.

Operating the tow nevertheless remained a challenge, something best left in experienced hands, and those hands generally belonged to people with some engineering ingenuity.

One such operator was John Hilton-Wood. He had been part of the rope tow construction team and, with Cedric Sloane, an Australian cross-country skiing Olympian, had supplied the differential from a troop carrier to help run it.

'I ran that lift in 1950 because I was the only one on the mountain who could splice the rope,' Hilton-Wood said, 'and it used to break regularly.'

He had studied mechanical engineering at Swinburne Technical College and had a touch of the daredevil in him as a motorcycle racer. 'Unfortunately I had a few crashes which weren't my fault, people falling in front of me and that sort of thing.

'I was recovering in hospital with a broken pelvis when a friend said, "I've got a new sport – skiing".'

Hilton-Wood could sense the potential in ski lifts and was encouraged to build Buller's second lift by Ernest Forras, who said he would find him the backing and arrange the necessary permits. It was another rope tow. Hilton-Wood had it operating for the 1953 season and it ran on Bull Run down to the Funnel in the centre of the bowl, a naturally clear area of rock scree.

'I was operating the lift on top of Bull Run and the [Forests Commission] officer, Ken Gibson, came up and said, "You haven't got a licence to operate this lift" and I said, "Ernest told me he had the licence".

'Well, he hadn't … so I said, "Oh well, I'll apply for a licence".' They were simpler days in a bureaucratic sense.

Rob Summers, outside the BMW lodge with the Bourke Street Rope Tow engine house in the background, in September 1958. His vision and enthusiasm led the SCV volunteers who built the tow. MERRICK SUMMERS

Looking up the line of the Bourke Street rope tow in 1954, before the run was cleared of its snow gums. The rope tow was replaced by a T-bar in 1959, built for the fledgling Ski Lifts Mt Buller/Orange Lifts company. JOHN HIRAMS/FORRAS

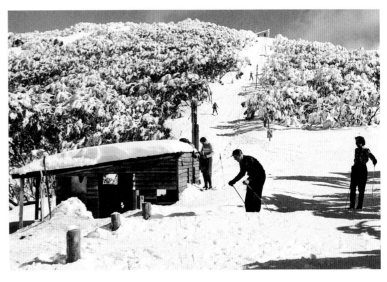

After the first season operating what was essentially a portable rope tow, Hilton-Wood extended the tow to the bottom of Bull Run and built a shed for the motor and a shed for the fuel at the top. 'We could never find the fuel drums – there were heavy snowfalls in those days,' Hilton-Wood said.

It is important to get a sense of the difficulty in riding the tows and in the terrain they were covering. Bull Run has a dramatic pitch; it's a steep run and it becomes more treacherous in hard or icy conditions. Compared with the ease and relative luxury of a chairlift, riding a rope tow could be almost as challenging as the skiing it delivered.

Some used nutcrackers, a device attached to the skier's body that is flipped over the rope and, hopefully, grips to it (they're still in use at some New Zealand club fields).

'It took all your strength to attach [the nutcracker] and keep upright,' Ed Adamson, son of the photographer Edwin Adamson and a long-term Mt Buller skier said.

'The wet or icy rope had to be held by hand while you flipped the open nutcracker shut with your forearm. If you missed the opportunity, you most often lost your grip and rocketed back down the slope in a splayed heap. The steep slope of Bull Run added to the challenge of the ride up.'

Bourke Street in 2003 (right) served by two chairlifts, a small drag lift and snow carpet lifts for beginners. JEAN-MARC LAROQUE

Bourke Street in the late 1950s (below); its popularity led to it being named after the busy Melbourne street and also the clearing of the run to make more room for skiers. The building at top right is Arlberg House. ERIC BURT

John Hilton-Wood bought out the Forras brothers, Aurel and Ernest, and ran the rope tow until 1962, when he replaced it with the Bull Run T-bar.

Varying quantities of skier demand and entrepreneurial enthusiasm had attracted Aurel and Ernest Forras to the mountain. After building the Bull Run Canteen in time to operate for the 1952 season (they were issued a building permit in May, so it was a tight building timeframe), they built the much bigger Kooroora, which opened in 1957, and ran their own portable rope tow from 1957 to 1961.

IN 1956, THE FCV approved a proposal by Maurice Selle to build a ski tow and canteen. The Little Baldy tow, as the Committee of Management referred to it (minutes, May 1956), opened in 1957 and ran until 1962.

Selle, who was said to be 'very British' was an accomplished skier and instructor who taught SCV members and others at Mt Buller and was credited with starting Victoria's first ski rescue service at Mt Buller in 1950 (see chapter 7). He was also a manager of the SCV's Ivor Whittaker Memorial Lodge.

Selle's tow ran on the area now known as Tyrol, from Tyrol Lodge down the current Tyrol lift line. The original Tyrol Lodge housed the engine for the rope tow. The tow ran down about 300 metres from the lodge, not far below the existing track between Spurs and Bourke Street.

In 1959, Hilton-Wood, who went on to operate under the Blue Lifts brand, expanded his ground, opening the Skyline rope tow which ran until 1962 when he replaced it with a T-bar on the same line it still follows.

The BMW Ski Tow Group built the Transportation or Koflers rope tow in 1959 (below) to move skiers from Baldy to the new Koflers hut in the summit area. It was built in part from material salvaged from the Bourke Street rope tow and, according to Merrick Summers, 'it ran without operators and most of the time for no charge.' MERRICK SUMMERS

After playing such a role in building Buller's first lift, some BMW Ski Club members retained their enthusiasm for lift construction and, discovering the next phase of technology – drag lifts like T-bars – secured the Australian agency for the Austrian manufacturer, Doppelmayr.

'We were known as the BMW Ski Tow Group, it was separate from the club, we just used the club as a site office when it was empty,' Merrick Summers said.

The BMW group applied for a permit to build a T-bar on Bourke Street. Around the same time, members of the Yurredla Ski Club applied to build a lift on Federation.

However, in 1959 some of the people behind these projects and others with interests on the mountain formed the non-listed public company Ski Lifts Mt Buller – which later became known as Orange Lifts – and convinced some of the groups applying to build lifts to join them.

Most did, apart from Hilton-Wood and Konrad Koch. In 1959, Koch applied to put in a rope tow in the Chamois area, which was later bought by Hilton-Wood.

Ski Lifts Mt Buller was incorporated on March 26, 1959 with its prospectus issued on April 28, 1959. Its founding chairman was George Chisholm who managed the Australian team for the 1952 (Oslo) and 1956 (Cortina d'Ampezzo) Winter Olympics and was president of the Victorian Ski Association.

Bruce Bretherton, a World War II flying ace who also had a hand in ski retailing and indoor ski centre operations in Melbourne was managing director.

Other board members were Jim Nilsson, Barry Patten, Ian Sutherland, Dick Zatorski, Norman Rothfield, Henry Simon, Eric Burt, Lance Riordan and Griff Morgan.

The 1959 season was preceded by an intense period of activity for Ski Lifts Mt Buller. It bought the Forras brothers' portable tow and the SCV's Bourke Street tow, which was by then operated under lease by Max Otter. It also built the Koflers rope tow,

Merrick Summers (left) and Jim Nilsson riding a T-bar assembly imported from Doppelmayr in Austria after problems with the Australian-made T-bar spring boxes. SUMMERS

two T-bars – Bourke Street and Federation – and an A-frame building to house two slow-running Blackstone diesel engines that generated the electric power for the whole system.

The A-frame was just above the top station of the Bourke Street T-bar and immediately above the A-frame was the start of the Koflers rope tow.

The Koflers (also called Transportation) tow was the precursor of a signature Mt Buller feature – the two-way lift. Skiers could use the same lift to ride up from Bourke Street and ski the Howqua Bowl beneath the summit and ride the lift back over the ridge to ski the Bourke Street or Skyline areas.

In addition to the lifts on the areas it took over and the expansion on Bourke Street and down Federation, Ski Lifts Mt Buller also had the stated objective to 'under contract to the Forests Commission, construct and operate a canteen/refuge on or near Koflers Flat.' (Prospectus, p3)

This was integral to its plan to develop lifts in the area around the summit, claiming as much terrain as it could, for even though it had bought out most of Buller's lift operators it still had a competitor in Hilton-Wood's Bull Run Enterprises (later known as Blue Lifts).

But Ski Lifts Mt Buller had some problems, chiefly of its own making. Technical difficulties with its new T-bar lifts were a substantial drain on the company. 'The T-bar spring boxes were hopeless,' said David Hume, a Melbourne businessman and an original guarantor who went on to become company chairman. 'Every time you got ice on them, the cable would spin out of the box and then they wouldn't retract … the electrical problems were also enormous. It was an absolute disaster,' Hume said.

Within the disaster lay an opportunity for the BMW group. 'We knew the lift company couldn't keep that up so we air-freighted a Doppelmayr [spring box] outfit from Austria and got it on the

The BMW Ski Tow Group's plan (below) for the Transportation or Koflers rope tow was prepared so Ski Lifts Mt Buller/Orange Lifts could cost the project. Even though this was prepared in May 1959, the tow was operating in the 1959 season, towing skiers to the Koflers/summit area and back again. SUMMERS

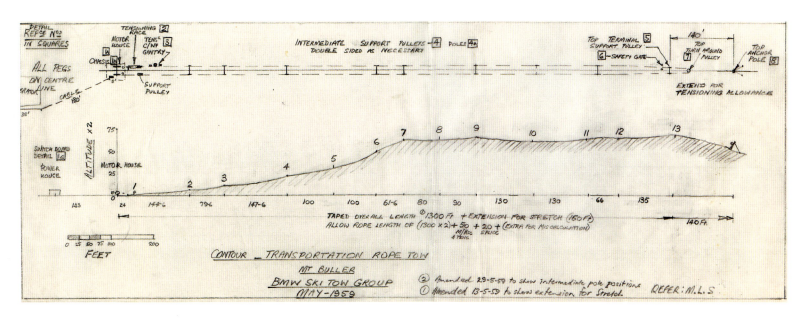

line before the end of the 1959 season,' Merrick Summers said. 'Come 1960, we got the order to replace them all [the T-bar spring boxes]. It was valuable to the company because they didn't get trouble from there on.'

Nevertheless, Ski Lifts Mt Buller was struggling for finance and sought investor funds by expanding its shareholder base. Among the drawcards were a lifetime lift pass and a shareholder-only lift queue. The former feature endured but '… public revolt brought the [exclusive lift queue] to an end,' David Hume said. The financial strains, along with some poor seasons following such an intense period of investment, were a catalyst for change at Ski Lifts Mt Buller. In January 1961, the chairman, George Chisholm asked Hume to take over as chairman.

Hume looked at the books and realised they were poorly positioned. 'I looked through the list of guarantors … and from these I selected a number who had the financial horsepower and, hopefully, the drive to take on the challenge,' Hume said.

It was a summer holiday interruption, with Hume and Jim Nilsson coming from Anglesea and Moggs Creek to meet with other guarantors at Portsea on the Mornington Peninsula, where many of them had houses.

'That meeting agreed with the proposal and

Orange Lifts' not-so-subtle A-frame shed in 1981, with one of the Baldy Pomas in the foreground. MARK ASHKANASY

we then played musical chairs with the board at the annual general meeting. That board had sufficient wit between them, and financial respect, to allow the company to turn around and prosper.'

Bruce Bretherton resigned as managing director and remained a director. Barry Patten also remained as a director, as did Jim Nilsson who was also a member of the BMW group. Griff Morgan remained the company secretary, later becoming a director and Kurt Geiger became chairman, a position he held until moving to London in 1964. (Hume, p4)

ON THE MOUNTAIN, two people who would continue to play a key role in the company's operations emerged as managers of Ski Lifts Mt Buller, first Ernest Forras and then Hans Grimus. Aurel and Ernest Forras had built Kooroora Lodge together (see chapter 15 for more on Kooroora and the Forras brothers) but Aurel bought Ernest's share and Ernest moved into a role managing Ski Lifts Mt Buller's mountain operations for the winters of 1961 and 1962.

SKI LIFTS —
Mt. BULLER LTD.

6d

4 tickets for one T-Bar Lift ride.
2 tickets for one Bourke St. Rope-Tow ride.
1 ticket for one Baldy Rope-Tow ride

Ernest lived at Koflers with his wife Judy, taking in guests on the sly (Hume, p6) and managed the company from loss into profit. He could be an unpredictable manager, however.

'One busy Sunday mid-season a stocky, round-faced Austrian … asked me for a job,' Forras wrote in his autobiography.

'He was lucky. At that very moment I needed a casual worker for a few hours to help out on the Bourke Street T-bar. Although it was snowing, all he had was a jumper – no jacket, no gloves and his backside was hanging out of his pants. I put him to work and went off about my business.

'… at 5pm closing time I suddenly remembered my man on trial at the T-bar. I quickly raced down to Bourke Street and there he was … looking just like a wet, bedraggled snowman. He told me he had missed his lift back to Melbourne and was stranded so I gave him a permanent job and settled him up in the little Black Hut next to the Bull Run Canteen.' (Forras, pp146-147)

The Austrian was Hans Grimus who had a slightly different recollection of the hiring process. Grimus, then a soccer player with little skiing experience, was spending his weekends helping friends build Enzian Lodge when he met Ernest Forras and asked him for a job on the lifts.

Forras said he would send him a telegram and even though it never came, Grimus continued his weekend visits to Mt Buller in winter 1961 and picked up some skiing technique on Bourke Street.

One morning he came across Forras on the mountain. 'I said, "Hey, what about the job?"' Grimus recalled. 'And he said to me he was very busy with a lot of snow and so forth, anyway, he asked me, "Can you ski?"

'I said, yes I could a little bit, so he got me some big goggles and a hat and took me down Federation.

'I nearly died. Halfway down Ernest left me,' Grimus said.

This is the surfing equivalent of taking a novice out at Bells Beach in a six-metre swell and leaving them to work out how to catch the wave and then ride it.

Federation is seductively clear on the ridge top, but once it sucks skiers into its bowl, it is very steep and difficult to navigate.

The bottom station of the T-bar was perched precariously above a steep drop – a net was positioned there to catch unfortunate skiers who failed to stop and was put to use on many occasions. But Grimus survived. 'Somehow I worked my way down and got the T-bar back to Bourke Street.

'He [Ernest] couldn't believe it when he saw me there and so he gave me a job on the Bourke Street T-bar.

'He just said, "Push and smile, push and smile". He didn't tell me there was a stop button; didn't tell me there was a phone.

'Then some bad weather came through, it started raining, I had no lunch and no one came to relieve me.

'At five o'clock everyone went home, so I thought I may as well go home too.'

In the 1950s, before there were lifts in the area, John Hilton-Wood used his Tucker Sno-Cat to take skiers from Bourke Street to ski the summit slopes for 10 shillings a ride. ERIC BURT

An illustration from the 1959 prospectus of Ski Lifts Mt Buller and a unique, arched T-bar tower concept that didn't quite take off. GADSDEN Inset (below) is the pass of one of the company guarantors, Bruce Dyson. NAMA

hood wasn't easy – he met his father for the first time when he was 14, when he went to live with him – and it was tough-going in post-war Europe.

Grimus and some friends made a pact to travel to Australia and after he completed his national service for Austria, he was ready to go. His friends weren't. Grimus made the trip alone and recalls the ship docking in Port Melbourne in early 1960. Soccer club officials met the ship, as was their practice, to spot some recruits.

'We were like cattle,' Grimus said. 'If you had a blue mark someone was going to pick you up, if you had a yellow mark you go to Bonegilla [the migrant reception centre near Wodonga].

'Some people had seen me playing in Austria and they said, "The fellow with the beard plays a reasonable game."

'So these Yugoslavs chased me around. I had already been marked to go to Bonegilla, and this fellow explained to me that they ran a soccer club and said if I played for them, he could guarantee me a job.

'So I went with them, I went up to Olympic Park and had to sign something, I didn't know what I signed and then they took me to Young and Jackson's [the hotel on the corner of Flinders and Swanston Streets in Melbourne] and then they took me off to Geelong.'

The club was Croatia. Grimus said playing soccer in those days 'was like a war – it was shocking,' but life was an adventure for a 19-year-old Austrian in a new land.

He played for the club for a time and worked at a refinery in Altona in his trade of carpentry, hitchhiking backwards and forwards from his home in North Geelong.

He had heard about the Snowy Mountains Scheme and soon made for Cabramurra via Cooma, working on the scheme from January to October in 1960.

He returned to Melbourne to play soccer again, first for the Croatian club and then for the Austrian club, when he met some of the founders of Enzian Lodge, who gave him his introduction to Mt Buller.

Grimus became a capable skier and a crucial part of the operation at Mt Buller.

Ernest Forras took him to the Kinnears rope factory in Melbourne where they learned to splice ropes, an essential skill to keep the cantankerous rope tows in operation.

Then, during the 1962 winter, the great Norwegian skier Stein Eriksen appeared on the mountain as part of a world tour for the making of John Jay's movie, *Winter Magic Around the World*. 'And Ernest just took off,' Grimus said. 'He went to Albury to play tennis with Eriksen and then went with him to Thredbo. He didn't say a word, didn't say what was going on or who should be running the show … and then the rope broke and we had to run up a new rope.

The next day, Sunday, Grimus reported for work again, interested in Forras' offer of a permanent job. He thought he should at least straighten out the job conditions.

'I said, "Look Ernest, I know I can't have lunch the way this show operates, but if I take the job I have to go home at three o'clock. My friends, they're going home at three o'clock, and I'll go home to Melbourne to pick up my gear and come back up."

'He said, "Yeah, yeah, yeah," and he was off again. I pushed and smiled and there was no lunch, three o'clock and no one relieved me, you had to push the people, you just couldn't run away.

'At five o'clock the lift stopped, so I went over to Enzian. All my mates had gone home so I had to hitchhike back to Melbourne.'

Grimus wondered if he should take the job, but he was enchanted by the mountain and its people and returned for the season, living some of the time in Enzian, some of the time in the youth hostel, some of the time in the Bull Run Canteen.

As a lift operator, he would collect tickets and load skiers who paid sixpence a ticket and handed him one ticket for a rope tow ride and five tickets for the T-bar.

Although Austrian, Grimus was not a skier. He was born in Austria's north, near the Czech border, one of the rare parts of Austria that isn't entirely surrounded by mountains. His child-

'After a few days who comes back, but Ernest. He started screaming and I said, "Look Ernest, you haven't been here, you don't know what's happening, we had to run a new rope, splice it, everything is going now so don't come and scream at us".'

Despite the occasional friction, Grimus believes Ernest Forras deserves more credit than he ever received for the success of Ski Lifts Mt Buller.

'In 1961 we took £16,000 … and then in 1962 we took £32,000; doubled it, suddenly, from everything going wrong it's very rosy.'

Forras moved on from Mt Buller, heading for Smiggin Holes, the neighbouring resort to Perisher Valley in the Snowy Mountains, to run a new hotel there.

The improvement in Ski Lifts Mt Buller's financial health underpinned the investment in the Shaky Knees T-bar for the 1963 winter, by which time Grimus was in charge of lifts and ticketing.

'That lift (Shaky Knees) used to be called Swanston Street,'

A tunnel was used by skiers for access from Bourke Street, underneath Orange Lifts' Baldy Pomas, out to the terrain served by Blue Lifts' Bull Run lift. The building is the Bull Run drive station which also served as Blue Lifts' staff accommodation. Near that building was the Bull Run Canteen and, later, the Fawlty Towers staff accommodation. This photograph was taken in 1974. CHRIS HILTON-WOOD

Grimus said. 'And people got really uptight about it, they accepted Bourke Street but not Swanston Street.

'Then Blue Lifts put Skyline in and that used to be called Little Collins Street … there was a real uproar and we had to rename it, so Swanston Street became Shaky Knees and then Little Collins Street became Skyline.'

Shaky Knees was an adoption of the ski run it served, a name given to it by Helmut Kofler. It was a statement on the condition of a skier's legs when they finally arrived at Chalet Creek.

Colour code

BEFORE THEY WERE united in 1985, the two lift companies were known as Blue and Orange, a simple enough distinction for skiers based on the colour of the respective company's lift towers.

But it wasn't always as clear-cut. John Hilton-Wood (of Bull Run Enterprises/Blue Lifts) initially painted his lift towers orange for the simple reason that he 'got a cheap rate on orange paint.'

However, when Ski Lifts Mt Buller was established in 1959, he wanted to distinguish his lifts from theirs and so he started to paint his lift towers blue. It wasn't until 1976 that orange became the overall colour of choice for Ski Lifts Mt Buller (until then, it was known locally as 'Ski Lifts'). One of its directors, Jim Nilsson, was behind the colour choice. He had attended a lecture by the Australian explorer and scientist Dr Phillip Law who explained that equipment and clothing in the Antarctic were coloured orange for better visibility. (Hume, p2)

For this reason, the company started painting all its towers orange, leading to the name Orange Lifts.

LIFT TECHNOLOGY WAS on the march. David Hume recalled a visit to Perisher in 1963 along with Kurt Geiger and Jim Nilsson to look at a new style of drag lift manufactured by the French company, Pomagalski.

There are few still in operation in Australia (Falls Creek's International Poma is the best example) and none at Mt Buller any longer, although some of its Poma lifts have found a new life at Ben Lomond in Tasmania.

The Poma lift also had the quality of being able to change direction, take dog-leg turns along its line, something aerial lifts cannot do and something that can be done with a T-bar, although it creates big challenges for their paired-up riders.

Also in those early years, the initial failure of the Bourke Street and Federation T-bar spring boxes added to the appeal of the Poma lift. The Poma hangers are spring-loaded for comfort with a button (like a frisbee) on the bottom to pull the skier along. An advantage for Mt Buller was that they detached from the main cable for storage, whereas the T-bar spring box remained in a fixed position on the lift cable.

In Mt Buller's climate, extreme ice overnight could 'build an immense weight on the cables,' David Hume said.

With the Poma hangers stored off the cable, they could be kept out of the worst of the icing weather. Mt Buller also joined other Australian resorts in the practice of running lift cables slowly overnight to prevent icing.

Looking down Bourke Street to the village in the bumper 1964 winter. ERIC BURT

'Both Doppelmayr and Pomagalski took convincing as to the severity of the ice build-up until they were sent photos,' David Hume said. Doppelmayr found it so remarkable it reproduced one of the images as a Christmas card.

Grimus adapted well to the mountain operations. Force of character and his early training in carpentry underpinned the skills he gained in lift construction and operation.

'I remember him appearing out of an ornery lift engine room covered in grease but with a smile on his face and a cheery word once the lift was working again,' skier Ed Adamson said.

One early task was to replace the Koflers rope tow with the Summit Access/Howqua Poma in 1964 which, like its predecessor, lifted skiers in both directions.

Improved access into the area also enabled the development of the summit slopes for the first time in 1964, with the construction of a Poma lift.

Lift construction was difficult and demanded some creativity. Grimus recalls using a tractor to run out the long cable for the Summit Access/Howqua Poma. It was crucial the cable wasn't kinked on the ground before it was spliced and tensioned into position.

Hans Grimus and his dog Captain (on skis) in a publicity shot for the Melbourne *Herald* newspaper in 1972. The irony is that Grimus, then Orange Lifts' general manager, is riding Blue Lifts' Bourke Street chairlift. GRAHAM WELSH/*HERALD*

They had portable radios, walkie-talkies, but these early models had very limited cover, so to call an emergency stop on the cable-lay, warning shots from a .303 rifle were used.

There were other problems leading into the 1964 season. It was an embarrassment of riches with heavy snow falls starting in May and pre-winter construction work incomplete.

Orange lifts had bought the old Tyrol Lodge, which had gone into receivership. The purchase was more to secure the site and the profitable Shaky Knees lift against the risk of Hilton-Wood's expansion than to get into the accommodation game.

'We had to buy it, firstly to protect our Shaky Knees territory and secondly to expand our north side development,' Hume said.

Grimus and some of his colleagues lived in the draughty old building in the 1964 season.

'There was no heating, no firewood. We used to dig down to get into the door and when you got up in the morning your boots were still icy,' Grimus said.

'A couple of mornings we woke up and it was all blown in, we had to shovel the snow inside in the lounge room so we could get out to work.'

The heavy winter had a compounding effect and towards its end, Grimus developed pleurisy and pneumonia.

He couldn't be moved to Mansfield, for fear of the effect of the change in altitude and air pressure so he spent a few weeks recuperating in the staff quarters.

The 1964 winter proved abundant but tough. Over the following summer, Tyrol Lodge was repaired and expanded to provide additional staff accommodation for Orange Lifts.

Bull Run Enterprises was also expanding, replacing its Bull Run rope tow with a T-bar in 1962 and installing the Skyline T-bar in 1963 – the latter is essentially operating as the same lift today.

For the winter of 1964, Hilton-Wood installed the Bourke Street chairlift. 'It was the first Doppelmayr double chair in the world,' he said. 'They were all single up to that date.'

Like many in the field, Hilton-Wood delights in the engineering of ski lifts, but the Bourke Street lift had its challenges.

'The loading ramp was only 20 feet [six metres] long which was all right for a single chair, but [for a double chair] we had to double the length of the ramp and chop the first and top towers and move them the next year.

'In other words, Doppelmayr learned at our expense. They supplied the running gear, we built everything ourselves, all the towers and everything,' he said.

Stylish 1960s skiers, Jon Hutchison and his wife-to-be Jill Hobson on the Bourke Street chairlift. TREVOR LEMKE/NAMA

Hilton-Wood even had the wire rope cable manufactured locally, from Inglis Smith who said they would guarantee it for 20 years.

'In America they reckon in the early days if you got six or seven years that was a good life. This one was a galvanised cable with a steel core, which was very unusual in those days – most of them had a hemp core and they were not galvanised, they were just black.

'Well, that lift ran from 1964 to 1983 and we never had a moment's trouble with the cable. Never.

'We ended up cutting it up into 100-foot [30-metre] lengths and selling it to the local tractor operators for their winches and it was still in beautiful condition,' Hilton-Wood said.

WITH ITS OWNERSHIP limited to John Hilton-Wood and his wife Marjorie's family, the Alstegrens, Blue Lifts remained stable at the top, even if it didn't expand at the same pace as Orange Lifts.

By contrast, Orange Lifts had a transformation in ownership in the 1970s. With the 1972 purchase of the magazine publisher, KG Murray Publishing, Kerry Packer's Australian Consolidated Press found itself owner of the lifts and other assets at Perisher Valley in the Snowy Mountains.

In early 1977, Harold Droga, Packer's manager at Perisher, made an approach to Orange Lifts with a $1.5 million takeover offer for the company. The deal would have been completed after the 1977 winter.

David Hume was by then vice-chairman of Orange Lifts and was also a member of the Melbourne Stock Exchange – he knew the value of Orange Lifts shares and knew that this represented the best value ever offered. He also understood the potential.

Bruce Wenzel, the company chairman, asked Hume for his opinion of the offer.

'And I said, "Well, Bruce, I've been running the book on all of our share transfers since the beginning and we have never seen the price equal to this, so therefore I am bound to say that I have to recommend the bid.

"On the other hand, you couldn't replace the assets on Mt Buller for $1.5 million, if you'd get a permit to do it, so I'm going to get about counter bidding it".'

Hume kept the board informed of his bid to avoid any conflict of interest and argued that, at worst, it would motivate Packer to increase his offer.

Hume spent the 1977 winter attempting to secure investors for his $2 million bid and struggled. Hume, Griff Morgan and Hans Grimus each committed to invest $100,000.

'Jim Nilsson agreed also, but for a smaller amount, and Barry Patten said he would think about it. The rest of the board had no interest in the scheme,' he said. 'I must say that I was getting pretty desperate about this stage,' Hume said. 'I thought, well, I've given it the best shot I can and I'm not going to get there.

'Then Garrick Gray (a Melbourne solicitor) rang and said he was interested.'

Together they created a scheme where each $10,000 investment unit had a Gold Pass, a transferable pass to use Orange Lifts, attached to it.

This appealed to investors. To make up the shortfall the new company borrowed $500,000 from Veall's Securities, a Melbourne-based business that later bought the Cardrona ski field in New Zealand's South Island.

BLUE SKI LIFTS MT. BULLER
BULL RUN ENTERPRISES PTY. LTD.
CHAIRLIFT   BULL RUN   SKYLINE   WHITTAKER   CHAMOIS

PRICES 1969 SEASON

DAY TICKETS, $3 ADULTS.
CHILDREN (Under 13), $2 DAY TICKET.
SINGLE RIDES, 20 cents ALL LIFTS.
MORNING ONLY TICKET, 9 - 1, $2.00.
AFTERNOON ONLY TICKET, 1 - 5, $2.00.
WEEKLY, $17 ADULTS, $11 CHILDREN.

CLUB CONCESSION

Any Bona Fide Club purchasing 16 or more Day Tickets, $2 per day each

PACKAGE DEAL

Mid-week MONDAY to FRIDAY, Daily Lift Tickets including Instruction from FRENCH SKI SCHOOL, $3 per day (to 18th July).

FRENCH SKI SCHOOL

14 Instructors catering for all standards from beginners to racing.
CLASS LESSONS, $2 for 2 hours, at 10 a.m. and 2 p.m., every day. Assembly point, Chair Lift Station opposite Kooroora.

PRIVATE LESSONS, $6 per hour, by appointment.

Blue Lifts' ticket options in 1969. NAMA

'We stuck our bid in,' David Hume said, fully expecting Packer to outbid it. 'Well, Kerry didn't come over the top. He withdrew, said "see you later", and we got it.'

That was the end of Ski Lifts Mt Buller and the birth of Mt Buller Ski Lifts, with a board comprising Garrick Gray, Rodney Davidson, Colin Coghill, Griff Morgan, Hans Grimus and David Hume as chairman. Later directors included John Clemenger, Jim Nilsson and Colin Toll.

THE 1970s AND early 1980s were a period of enormous growth in Australian skiing and resort infrastructure expanded accordingly. Even so, the pace of development at Mt Buller probably outstripped the rest of the country, partly because of the competition between lift companies.

'It was a bloody punch-up all the time really,' Dr Ron Grose, the Forests Commission's chairman of Mt Buller's Committee of Management from 1967 to 1981 said.

'There were some pretty high-flyers on the board of Orange Lifts and they knew how to make things happen.

'John [Hilton-Wood] was a nice fellow but he didn't have the punch that those other buggers had.'

Hans Grimus recalls the battle fondly. 'I always said it was the best thing ever. When you had two girlfriends coming up, you bought one a ticket on the Blue Lifts and got the other one on the Orange Lifts!

'But what many people don't realise is that it was such an important factor for the Australian ski industry because the two companies pushed each other. Blue Lifts put in the first chairlift in 1964 and we wanted something better,' Grimus said.

John Hilton-Wood agreed both companies were inclined to invest to keep up with each other.

'That's why Buller actually developed far faster than any of the other resorts, because we went lift for lift for lift,' Hilton-Wood said.

David Hume said Orange Lifts' growth came more from the coincidence of new lift technology and a crucial economic and political decision. The Federal Government brought the tourist industry into its investment allowance scheme and that had the effect of allowing a company such as Orange Lifts to claim a 120 per cent depreciation for a ski lift over five years. It had previously been restricted to an annual rate of 7.5 per cent.

At the same time, Doppelmayr invented the triple chairlift. Up until then, a double chair cost twice as much as a T-bar but had the same capacity. 'We therefore stayed with T-bars to preserve our scarce capital, but now you could buy a (higher capacity) triple for not much more than a double,' Hume said.

So Hume developed a plan that Orange Lifts adopted where they built a major new lift each year.

Lifts lining up everywhere; the revolution with chairlifts was to remove uphill transport from the slopes and give skiers and boarders much faster turnaround. Here, in 1978, most people are riding the Summit Pomas or are in the queue; relatively few are on the slopes. BILL BACHMAN

'By 1984, we had the largest lifting capacity in Australia, with the most modern equipment. We took the view that if one provided the new capacity, the skiers would come. And they did,' Hume said.

Ironically, the same breakthrough that brought in the triple chairlift would have allowed the immediate implementation of quad chairlifts.

David Hume later asked the creator of the triple chair, Artur Doppelmayr, why he didn't move straight to the four-seater.

'He said it was because the Austrian Government wouldn't let him build them, they told him the jump from two to four was too big, he had to start with three … and that cost the whole world.'

Nevertheless, the creation of the triple chairlift underpinned the creation of one of the world's highest capacity lift systems at Mt Buller.

molony's
SKI SHOP

Skis   Clothing
Boots   Hire
110 KING STREET MELBOURNE
TELEPHONE 62-7387

The first of the lifts was the Grimus triple chairlift, which opened in the 1979 winter, followed by Burnt Hut in 1980 and Federation in 1981. The Federation lift went much lower than the T-bar it replaced, thus opening up Little Buller Spur for skiers.

By this time, Blue Lifts had built its Baldy double chairlift (1974) and maintained its investment in surface lifts, such as Enzian Poma (1979), Sun Valley Poma (1980) and the Village T-Bar (1982) replacing the Whittaker Poma and running further down towards Chalet Creek.

It was this latter area on the northern slopes that saw a development proposal that reflected most dramatically the intensity of competition on the mountain.

THE COMPLEXITY OF interests in a mountain resort is one of its most fascinating features, even if it can be one of the most frustrating features for the people entwined in those interests.

It is in the nature of business that competitors will push for an advantage or attempt to defend the ground they believe they have gained. No event illustrates this struggle as well as the development of the Horse Hill lift and associated businesses.

A Horse Hill lift had been contemplated as early as 1959, in a proposal put to the Committee of Management for a chairlift from Horse Hill to an area near the Ski Club of Victoria's lodge in the village. (minutes, October 1959)

Bob Pullin, a Mansfield resident with a local car dealership, recalled approaching the Committee of Management, in the late 1970s, with another plan.

'I knew that the car parking at Buller was eight miles long and one car wide, so I thought there must be a different way.'

To Pullin, Horse Hill was the logical location for denser car parking and he envisaged a development that included transfer facilities for overnight visitors, a lift, petrol station and skating rink in one location.

The lift, to be built by John Hilton-Wood's Blue Lifts, would have run from the Horse Hill car parking area to the village. 'People would unload their gear (luggage and supplies) into a sled and Billy Heathcote would pull the sled up,' Pullin said.

'We were going to have a petrol station there as well, at the base of the chair.

'So I went to the Committee of Management and they said it couldn't be done. I'd done a lot of work on it, had surveys done and so forth, had involved engineers. They said they couldn't give me a permit to do it and then the following year they did it themselves,' Pullin said.

The construction of the Horse Hill car park was undertaken and completed by the Committee of Management. With that project under way, the committee received another proposal at its October 1979 meeting.

David Hume credits Hans Grimus with the refinement of the idea for Orange Lifts. Most related proposals included car parking and a staging area for day visitors in the Horse Hill/Skating Rink area but the Orange Lifts plan was for a new lift operating from that point to the top of Dam Run.

It meant day visitors wouldn't have to go through the village to start skiing, reducing congestion in the village and accelerating day visitor access to the slopes. The plan called for a detachable chairlift that would have been Australia's first. On such a lift, the chair detaches from the main cable for loading, unloading and storage, vastly increasing cable speed and overall capacity.

David Hume said they were given support for the concept by their landlord, the Forests Commission, so his board opted for

Mountain politics forced the Horse Hill chairlift to be a fixed-grip triple in its first incarnation, rather than the higher speed detachable quad that was originally planned for the site and that it later became.
BILL BACHMAN

SKI LIFTS — MT. BULLER LIMITED

(Incorporated under the Companies Act 1938 of Victoria on 26th March, 1959)

PROSPECTUS

of an Issue at Par of 40,000 Shares of £1 each
Payable in Full on Application

AUTHORISED CAPITAL

100,000 Shares of £1 each	£100,000

SHARES TAKEN BY THE SUBSCRIBERS TO THE MEMORANDUM OF ASSOCIATION

5 Shares of £1 each fully paid	£5

SHARES NOW OFFERED FOR SUBSCRIPTION

40,000 Shares of £1 each	£40,000

UNISSUED SHARES

59,995 Shares of £1 each	£59,995
100,000	£100,000

This Prospectus is dated the twenty-eighth day of April, 1959.
A Copy of this Prospectus has been lodged for registration with the Registrar of Companies of the State of Victoria.

The operators

DATES INDICATE THE year of establishment of the group or company or the year of a change in ownership.

1948 – Ski Club of Victoria ski-tow sub-committee.

1953 – Hilton-Wood Enterprises.

1959 – Bull Run Enterprises (previously Hilton-Wood Enterprises, later known as Blue Lifts).

1959 – Ski Lifts Mt Buller (later known as Orange Lifts).

1977 – Mt Buller Ski Lifts takes over Ski Lifts Mt Buller, still known as Orange Lifts.

1984 – Bourke Street Ski Lift Company/Buller Ski Enterprises (owned equally by Macmahon Holdings and Blue Lifts).

1985 – Buller Ski Enterprises buys Orange Lifts.

1991 – Macmahon Holdings buys out Blue Lifts to become sole owner of Buller Ski Enterprises.

1992 – Rino and Diana Grollo's Mt Buller Investments buy 80 per cent of Buller Ski Enterprises.

1993 – Grollo family buys remainder of Buller Ski Enterprises, renaming it Buller Ski Lifts.

---

a detachable triple with detached load/unload points near Chalet Creek and at the halfway point, virtually level with the Tyrol T-bar's current mid-load point.

With these added load points, the lift could be as much a ski lift as an access lift.

Also integral to the plan were a restaurant, ski hire, ski and storage lockers and other facilities split between the base and a terminal building located between the top stations of what are now the Burnt Hut Spur and Horse Hill chairlifts.

The Orange Lifts board put in an order with Doppelmayr for a detachable triple chairlift with four separate loading/unloading stations along its line – a technically very complex and sophisticated lift.

There were numerous ski hire and restaurant operators on the mountain at the time and they united to oppose the development. Ironically, Hans Grimus, who had left Orange Lifts in 1980 and was running Pension Grimus with a restaurant and ski hire of its own, was among the objectors. They weren't necessarily against the lift, but they saw Orange Lifts' entry into the ski hire and restaurant businesses, particularly at these locations, as giving it too strong a hand.

Hume argued that an expected growth rate of 10 per cent for five years would mean 'all ski hirers will have increased business and any possible effect of the proposed Horse Hill ski hire on the village ski hirers will be absorbed.' (minutes, July 1980)

To combat the objections, which were being heard through the Committee of Management meetings but culminated in the form of a writ, Orange Lifts sought an opinion from a senior barrister, a Queen's Counsel.

'The QC's opinion was very simple,' David Hume said. 'All the Forests Commission had to do was tell the objectors that they had listened to their objections and they were being overruled and we were to go ahead and finalise the contract.'

Hume contacted the resort management board chairman Ron Grose and showed him the QC's opinion.

Hume maintains Grose had initially been an enthusiastic supporter of the project, however by this point he had turned against it as a result of the objections – something Grose was authorised and entitled to do in his position. 'He never discussed that with me, he just said, "I'm just not going to do it".'

The Committee of Management also had reservations about the safety of non-skiers who would use the lift.

The ski hire and restaurant – and their revenue – were central to the project. Without them, Orange Lifts was forced to go back to Doppelmayr, cancel the order for the detachable lift and replace it with an order for a fixed-grip triple chairlift.

'We saved about $1.25 million. We all knew it was a terrible decision on day one but we did it anyway. We very nearly lost Doppelmayr as a friend,' Hume said.

The battle and its fallout accounts for the bizarre location of the current load station of Horse Hill – a few formidable flights of stairs below the car park and the ski hire.

The ski hire that eventually went ahead was a cooperative venture of the mountain's ski hire operators, excluding Orange Lifts. It was located at the base of the lift rather than its top terminal, as originally proposed by Orange Lifts, and has now become part of Buller Ski Lifts' Buller Sports operation.

To underline the fit of lift and location, one of the first projects of Buller Ski Enterprises, when it had bought both Buller lift companies, was to replace the Horse Hill triple with a quad detachable chairlift. However, the detaching mid-load/unload stations have never been installed.

THERE ARE NUMEROUS examples throughout the skiing world, particularly in Europe, of separate companies owning lifts within a resort, but in almost all cases, they negotiate a single ticket for the convenience of customers and divide the spoils according to an agreed formula, or more recently, using tracking technology.

John McDonald, who with John Hilton-Wood created the Bourke Street Ski Lift Company and Buller Ski Enterprises that in 1985 bought out Orange Lifts to create a single lift company, after 32 years of division.
MARK ASHKANASY

Blue and Orange did occasionally agree on a split and sold a joint ticket, but David Hume said the price was 'always set a little too high, so ticket sales were never large.'

Hume said he approached John Hilton-Wood every year for 18 years to see if they could turn their two companies into one but they could never agree on terms.

'We were at school together and were never close friends but were never enemies, Hume said.

Hilton-Wood eventually responded to another move: 'I was approached by Macmahons to sell them half the company, which I did,' Hilton-Wood said. The new business was known as the Bourke Street Ski Lift Company.

John McDonald, then chief executive of the South Australian mining and construction company, Macmahon Holdings, was a Mt Buller enthusiast. Under McDonald, Macmahon Holdings invested in Breathtaker Lodge and later the Pinnacle Valley complex. Macmahon Holdings succeeded, where others had failed, in negotiating a stake in Blue Lifts.

McDonald purchased some parcels of shares in Orange Lifts and this gave him a better understanding of the way the mountain operated. The Horse Hill debacle was soon overshadowed by the creation of the Bourke Street Ski Lift Company and its stunning investment, for the time, in the Blue Bullet 1 and 2 quad detachable chairlifts on the Bourke Street to Baldy route.

Around the time this project was receiving Government approval – in 1983 – David Hume, still chairman of Orange Lifts, was called in to see Rod Mackenzie, the Victorian Cain Labor government's minister for conservation, forests and lands. Mackenzie explained that he was going to give Blue Lifts/the Bourke Street Ski Lift Company a permit for their new lift and he was willing to grant Orange Lifts a permit to build a similar lift.

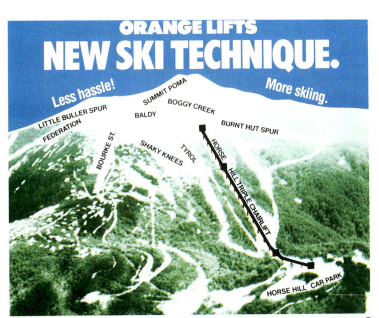

Lift company marketing in the 1980s. NAMA

David Hume; the guiding hand for Orange Lifts as its chairman and later a guiding hand for the industry as chairman of the Australian Ski Areas Association and the Alpine Resorts Commission. He is pictured here in his early years as Orange Lifts' chairman. HUME

FOR THE 1984 season, a joint lift ticket was offered to skiers – $25 a day to use both companies' lifts, compared with $22 for an Orange day ticket and $19 a day on Blue Lifts.

In November 1984, Macmahon Holdings announced a $12.7 million takeover bid for Orange Lifts. Each of the 137 $10,000 parcels that investors had bought in 1976 were bought for $92,500 by Macmahon, with their Gold Passes intact (although the status of those Gold Passes has fluctuated in the years since). The offer was accepted unanimously. Including the value of the Gold Passes, 'the shareholders … multiplied their money more than 11.5 times in eight years, tax-free,' David Hume said.

At the time of the Macmahon takeover, it was 'ascertained that Orange had enjoyed about 85 per cent of the trade and Blue Lifts 15 per cent.' (Hume, p25)

Given the balance of business over the years, with Blue buying Orange there was a sense that David had taken over Goliath.

Even if that discounts the capability of a business the size of Macmahon Holdings, it does acknowledge John Hilton-Wood, a Mt Buller pioneer.

'Buller would never be anything without bringing those two lift companies together,' John McDonald said. 'I would regard that as the principal difference we made, that and bringing the professional engineering skills of Macmahon Holdings to the mountain.'

Hume didn't believe there was sufficient demand or space to justify duplicated chairlifts along Bourke Street from Cow Camp to Baldy, but he countered with another proposal. He explained that his competitors would have to build two lifts, not one, because they couldn't find a straight line between Cow Camp and the site they were entitled to use on Baldy.

Hume offered to remove Orange Lifts' duplex Pomas on Baldy, creating a clear line for the new lift, if the two companies could come together and jointly own the new lift.

He was asked to 'come back tomorrow.' So he returned the following day to see the minister. As Hume recalled: 'Mackenzie said, "I've given them a permit to do it and I want to give you a permit to build the same thing." and I said, "We're not going to apply, Minister, thank you very much, but I want you to know you've made a terrible mistake today".

'If we'd taken our lifts out of there we could have put a straight line in. We would have owned half of it each, which would have been the starting point to amalgamate the two companies on some sort of a sensible basis,' Hume said.

With their permit in hand, Hilton-Wood and McDonald were under enormous pressure to get the lift built. Given that it was late November 1983, their construction window was small and closing. Doppelmayr eventually offered them a two-part quad detachable chairlift that had been ordered for Breckenridge in Colorado, managing to delay delivery to that resort given the later starting date of the northern season.

It was a busy summer on the mountain. Orange Lifts built two fixed-grip quad chairlifts, Howqua and the Summit, which, like the Blue Bullet 1 and 2 lifts, opened for the 1984 winter.

Despite his disappointment with the outcome on Bourke Street, Hume conceded that 'Macmahons did a good job from an engineering point of view.'

The balance was shifting.

A dashing John Hilton-Wood and his wife Marjorie (Alstegren – a family successful in business in Melbourne). HILTON-WOOD

Hans Grimus recalled the landmark. 'When they bought Orange Lifts, the next day he [John Hilton-Wood] bought paint brushes and blue paint and every man on the mountain had to paint the towers blue! That was the happiest day in his life.'

After years of competition, Mt Buller had a world-class lift system, even if the battle had left it with some scars like an unnecessarily disjointed pair of Blue Bullets and an inconvenient load at Horse Hill.

At the time of the two companies coming together in 1985, they had a combined stable of 23 lifts capable of moving more than 20,000 people per hour – a capacity similar to some of the larger US resorts such as Vail in Colorado.

'The existence of two lifting companies on the mountain was strongly supported by the Forests Commission in the mistaken belief it would lead to better service and cheaper prices,' David Hume wrote.

'It did neither. Some of the lifts on the mountain were built to prevent the other [company] from expanding and a study of lift prices in Australia shows that Orange Lifts did not place its prices below those of competing areas.' (Hume, p25)

Following the departure of Hans Grimus as Orange Lifts' general manager in 1980, Bob Bateup – who became mountain manager and operations manager – filled the role temporarily. Grimus' eventual replacement was an army colonel, a Vietnam veteran and former tank commander, Colin Toll.

Michael Monester, photographed in 1989. The former ski patrol captain returned to Mt Buller as the chief executive of a united lift company, bringing new levels of customer service, partly as a result of his North American experience. MARK ASHKANASY

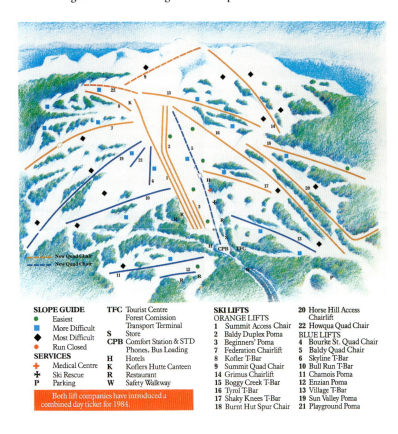

Part of the mountain's welcoming of a joint-ticket in 1984 was a joint trail map. There was some anticipation at the time that some unity might be created among the lift companies. NAMA

SLOPE GUIDE
- ● Easiest
- ■ More Difficult
- ◆ Most Difficult
- ● Run Closed

SERVICES
- ✚ Medical Centre
- ✢ Ski Rescue
- P Parking

TFC Tourist Centre
Forest Comission
Transport Terminal
S Store
CPB Comfort Station & STD Phones, Bus Loading
H Hotels
K Koflers Hutte Canteen
R Restaurant
W Safety Walkway

SKI LIFTS
ORANGE LIFTS
1 Summit Access Chair
2 Baldy Duplex Poma
3 Beginners' Poma
7 Federation Chairlift
8 Kofler T-Bar
9 Summit Quad Chair
14 Grimus Chairlift
15 Boggy Creek T-Bar
16 Tyrol T-Bar
17 Shaky Knees T-Bar
18 Burnt Hut Spur Chair

20 Horse Hill Access Chairlift
22 Howqua Quad Chair
BLUE LIFTS
4 Bourke St. Quad Chair
5 Baldy Quad Chair
6 Skyline T-Bar
10 Bull Run T-Bar
11 Chamois Poma
12 Enzian Poma
13 Village T-Bar
19 Sun Valley Poma
21 Playground Poma

Both lift companies have introduced a combined day ticket for 1984.

He 'took command on April 1, 1981 and soon earned the respect of those about him … he was a remarkably competent manager and took the company through the next growth stage.' (Hume, p22)

Toll resigned after the 1986 ski season, having managed first Orange Lifts and then the Bourke Street Ski Lift Company through the transition. He was replaced by a former Mt Buller ski patrol captain, Michael Monester.

Monester's profession was law but a passion for the mountains saw him pursuing a career in the ski industry, first in Canada and then at Silver Creek, a small resort in Colorado, which he was running when the Mt Buller job became available.

The interviewing process involved a telephone conference call, unusual at the time. 'We had a chat for a while and they said, "Can you send us a 20-minute video, a day in the life of Michael Monester".

'This was a John McDonald creation, at the time I thought it was absurd but in retrospect it was a touch of genius. I think it is probably one of the best ways to interview someone from afar,' Monester said.

He started as the general manager of the Bourke Street Ski Lift Company in February 1987. He'd had a five-year absence from the mountain since his patrolling days and on his return, he found the change remarkable.

'Colin [Toll] had revolutionised Buller. He was military and he set up systems and made people accountable,' Monester said.

The emphasis Monester sought to bring to Mt Buller when he returned was on customer service. It was due for an overhaul; when he'd left Buller in 1981, there was a sign on the ski patrol door saying 'No turkeys (tourists) allowed'. By the time he returned, Australian ski resorts were facing growing competition from New Zealand snow fields and Queensland resorts. It was time to make the mountain operate more for the customer than the staff.

Monester had won US recognition at Silver Creek for customer service. He applied some of the principles at Mt Buller.

'First of all I employed people on the basis of their personality. I focused on people who were going to be good to the guests; the right attitude is the essence of good customer relations.

'You can't tell people to be nice, but you can demonstrate the power and rewards generated from a smile or a good deed. I had 300 staff on the mountain; if each one only gave three favours a day to customers, that was 900 good things happening each day. That generates a good feeling which is the best marketing you can have. There's no effort required, just an attitude, and the rewards on both sides are exponential,' Monester said.

The problem was, people who were good with guests often did not have the disposition to be good with equipment. This initially drove the maintenance crew to distraction.

'But I persevered, I explained to the maintenance people that you can train people to do the mechanics but no one can train someone to smile.'

Monester oversaw the construction of the South Side quad chairlift in 1990, a lift notable for its location as much as the terrain it covered – South Side has a much higher-altitude base sta-

When it was rebuilt as a quad detachable chairlift in 1985, the Horse Hill lift also started to run gondola cars, the first ski lift in Australia to do so. MARK ASHKANASY

tion than its immediate neighbours in the Federation or Bull run chairlifts.

It was built before snowmaking was truly established on the mountain, but also after experience had taught the operators that the reliable natural snow line was significantly higher than Mt Buller's pioneers might have hoped or believed.

After the 1991 winter, Monester moved on to establish his own ski area consultancy and become executive officer of the industry body, the Australian Ski Areas Association.

SOON AFTERWARDS CAME another transition when the Grollo family bought 80 per cent of the Bourke Street Ski Lift Company. Given the timing of the purchase – just prior to the 1992 winter season – Macmahon Holdings was contracted to remain as manager of the lifts with its chief executive, John McDonald as executive chairman.

In 1993 Rino and Diana Grollo bought the remaining 20 per cent of the company, renaming it Buller Ski Lifts. It was an extension of a long association with the mountain for the Grollos. In the early days of his construction company, Rino Grollo's father Luigi

Brad Spooner took over as chief executive of Buller Ski Enterprises after Michael Monester in 1991.
MARK ASHKANASY

Bruce Dowding followed Philip Bentley as lift company chief executive and in turn recruited Laurie Blampied as his own replacement. RMB

The lift company's part-owners in 1992 and full owners since 1993, Rino and Diana Grollo with Bob Bateup at the opening of the Bob Bateup Workshop, named after Mt Buller's enduring mountain manager. BSL

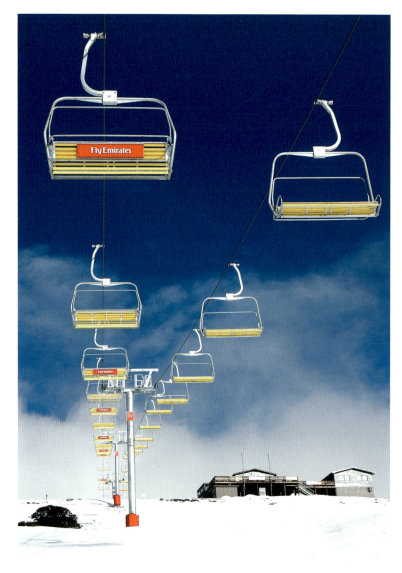

The Emirates Discovery quad chairlift, opened in 2005 and opening up new terrain on the run Helmut Kofler named Shaky Knees.
ANGELO MARCINA

had built Mt Buller's main water supply, the reservoir near Burnt Hut Spur, between Tyrol and Boggy Creek.

That project brought a 16-year-old Rino Grollo to the mountain and he became a regular visitor to the region, first in summer and later in winter to ski.

'As a teenager I camped with my father around Myrtleford, Porepunkah, Mt Buffalo, and Bright and on the Delatite River and at Sawmill Settlement,' Rino Grollo said.

He and his wife Diana (Ruzzene) continued to go camping in all those areas 'and we used to go to Buller on day trips in summer and winter before we got married.

'We always had that love affair for the mountains and the wilderness and the rivers,' he said.

They bought some land at Sawmill Settlement – from Harold Doughty, a local sawmiller and road builder who was SCV president for a time.

Sawmill Settlement became the Grollo's initial base for winter visits, first on cross-country skis at Mt Stirling in the mid-1970s and then on alpine skis at Mt Buller in 1978.

'We all pretty much learned at the same time,' Diana Grollo said, 'I put the children into ski school, including our nephews and nieces.'

'We'd go up for the day from Sawmill Settlement and get into ski school and do our skiing and come back of a night time.

'After doing that for three or four years, we decided we should buy a lodge. We bought a flat in Snowflake and that got too hard so we bought a little lodge, we bought Ullr, it was a doll's house – all the kids called it a doll's house. It was the smallest lodge on the mountain,' Rino Grollo said.

'We just had a love for the sport, it was pure passion,' Diana Grollo said. 'And when we brought friends up they would catch on and say, "This is fantastic, oh, this is such a wonderful time" and they'd

Hooked

OCCUPATIONAL HEALTH AND safety professionals in the 21st century would shudder at some of the shaky situations ski lift staff got themselves into in the early days. They would clamber up towers in ski boots with no harness to de-ice lift pulley batteries and cables, hanging on with one hand and belting the ice with an aluminium hammer in the other. The risks were exacerbated by the extreme icing conditions that could be encountered. Climbing harnesses were looked at, but as Mt Buller's mountain manager Bob Bateup put it, 'Because the ladders and towers were ice covered, any fall protection equipment that was available on the market just wouldn't work. So we decided to come up with something that would work in icy conditions.'

Bateup was talking to former lift company general manager Michael Monester about the problem, saying new safety regulations meant tower climbers had to be attached to the tower at all times, meaning they needed two lanyard hooks, climbing a couple of rungs on the tower ladder and moving one of the hooks up and so on.

Monester, a climber, suggested climbing by holding on to hooks shaped like karabiners, much as you do with ice axes – one axe is always in contact with the ice, then you dig the next one and move up. Instead of using the rungs, the lift tower climber would hold on to the hook.

'It went on for 18 months,' Bateup said. 'There were probably 50 different prototypes and all types of testing – what seemed to be such a simple idea ended up being very complicated to meet the standards.

'To get them light enough but strong enough was very, very difficult. They had to be light and they had to feel right, you had to feel safe with them – it was a lot more difficult than we first thought.'

The system comprises two personal climbing hooks that have pistol-style handles and are attached to the front of the user's harness by a connecting device and two energy-absorbing lanyards.

The climber uses each hook as an extension of their hand, locking it over each rung as they climb. The hook is closed off with a safety latch that is unlocked and opened by gripping the handle of the device.

The pistol grip ensures each hook can be released quickly so the device

does not impede climbing speed, but it also ensures the user is attached to the ladder by at least one device at all times. The Buller Climbing Hook, which is manufactured by a Melbourne engineering company, won a 2005 Victorian Engineering Excellence Award and a WorkSafe Victoria award.

The method has changed but the challenge has endured. In 1959, the BMW Ski Tow Group's Graham Hoinville (below) holds tight with his legs as he cuts through a frame in the construction of the Transport or Koflers rope tow. In 2004 Nick Reeves (above) uses the award-winning Buller Hook to climb a lift tower for maintenance. Rime ice (below left) and its weight is an ongoing problem for the mountain's operators. MERRICK SUMMERS/BOB BATEUP

have a great day and of course they in turn would introduce other people to it.

'I think we've introduced quite a lot of people to this skiing.'

Their first commercial investment was the Abom restaurant in 1987 ('Everybody used to ski and there was nobody left to cook,' Diana Grollo said – see chapter 17 for more on the Abom).

In 1992, Rino Grollo had an approach from John McDonald. 'He came to see me because Macmahons wanted to get out of the skiing industry and concentrate on their mining.

'We bought 80 per cent of the company in 1992, then we bought the other 20 per cent in 1993,' Rino Grollo said.

Their first major investment was the Wombat quad chairlift for the 1993 winter, to serve the supertrail-style Wombat and Little Buller Spur runs.

At the same time, the Chamois double chairlift replaced the Enzian and Chamois Pomas on the slopes that would become the World Cup aerials site.

Since then, apart from the Abom six-seat chairlift which replaced the Abom triple and Blue Bullet 2 quad chairlifts for the 2008 winter, and the Northside/Emirates Discovery quad chairlift which replaced the Shaky Knees T-bar for the 2005 winter and some smaller access rope tows and snow carpet lifts, much of the capital investment has gone into less obvious but increasingly important snowmaking infrastructure (see chapter 6 for more on snowmaking).

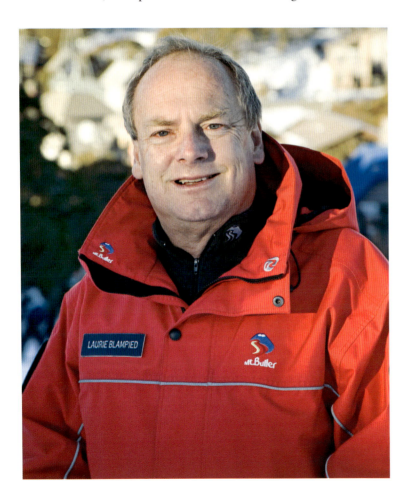

Laurie Blampied, Buller Ski Lifts' general manager since 1996.
MARK ASHKANASY

BULLER SKI LIFTS' current general manager, Laurie Blampied, arrived on the mountain in 1996, having been assistant general manager of the lift company at Falls Creek and prior to that working in the building industry in Melbourne. Blampied has overseen Mt Buller's snowmaking investment and has also, more recently, developed a master plan for the mountain. 'Clearly we need to consolidate some of the lifts that we're operating. We're currently operating 24 or 25 lifts – it depends on how you count them – and that's about the same number of lifts that Vail resort operates in Colorado.

'The only difference is they're skiing 1,500,000 people and we're skiing 300,000 so, there's a real economic imperative to rationalise our lifting system. But the compounding problem is that we don't have as much vertical [metres to ski or board] and with the peak visitation we have, we need to have the capacity to get a lot of people up the hill quickly, so we've just got to be very careful with that consolidation.'

Part of the consolidation has begun, moving grooming and maintenance facilities from the Blue Bullet mid-station on Bourke Street and other locations to a central point at the Snowflake Factory near the South Side and Bull Run top stations.

Blampied has some other ideas to make the mountain work more efficiently for its operators and its guests.

One idea that became possible following the relocation of the maintenance facilities from the Blue Bullet mid-station area was the relocation of some of the Ski School activities, reducing congestion on Bourke Street.

'That's a natural launching place for skiers of all abilities and it's a much easier place to get to for novice skiers,' Blampied said.

The type of lift can also change the pattern of people's movements on the mountain.

'When we built the Emirates Discovery lift to replace Shaky Knees [T-bar] that really changed the face of skiing on the northern side of the mountain. There's a lot of terrain there that wasn't skied.

'The Shaky Knees top station was too low to be able to effectively get to the south side of the mountain. Now, by lifting people up on to Tyrol Flat they're able to get back into the village a hell of a lot easier.

'People have much higher expectations of modern ski lifts. T-bars and snowboarders aren't a particularly good mix for example, but put them on a high-speed detaching chairlift and it's a whole new ball game,' Blampied said.

Applying that principle to the Horse Hill lift could be another improvement to the way the mountain works for skiers and boarders and would also realise the original intention for the lift.

Horse Hill currently has a station in the valley floor at Chalet Creek, however, because the chairs don't detach from the cable at that station (as they do at the top and bottom stations) when it is in use, the cable speed has to be lowered significantly.

'That reduces capacity appreciably. If we had a detaching station

A Doppelmayr six-seat chairlift, in operation in Europe. DOPPELMAYR

in there, it would be a detaching chair all the way through,' Blampied said.

That would make Horse Hill not just an access lift but also a lift for skiers and snowboarders to use Cow Camp and Dam runs and all the terrain in between.

The Tyrol T-bar could be dispensed with, further opening up the terrain on those slopes.

Another improvement to the Horse Hill lift would be a better-located bottom station.

'It's in the wrong place; it's apparent to anybody who visits Buller that it should have been at the car park level – that was a political decision taken at the time.

'Maybe that's something we can revisit with the current resort management board, where we create a proper entry portal to the resort there, with better ticketing and ski hire and day visitor facilities,' Blampied said.

But as he says, the lift base location is a minor negative amid a major positive, considering the ease of access from the Horse

Hill car park, where skiers and boarders can be on the summit of Mt Buller after riding just two lifts and others can use the shuttle bus service for fast access to the village.

The new Abom six-seat detachable chairlift is another example of lift consolidation.

'This new lift, another Australian first for Buller, increases capacity, reduces the trip time and congestion dramatically and improves the visual amenity of Baldy,' Blampied said. (see chapter 20 for more)

Despite their ambitions and energy, even the SCV's ski tow enthusiasts, the people who started it all in 1948, could hardly have imagined how the combination of Mt Buller's popularity and the advances in ski lift technology would allow the mountain to be climbed so easily by so many.

The 1987 grooming crew. In the back row are Grant Dickinson (left), Angus Syme and Andy Weingott. In the front row are Craig McDonald (left), Oliver Chords, Tony Gardiner and Ray Brinkley. MARK ASHKANASY

Peter Rose (centre) and Craig Burnside (right) and another maintenance crew member in the late 1980s. MICHAEL MONESTER

General manager Hans Grimus (left) and snow groomer, later mountain manager, Bob Bateup in 1974. BOB BATEUP

Snowmaker Ewen Macaskill in 1995. MARK W ASHBY

Lift operator Michael Ford in 1989. MARK ASHKANASY

The mountain operations team in 1987. MARK ASHKANASY

Nick Reeves in 1989. MARK ASHKANASY

Dwayne O'Dwyer working on the Wombat drive in the 1990s. MARK W ASHBY

Tim Gerrish gets behind the dash in a grooming machine in the 1990s. MARK W ASHBY

Snowmaker Mick Sheedy on the summit in 1995. MARK ASHKANASY

Tracey Mears de-icing. BOB BATEUP

The summit area lift crew get a lift to work in 1988. MARK ASHKANASY

The ski school and mountain operations teams in 1990. MARK ASHKANASY

The 1989 grooming crew. On the skidoo, clockwise from the front are Andy 'Spook' Kelly, Ray Brinkley, Des Lemin and Mick Feeney. In the second row are Ross Linscott, Wayne Talbot, Kevin Kastin, Tim Gerrish and Andrew Fraser. In the third row are Tony Gardiner, Ash Gregory, Scotty Drayton and Will McDonald. In the back are Andy Weingott and Angus Syme. MARK ASHKANASY

The lift company's outside operations team in 1991. MARK ASHKANASY

Maintenance crew member Geoff Schulz in 2007. MARK ASHKANASY

Darren Lochridge de-icing.
BOB BATEUP

Guest Services in 2007. At the back are Stan Staugas (left) and Rich Eason, in the centre are Frank Pannia (left), Alan Bennett and Rhiannon Lodge, in the front row are Ken Wallbridge (left), Wilma Johnson, Anne Bloomfield and Felice Morris. FUN PHOTOS

Grooming and maintenance staff in 2007. In the back row are Carl Hoffrichter (left), Will Macdonald, Jason Campbell and Rod Sargent. In the middle are Scott Drayton (left), Neil Peet, Geoff Schulz and Glen Andrews. In the front are Peter Laurence (left) and Mark Angliss. MARK ASHKANASY

In the snowmaking air compressor shed, Ben Hazelwood (left), Paul Richmond, Daniel Roberts, Stuart Burns and Greg Sheppard. MARK ASHKANASY

Kassbohrer maintenance in 2007. MARK ASHKANASY

Jane Swinburne (left) and Kat Gannon in the control room in 2007.
MARK ASHKANASY

In the control room in 2007, Rod Sargent (left), Kaisie Rayner and
Bob Bateup. MARK ASHKANASY

The 2007 mountain operations team. FUN PHOTOS

BSL administration and marketing staff in 2007. In the
back row are Sharon Rainsbury (left), Jacqui Whitby,
Helena Hradil, Leanne Drake and Louise Brannan. In
the front row are Helen Vatzakis (left), Will Walker and
Carmine Mancuso. MARK ASHKANASY

The 2007 BSL tickets team. Standing are Karen
Shepard (left), Kate Raidal, Sue Anthony, Stan Staugas
and Leeroy Johnson. At the front are Angela Parker
(left) and Sue McGregor. MARK ASHKANASY

Nathan Dalley (left) and Palo Galko working on
information technology in 2007. MARK ASHKANASY

Lift lines

DATES INDICATE THE first, and where applicable, last winter of operation. The organisation or person/people that built and operated the lift is also indicated.

1949 – 1958	Bourke Street rope tow, Ski Club of Victoria.
1953 – 1954	Bull Run portable rope tow, Hilton-Wood Enterprises.
1955 – 1962	Bull Run permanent rope tow (extended), Hilton-Wood Enterprises.
1957 – 1961	Forras portable rope tow, Aurel and Ernest Forras.
1957 – 1962	Tyrol (Little Baldy) rope tow, Maurice Selle.
1959 – 1961	Skyline rope tow, Bull Run Enterprises (formerly Hilton-Wood Enterprises, later known as Blue Lifts).
1959 – 1963	Koflers rope tow (also known as Summit Access or Transportation rope tow) Ski Lifts Mt Buller (Orange Lifts).
1959 – 1968	Bourke Street T-bar, Orange Lifts.
1959 – 1980	Federation T-bar, Orange Lifts.
1961 – 1963	Bourke Street double rope tow, Orange Lifts.
1961 – 1963	Konrad Koch rope tow (bought by Blue Lifts from Konrad Koch and replaced by Chamois Poma in 1965).
1962 – 1984	Bull Run T-bar, Blue Lifts.
1963 –	Skyline T-bar (originally called Little Collins Street), Blue Lifts.
1963 – 2004	Shaky Knees T-bar (originally called Swanston Street), Orange Lifts.
1964 – 1983	Bourke Street double chairlift, Blue Lifts.
1964 – 1983	Summit Poma, Orange Lifts (duplicated in 1968).
1964 – 1983	Summit Access Poma/Howqua Poma, Orange Lifts.
1965 – 1987	Chamois Poma, Blue Lifts (extended in 1969 giving an alternative to the Bull Run T-bar as a return from Standard Run).
1967 –	Boggy Creek T-bar, Orange Lifts.
1968 – 1983	Summit Poma duplicated.
1969 – 1981	Whittaker Poma (replaced by the Village T-bar in 1982), Blue Lifts.
1969 – 1985	Baldy duplex Pomas, Orange Lifts.
1972 –	Tyrol T-bar, Orange Lifts (original line went all the way to Baldy, it was shortened to create a lower top station in 1987).
1974 – 1983	Baldy double chairlift, Blue Lifts.
1974 – 2003	Bourke Street Beginner's T-bar, Orange Lifts (replaced by Bourke Street snow carpet in 2004).
1976 – 1977	Beginner's Carousel at Helicopter Flat, Orange Lifts.
1977 –	Koflers T-bar, Orange Lifts.
1979 – 1996	Enzian Poma, Blue Lifts.

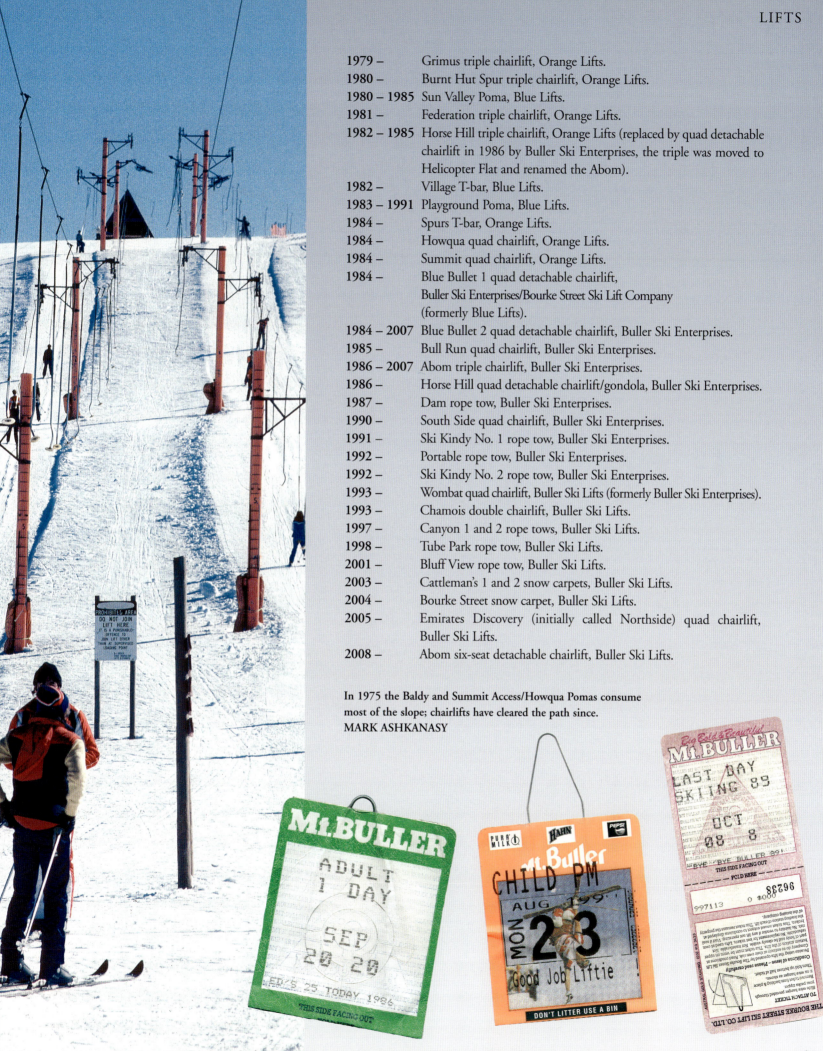

1979 –   Grimus triple chairlift, Orange Lifts.

1980 –   Burnt Hut Spur triple chairlift, Orange Lifts.

1980 – 1985 Sun Valley Poma, Blue Lifts.

1981 –   Federation triple chairlift, Orange Lifts.

1982 – 1985 Horse Hill triple chairlift, Orange Lifts (replaced by quad detachable chairlift in 1986 by Buller Ski Enterprises, the triple was moved to Helicopter Flat and renamed the Abom).

1982 –   Village T-bar, Blue Lifts.

1983 – 1991 Playground Poma, Blue Lifts.

1984 –   Spurs T-bar, Orange Lifts.

1984 –   Howqua quad chairlift, Orange Lifts.

1984 –   Summit quad chairlift, Orange Lifts.

1984 –   Blue Bullet 1 quad detachable chairlift, Buller Ski Enterprises/Bourke Street Ski Lift Company (formerly Blue Lifts).

1984 – 2007 Blue Bullet 2 quad detachable chairlift, Buller Ski Enterprises.

1985 –   Bull Run quad chairlift, Buller Ski Enterprises.

1986 – 2007 Abom triple chairlift, Buller Ski Enterprises.

1986 –   Horse Hill quad detachable chairlift/gondola, Buller Ski Enterprises.

1987 –   Dam rope tow, Buller Ski Enterprises.

1990 –   South Side quad chairlift, Buller Ski Enterprises.

1991 –   Ski Kindy No. 1 rope tow, Buller Ski Enterprises.

1992 –   Portable rope tow, Buller Ski Enterprises.

1992 –   Ski Kindy No. 2 rope tow, Buller Ski Enterprises.

1993 –   Wombat quad chairlift, Buller Ski Lifts (formerly Buller Ski Enterprises).

1993 –   Chamois double chairlift, Buller Ski Lifts.

1997 –   Canyon 1 and 2 rope tows, Buller Ski Lifts.

1998 –   Tube Park rope tow, Buller Ski Lifts.

2001 –   Bluff View rope tow, Buller Ski Lifts.

2003 –   Cattleman's 1 and 2 snow carpets, Buller Ski Lifts.

2004 –   Bourke Street snow carpet, Buller Ski Lifts.

2005 –   Emirates Discovery (initially called Northside) quad chairlift, Buller Ski Lifts.

2008 –   Abom six-seat detachable chairlift, Buller Ski Lifts.

In 1975 the Baldy and Summit Access/Howqua Pomas consume most of the slope; chairlifts have cleared the path since.
MARK ASHKANASY

6

Trails

The nature of Mt Buller's terrain meant some runs above the tree line – about the 1750-metre mark – were naturally clear, while below the tree line, new trails were cut with equal amounts of enthusiasm, effort and passion but sometimes little in the way of planning. Trail and slope management has evolved to incorporate new technology and accommodate environmental understanding.

IN A BUMPER snow year, trails are everywhere. Skiers and snowboarders are limited only by their imagination and the density of the trees they're moving through. Unlike the northern hemisphere, where firs and conifers are easier to navigate as the snow gets deeper, the cauliflower-shaped snow gums become more complex as increased snow depth puts a skier or boarder higher in the canopy. In a good year, or after good snowfall, Mt Buller's snow riders can make the journey deep into the woolly butt forests, the mountain ash and alpine ash that grow tall and straight in the sub-alpine zone. Adventurous skiers have made the trip from Mt Buller's summit to Mirimbah, from Boggy Creek down to White Bridge and from runs like Moonlight or the Summit Chutes down deep towards the Howqua.

Trails make sense on many levels; they keep people from becoming lost in what can be a hostile environment, they enable some quality control of the snow surface and, when cut properly, provide shelter and encourage snow drift.

Moonlight is an area beyond the resort boundary, past the Summit Chutes, named by patrollers Brian Singer and Brian McMahon who first skied it in fresh powder snow under moonlight. They later discovered the nearby slope now called Frenchman's had been skied in the 1940s and named Veloce. This photograph, of patrollers Andy Laidlaw and Rolf Denler skiing Moonlight was taken around 9am on August 26, 1990.
MARK ASHKANASY

They're created in many ways, sometimes on the back of natural clearing such as bushfire, sometimes through the endeavour of the skiers who would get to use them, more recently as part of a slope management plan.

Helmut Kofler was probably the first to clear a run on Buller – Shaky Knees and then another run from the Chalet to Cow Camp. (Stephenson, p212)

Later efforts were made by working parties related to bodies such as the Ski Club of Victoria (SCV). Joe Guss, the father of Olympic skiers Antony, Marilla and Alistair recalled clearing trees and rocks from Bull Run in the 1950s, 'just because we wanted to ski it so much.'

Mick Hull had fond recollections of the mountain's trails when it still had few lifts:

Either side of Bull Run there were untracked slopes like Lois's Run and the Wombat Spur, Fanny's Finish was won-

Northern slopes

Even though its ridgeline gives it the appearance of a shoulder, McLaughlins Shoulder (to the right of the chairlift in this photograph) was named after a US ski team member, James Loughlin (*ASYB* 1938/*Schuss* 1937) because he fell and injured his shoulder on the site in 1937 (also McLoughlin's and McLaughlan's). Mick Hull skied with Loughlin and described him as coming from a prominent US steel-making family, who was '… a member of the four-man American team from Dartmouth College New Hampshire that visited Australia in 1937, led by Dick Durrance, with Dave and Steve Bradley.

'A Victoria versus USA match had been arranged for Buller, and in the downhill on an impromptu course … Jim Loughlin broke his shoulder while schussing part of it. 'These happenings were fully described in *Schuss* for September 1937 and the signposting of the locality today as "McLaughlin's Shoulder" is a more recent

misnomer.' (Hull p235) The years have certainly had their way with the spelling of the run.

Along Klingsporn's Bridle Track for walkers or at the top of the Horse Hill chairlift for lift riders, Burnt Hut Spur (to the left of this picture) was named after the two huts built there – one by the Lovicks and one by the Mansfield Progress Association, both burnt down (Lovick's in 1924-25 and the MPA hut in 1933). Chalet Creek is the creek below the original Mt Buller Chalet and Shaky Knees was the name given to those ski runs by Helmut Kofler – it was a statement on the condition of a skier's legs when they arrived at Chalet Creek. The Playing Fields of Eton is the area between Boggy Creek and Shaky Knees.

The Home Trail was a run from the village to the car park that would lead to the car and then home (to Melbourne or other destinations).

MARK ASHKANASY

drous in July powder. Kofler's run farther out than Tyrol, the *Knaesknaggler* (Shaky Knees) which had been carved through the trees down to the creek opposite Horse Hill had some fast schusses in between the corners.

Below the Ivor Whittaker Lodge there was an open kind of wood run that seemed always to hold powder for some days after a new fall.

Between the gully of Boggy Creek and Kofler's Shaky Knees there were several slopes leading through open timber, lovely wood-running that Freddy Derham christened the "Playing Fields of Eton," because there were so many choices.

In a heavy season you could ski Federation right to the woolly butts, 1750 vertical feet [533 metres] as measured by barometer on one glorious run with Malcolm McColl [Hull may have meant Fanny's Finish as it offered much more vertical before Federation was cleared].

And in the chute above the shoulder nor-nor-west of Boggy Creek, Ernest Forras and others in one very heavy year skied down almost to the road alongside the Delatite River, upstream from Sawmill Settlement. (Hull, pp254-55)

In the years before the establishment of the Committee of Management (December 1948) and its closer control of Mt Buller, clearing for ski runs did not necessarily pay a lot of attention to the natural environment. The population pressure wasn't there and the science wasn't there. Fortunately for the mountain and those to come, the equipment wasn't really there either. Modern earthmoving machinery could do in a day what it took the skiers of the early years weeks to do with their axes and saws and winches and explosives.

Even if Mt Buller's landlord, the Forests Commission (FCV), had a fundamental responsibility to oversee the harvesting of the state's timber as a resource, it was also a careful land manager. In its day, it held more knowledge within it about the natural environment and certainly the alpine environment, than virtually any other body in the state.

Southern slopes

Federation was named after the Ski Federation of Australia in 1950 and the nearby Yurredla was named after the ski club of that name. Yurredla originally sought to build a lift on Federation and gave up its entitlement to do so in exchange for a seat on the board of the company that became Ski Lifts Mt Buller (Orange Lifts). MARK ASHKANASY

This was complemented by the state's Soil Conservation Authority (SCA), which gained a seat on the Committee of Management and researched and developed revegetation programs for alpine regions and their ski runs.

David Hume recalled skiing Little Buller Spur late in the 1979 snow season with Hans Grimus and the SCA's Rob Patrick to research a line for the new run. Grimus and Hume disagreed on the depths to which the run could reach, 'I went to the Lands Department in Melbourne … they showed me the stereos [aerial photographs] of the area, and we were able to agree that we could get out from the bottom. 'After some calculations, we agreed that we could do it using a 5 per cent grade. That angle is ideal for traverse tracks.

'After the thaw, my wife Berna and I walked down the newly surveyed lift line to where the bottom station would be. Berna started up the line I indicated, using my inclinometer to get the grade right.

'At the first point, I got her to adjust her position vertically; she then tied an orange ribbon on a branch. I moved to that position, and so on, 'til we came out on what would be the Little Buller run.

'Bob Bateup and his crew cut the track, but they started a little

There are a few attributions for Fanny's Finish. Determined to win a race, photographer Edwin Adamson flew through the course and won, but landed on his rear-end (fanny) at the end creating the name Fanny Finish (SCV Yearbook, 1932) which popular usage has transformed to Fanny's Finish.

Then again, Dave Hume, a member of the old Moose Ski Club recalled a senior club member, Hamish Pearson (of Pelaco Shirts), telling him the run was named after 'Fanny' Strauss, who slid down it on his fanny. Strauss was in the RAAF and was killed in World War II. MARK ASHKANASY

Bourke Street was named in 1947 'when the opening weekend crowd made it as busy as its Melbourne namesake.' (Joss, p19) Helicopter Flat, located on Bourke Street, near the tow hut at the bottom right of the cleared area in this photograph, got its name when Squadron Leader Robertson landed a helicopter on the site on September 19, 1949. This photograph was taken in the late 1950s. ERIC BURT

uphill of our point, so the track was a bit steeper in parts. It has now been moved right to the saddle of Little Buller, and is one of the most popular runs on Buller,' Hume said.

The supertrail-style Little Buller Spur was cut in the summer of 1980-81, for skiers who would use the Federation chairlift that opened in winter 1981.

The crowd, funnelled in from the runs bounded by Fanny's Finish to the north and Family Run to the south, line up for the Howqua chairlift. MARK ASHKANASY

Every run in a day?

A MEASURE OF any mountain is how long it takes to ski. Can every one of Mt Buller's marked runs be skied in a day? The author attempted it in 2002 on a sunny August day with a full cover of snow and every lift operating.

The guide was ski patroller Ed Mahon, an accomplished skier who knows the mountain inside out. He was looking forward to the quest but was up front about it – 'I don't think we can do it, I think there's just too many runs,' he said.

For an overview, we skied the runs off the lifts on the northern slopes, with our first run out the back door of the patrol base and down Shaky Knees.

Next came Cow Camp, to the bottom of the Tyrol T-Bar, and then Dam Run, uniquely Buller runs. Most of the tree skiing in Australia is among the short, gnarly snow gums, but these runs drop right in among the spectacular woolly butt trees that dominate the lower altitudes. They also underline the potential of the skiing in a good season and just how low it can go.

We moved along through Burnt Hut, stopping to help a skier with a cut from a fall, and then over to Boggy Creek, Grimus and the summit area. While we'd covered almost every lift on the northern slopes, we'd skied less than a third of the runs.

'We're not going to get through it, but I've got an idea,' Ed Mahon said. 'We'll ski all the runs in the Bull Run Bowl and from that, we can work out how long the whole exercise would take.'

So, after a fuel-up at Koflers, we moved into Bull Run Bowl and first-up skied the steep, long and interesting Women's Downhill. Next run was Sun Valley – every area has one, named in tribute of the pioneering North American resort. After Sun Valley came Hog's Back, then Plug Hole and then the Funnel, the halfway point or centre of the bowl.

The bumpy and challenging Wood run, the site of the annual Abom Mogul Challenge was our sixth run, followed by Fall Line and then Standard. Eight runs, eight rides on the Bull Run chair. We skied hard and didn't have to wait in any queues and it still took us 95 minutes.

If you divided the mountain up into zones like this, there would be seven in all: Tyrol; Boggy Creek and Grimus; Summit and Howqua; Wombat; Federation; Bull Run; and Baldy, Bourke Street and Chamois.

Each area would take about as long as the Bull Run Bowl with Wombat probably taking twice as long. That's a minimum 14 hours skiing and considering the lifts open at 8.30am and are all closed by 5pm, one day just wouldn't be enough.

'Look, it just goes to show you, this is a big mountain,' Ed Mahon said.

'Even if you were a fully fit, very fast Australian ski team member, I don't think you could ski all the runs in a day.'

Nevertheless, riding the lifts as we did is a good way for accomplished skiers to get to know Mt Buller or for old hands to reacquaint themselves with it.

'The way we moved is the way to do it,' Ed Mahon said, 'starting on the north side and always moving to skier's left. It just flows better around the mountain doing it like that.'

Ed Mahon (left) and Jim Darby on the summit of a mountain that can't be covered in a day. MARK ASHKANASY

THE LEGEND HAS it that snowmaking was accidentally created in the 1950s by two American brothers, Joe and Phil Tropeano, keen skiers who worked in agriculture.

They were spraying a client's orange orchard with a mixture of water and compressed air, aiming to increase humidity and protect the crop from frost. The story went that they returned in the morning to find the crop ruined but covered in snow, so they approached some ski area contacts saying to them, 'Boy, do we have an invention for you …'

Later in life, an 84-year-old Phil Tropeano conceded that his brother Joe had invented the story 'to make it look like they hadn't stolen the patent.' (LeCompte/American Heritage)

That patent belonged to Wayne Pierce and Tey Manufacturing, a company that was a genuine snowmaking pioneer, which was also credited with the production of the first laminated aluminium skis. Pierce had actually contacted the Tropeanos because their company, Larchmont Farms, was an irrigation specialist with a background in moving large volumes of water. The Tropeanos eventually bought the patent rights from Tey and Pierce for their snowmaking technology and progressively improved the system of using compressed air and water under pressure, mixing them in the chamber of a 'gun' to be shot into the atmosphere, to create crystals that would fall as snow.

Snow is trucked in and spread over Bourke Street to keep the lifts turning and the skiers skiing in 1988. MICHAEL MONESTER

Mt Buller's John Hilton-Wood approached the Tropeanos and secured the Larchmont agency for Australia and New Zealand.

His first problem was encountered at Australian Customs: 'They didn't like anything called a gun, even then … so we got them changed to snowmakers,' Hilton-Wood said.

Snowmaking needs a combination of low temperature and low humidity. Hilton-Wood had some basic weather readings from around the mountain and found the temperature and humidity could work best on Chamois.

'It was actually drier there than anywhere else and it was on the south face and it wasn't windy, so we decided to make snow there.' The early 1980s experiment was agricultural, with four-inch (10cm) irrigation pipe installed above the ground to channel the air and the water.

'We ran the pipes here, there and everywhere and it made snow very, very successfully; it made a great big pile of snow there and what happened then, of course, was it snowed like hell and buried the lot.'

They then faced neighbourhood complaints about the noise of the compressor, so they built a soundproof shed at the top of Chamois. The experiment continued. A problem Hilton-Wood faced was that the air out of the compressor was too warm, so he would cool it using jacketed pipes, or radiators, or even liquid nitrogen.

'The liquid nitrogen was dicey because you could get a bad burn off it. It wasn't dear to buy because it's a by-product of liquid oxygen. I used to cart that up and that went very successfully, but it was a pretty dicey operation,' he said.

He eventually moved the system over to Bourke Street and found some success there.

In the lean 1982 winter, Orange Lifts' CEO Colin Toll despairs over the mountain's lack of snow cover. BILL BACHMAN

EVEN BEFORE HILTON-Wood's experiments, Orange Lifts had reached an agreement with Monash University to study Mt Buller's winter climate and determine its suitability for snowmaking, over a period from the late 1960s to early 1970s.

The results were not appealing – 'the energy cost to make snow under these average conditions was seen to be huge. These were the early days of snowmaking … The board took the view that the scarce capital would be better employed in building lifts and summer grooming.' (Hume, p10)

It was later in the 1980s and early 1990s that snowmaking technology for marginal conditions improved to the point where it could be seriously considered for major investment.

In February 1987, when he returned to Mt Buller from Colorado to become the lift company general manager, Michael Monester had some interesting objects in his luggage. Among them were four snow guns, a variety of heads or nozzles for the guns and an injection system for Snowmax, an inert bacteria developed in the United States and used internationally to enhance snowmaking productivity.

'There really was a perception at the time that snowmaking couldn't work at Buller, that it couldn't be done,' Monester said. He had worked with the technology in Colorado and was determined to make it a success at Mt Buller.

When temperature and humidity permit, every opportunity is taken to make snow. On a June morning in 2007, snow is covering the Emirates Discovery chairlift and the Shaky Knees run. BOB BATEUP

By the mid-1990s, snowmaking and snow grooming were securing the mountain's snow cover. This is the same location as the photographs on the page opposite. MARK ASHKANASY

Snowmaking at night on Bourke Street using the high-capacity airless fan guns. MARK W ASHBY

In winter 1987, Monester arranged for the hire of some air compressors and a water pump and installed the pilot system on Bourke Street. 'It just pumped out the snow, we ended up with two metres of snow on Little Bourke Street, it blew everyone's socks off and this led the way for further development,' he said.

Having proved the technology could work, the barriers Mt Buller had to overcome were in the availability of resources for snowmaking, particularly power and water.

A COINCIDENCE OF events underpinned the first major snowmaking investment at Mt Buller.

Sandie Jeffcoat, the resort's area manager from 1982 to 2005, recalled 1993 as an 'absolutely disastrous season with just over 100,000 visitors, compared with a normal year of 500,000.'

That coincided with the Grollo family completing their acquisition of Buller Ski Lifts and their willingness to invest in mountain infrastructure.

An issue all mountain resorts had to face was who would pay for snowmaking. Their position as the dominant business on-mountain meant lift companies had the most to gain from snowmaking or the most to lose from the absence of snow cover, but all businesses shared that interest to an extent.

At Mt Buller, the resort management, then part of the Victorian Government's Alpine Resorts Commission, agreed that the community input would be to supply the water and make an annual contribution towards capital infrastructure costs for snowmaking.

Buller Ski Lifts would cover the remaining costs, including most of the infrastructure costs and the operating costs other than water supply into the dam.

'It's important to acknowledge the contribution of the Resort Management Board of Mt Buller,' Buller Ski Lifts' general manager Laurie Blampied said.

Snowmaker Angus Syme (left) and mountain manager Bob Bateup in 1994 with a new snowmaking fan gun and the water supply from the new dam available to feed it. MARK ASHKANASY

'Since 1994, following the 1993 season, which was a disastrous year for the ski industry generally and Mt Buller in particular, the Mt Buller community and the Resort Management Board, really shared the vision with the importance of snowmaking.

'The Resort Management Board signed a long-term agreement with the lift company to provide funding for snowmaking infrastructure … significant sums of money for the continual expansion and development of snowmaking.

'That's been a real incentive for the lift company. It's always difficult to get boards to commit additional money for snowmaking, but

can produce and the amount of snow that you can produce.

'As systems get larger and larger, that becomes increasingly important.'

Technological improvements have meant Buller can still operate the original air/water snowmaking system with enhanced efficiency as well as take advantage of breakthroughs in airless or fan gun technology.

The air/water guns are the ones on towers or stands around the mountain producing snow from a nozzle at the end of narrow pipes. The fan guns are the ones that look like mobile cement mixers.

when you've got a carrot like that, that always makes it a lot easier,' Blampied said.

By the 1994 winter, Mt Buller had a 72-million-litre dam ready for the new system's pumps to draw on. One thing that hadn't been totally accounted for was the demand on the mountain's power supply. 'There were some major blackouts,' Sandie Jeffcoat said.

'When the snowmaking system was turned on, all the village lights would dim … there was so much draw through the power lines going to Buller, the insulation melted off the power lines.

'You could actually see smoke coming off them … it was like the proverbial toaster element with all the power lines glowing in the dark.'

Within a few years of commissioning the system, a second power line was provided, although it was installed in a trench along the Mt Buller road, rather than overhead.

SNOWMAKING NOW COVERS 18 kilometres of the resort's trails or 73 hectares – almost a third of Mt Buller's 236 hectares of patrolled terrain. Expansion and efficiency enhancements have followed the initial investment.

'The intellect and thought and research and development that has gone into snowmaking around the world has resulted in some enormous improvements in efficiency,' Laurie Blampied said.

'Automation, for example, typically gives you a 30 to 35 per cent improvement on efficiency, the quality of snow that you

The snowmaking dam under construction in 1994 (left) and with its own snow cover in 2003 (above). SANDIE JEFFCOAT/MARK ASHKANASY

'People really don't appreciate how much Australian snowmakers have been pioneers.

'We have to make a lot of snow in a very short period of time … people are blown away when we talk about the number of guns that we have and the pump capacity that we have to make snow,' Blampied said.

Even though it is at the source, at the watersheds, water remains a limiting factor for Mt Buller's snowmaking, not least because of its ridge-top location.

A $3.5 million water recycling and filtration scheme has been implemented and is being tested and is due to be fully commissioned for the 2008 winter season.

'Water's a limiting factor for every resort when they're making snow around the world,' Laurie Blampied said.

'You can't get too much of it. As you expand the network of trails that you service with snowmaking, obviously you've got to increase the amount of water that you have available.

'The (recycling and) filtration project is going to give us some respite over the next five years, but ultimately the snowmaking system will be constrained by the amount of water.'

THERE ARE VARIOUS ways to prepare a run or trail for skiers and snowboarders. Trail clearing and slope grooming are activities generally undertaken outside winter and can involve rock clearing, tree clearing, earthworks and revegetation.

Snow grooming involves moving snow and preparing the snow's surface during the snow season.

For winter snow grooming, Mt Buller claims the largest grooming fleet in Victoria, with 12 Kassbohrer PistenBully groomers. Three of them are Winch Cats for steeper terrain, one has a pipe cutter attachment to shape half-pipes for skiers and snowboarders and another has a track setter for cross-country trails.

It wasn't always that simple. Although David Hume and Hans Grimus brought the first dedicated grooming machine to Mt Buller in 1973 John Hilton-Wood claims to have started the process in the 1950s.

He even used it as part of an advertising campaign.

'I bought a snow cat off the disposals down in Salmon Street in Port Melbourne,' he said. It had previously been used by the State Electricity Commission in the Falls Creek area.

'I paid £800 for it, then I had to replace all the track rollers which had rusted up.'

He initially used it to take trips from the top of Bourke Street to the summit, charging 10 shillings a ride.

'We used to take 16 people. I think we had six on each rope and about four or five jammed inside it.'

When Hilton-Wood built the Skyline T-bar, there was some resistance from ski instructors to teach in the area.

The United Ski School, with instructors like Tony Aslangul and the Forras brothers, was telling him Skyline was too rough.

'So I got hold of one of the cutters they use to make dowel [cylindrical timber rods]. I got hold of one which was about 14 feet wide [4.3 metres] and we used to tow that up and down behind the old Tucker which used to break the crust and flatten out [the slope]. 'That was in about 1960. We used that for a few years and then I went overseas in 1968 and bought a Ratrac which was made in Switzerland. 'It had rubber tracks and it had a Ford Falcon engine and gear box in it. We used that for a couple of years.

Snow fences are used around the mountain to create snow drifts, like this one between Baldy and the summit. Stockpiled snow is used when required to cover high-wear areas. BOB BATEUP

'It was quite interesting; the price was exactly the price of a new Rolls Royce. So the first one I think was $16,000 and the next one we bought in '76 was a twin-track Tucker Sno-Cat for $28,000.

'Then we bought a Kassbohrer in the 1980s which I think was $90,000, about the same price as a Roller at the time.'

Not everyone remembers Hilton-Wood's oversnow machinery as fondly as he does.

Sandie Jeffcoat arrived on the mountain in 1982, and he recalls Blue Lifts' old Tucker Sno-Cat.

'John Hilton-Wood had bought this bloody big snow scoop thing and used to take them up to Tyrol and back down to Bourke Street or Little Bourke Street.

'He just made an absolute mess and there were always fights between Orange and Blue about the mess that John made at night.'

THE NATURE OF the competition between them meant that Orange Lifts always sought to match or improve any Blue Lifts innovation.

The first Orange Lifts attempt at grooming was in 1964 when it bought a Tucker Sno-Cat, but the nature of its tracks meant it was a very high maintenance vehicle, which was 'pensioned off to tow a hydraulic crane for tower maintenance.' (Hume, p11)

In 1972, the Orange Lifts board decided it was time to get serious about snow grooming, so its chairman David Hume and general manager Hans Grimus embarked on a national and international tour to find the best equipment available. They were fortunate to survive. They inspected a Thiokol machine working at Thredbo at night and were 'horrified to see it coming down the mountain sideways out of control.'

Next stop was Canada where they visited the Bombardier factory near Montreal and were taken for a test run with the gun groomer driver, Reggie, at a nearby resort.

Hume recalls them heading for a mogul field and Reggie boasting that he'd show them how the moguls were cut.

'The machine was fitted with a short straight blade and was vastly underpowered. It grunted through a few moguls, then clipped one.'

That forced the machine around and it started to bounce down the slope sideways. Reggie eventually pulled it around, but to face uphill, so it was sliding backwards out of control.

It eventually slammed into a snow wall near the base of the run. Hume recalls Reggie saying 'thank goodness I built that wall … there's a thousand foot drop off there.'

They moved south to the United States east coast where they came across a Kassbohrer groomer with a locally made U-shaped blade fitted to it.

A winch cat in operation in 2000. The cable coming over the cabin of the Kassbohrer is attached to a winch and anchored to a point on the slope above, enabling the grooming of steeper slopes. MARK W ASHBY

They had found what they were looking for. Even though the manufacturers had not designed or powered the machine to move snow, but rather to pack it as it fell, the U-blade meant it could do both.

The other advantage that struck them about the Kassbohrer was that it was hydraulically driven, meaning one track could be going forward and the other in reverse, so the machine could 'spin on the spot if need be,' a big advantage given their recent experiences.

They kept travelling, observing the groomers in Lech in Austria's Arlberg leaving a large area of 'mangled snow behind,' and going to a demonstration of a new Ratrac machine at Axamer Lizum, near Innsbruck. It was bogged when they got there and remained bogged for the afternoon.

So they ordered a Kassbohrer, along with one of the U-blades they had seen in the US.

'This was the first Kassbohrer imported to Australia, arriving at Buller in time for the 1973 snow season.' (Hume, pp11-13)

Bob Bateup, Mt Buller's mountain manager, was originally from Belingen on the NSW mid-north coast. He completed an apprenticeship in the Australian Navy before working at Perisher Valley on lift maintenance and then snow grooming.

Mt Buller was 'looking for someone to come down and drive their new grooming machine so I came down to do that. I arrived in April [1974] and helped them get some trail work done.

'That was one thing David Hume and Hans Grimus had worked on – getting a grooming machine that could do one-pass grooming.

'Prior to that, the grooming machines towed implements of some description, either rollers or smoothing blades, but they were towed behind the machine.

'The machines might have had a front blade, but it was generally a straight blade used for clearing around buildings, it wasn't good for grooming.

'The Kassbohrer was one of the first to come out with hydrostatic drive, so they were much more controllable and relatively advanced,' Bateup said.

However, because the early machines were still designed for packing snow and not pushing snow, they had trouble with the chassis owing to the forces involved with pushing snow.

They were also awkward to operate because the controls weren't set up for the use of a front-mounted blade.

'Because we had these [chassis] problems with the machine, they sent out an engineer from Kassbohrer – in the winter of 1974 – to see what was going on,' Bateup said.

'He couldn't speak English and in those days the Germans had this view that their machine was perfect and if anything went wrong with it, it was the operator's fault.

'So this engineer came out with me at night and we'd go grooming and I was thinking, "I'm not going to let this bugger find me doing something wrong."

'So I'd say, "I'm finished now for the night" and drop him off and then I'd go back out again.'

Bateup didn't discover until after the engineer had left that he was actually one of the machine's designers, and he'd never seen it used for moving snow the way they were doing it at Buller. 'They only used the machine for packing snow, not for moving it.' The following summer, Bateup went to Europe and met with the engineers who were discussing that particular machine and what they were going to do with it.

In a sense, a mountain resort is a farm, with its operators making the most of every opportunity the weather permits. Snow grooming attachments are as versatile and varied as those used in agriculture – here a pipe cutter is used to shape a half pipe. ED MAHON

Mt Buller's snow groomers are sought-after throughout the world for the skills they develop in Australia's marginal conditions. Ant Bateup (below right), from Mansfield, won an award in 2005 as a finalist in the Colorado Terrain Master titles. BOB BATEUP

Little Buller Spur follows the style set by North American resorts – long runs cut through the trees and well groomed in summer and winter for an easy ride. MARK ASHKANASY

'They were saying, "You shouldn't put the U-blade on it, you shouldn't use it for grooming, it was designed for packing and that's what you should do with it."

'And I was saying, "No, you've got to be able to groom with it" and the engineer who had come out here was on my side and he was saying, "No, you've got to use it for grooming, it's good for grooming".

'They then came out with a new model that was designed around the U-blade.'

That first Kassbohrer is still in operation. It was sold to Selwyn Snowfields in the NSW Snowy Mountains and was in turn sold to a commercial lodge in Perisher Valley, Peer Gynt, which uses it for oversnow transport.

Kassbohrer retains market dominance in Australia and Mt Buller's lift companies have been among its most loyal customers. The technical progression has been to build bigger and more powerful machines, but also to enhance their versatility, with better attachments such as tillers and other developments like the winching arm. The use of the winch and its cable anchored to a point at the top of a slope means virtually all runs can be groomed, no matter how steep they are. The impact of grooming can't be underestimated.

'People really enjoyed it. If you went back now and had a look at the grooming in those [1970s] days, you'd say it was a poor grooming job. 'If it was done in the right conditions it was not much different to what you get today, but it had to be the right snow texture at the right time – once the conditions were right you had to go like hell. If it was soft snow and it froze up, it was over,' Bob Bateup said.

Veteran skier Merrick Summers certainly noticed the difference. In the early days, a slope like Boggy Creek would 'go to glug. We had to be following the sun every day. You'd never ski a slope that had been knocked around by the sun because the grooming just wasn't there in the early days.'

Former ski school director Egon Hierzegger said the combination of machine-made snow and grooming could greatly ease his instructors' workload.

With snowmaking, 'the crystals are not as big so when they fall the content of air is less … and that makes it a lot more compact when it's groomed.'

That in turn makes it much easier to find an edge on carving skis. In soft snow, the resistance is much greater.

'When it's hard and the ski doesn't sink in, then it becomes a lot easier. All those things I think have contributed to a faster learning progression.'

The ski patrol is also an admirer. Terry 'Speaky' Lyons: 'There is basically not a run on Mt Buller these days that they can't groom and you'll notice that people go where the grooming is.

'People love the grooming and I think the grooming also makes things safer, it probably does make people ski a little bit faster at times but I think it's still safer to have it like that.

'The people that come in from overseas, the instructors and those guys are just amazed at what we can do in our conditions.

'Some of the groomers [drivers] at Buller go overseas and are seen as the best. Buller really has a worldwide reputation for grooming.'

Snow farming is another important strategy in keeping the trails open.

'The fact is, we have marginal snow conditions,' Bob Bateup said, 'and we have to do an enormous amount of work here on the snow to bring it up to a standard that other areas might have without doing anything.

'That involves a lot of snow farming. We farm more than you would in most resorts. In a lot of ways, in marginal snow conditions, we are probably the leaders, because we've had to do it … it's a matter of survival.'

Snow farming involves capturing, storing and moving snow. Knowledge and experience are essential, to position snow fences to catch the most snow possible as it drifts on the wind and to understand where natural drifts or deposits of snow are located so that groomer drivers can mine and move it to cover high wear and other high priority areas to keep people skiing and boarding.

7

Ski patrol

The fundamentals of ski patrol are unchanged – prevent injury however possible and treat it when it occurs. But the way patrollers go about their business and the equipment available to them have changed dramatically.

MT BULLER'S SKI patrol base is the beating heart of the operation: patrollers coming and going on skis and snowmobiles; equipment checked and fitted; radio buzzing; calls taken and calls made; training in progress.

The patrol base is also part-museum, its walls papered with patrol-related articles, photographs and correspondence.

In an article written at the time of the patrol's fiftieth anniversary in 2000, a patroller, Ed Mahon, wrote about the differences in ski rescue in the pioneering days and in patrolling today.

He based the pioneering side of the comparison on the recollections of the hardy Victorian skier, Mick Hull, at the Victorian skiing championships in 1935. There were no lifts, no queues, no crowds, but in the 1930s, with ski equipment that lacked any form of safety release, the risks were there and rescue was made all the more difficult by the remote nature of the mountains. The course for the state downhill titles was Fanny's Finish. It was the afternoon of Tuesday August 20, 1935.

Mick Hull recalled it this way: 'The weather was still fine with conditions hard and icy to Rocky Shoulder, but below the snow was soft and easy to control in the gully, though still very fast … later in the afternoon it became tricky and uneven on the lower part of the course.

'My starting signal came and I shot down the slope … as I came across into the sunlight there was this tremendous "hanging in your bindings" feeling as I hit even wetter snow.

'As I went head over heels … my right ski dug into the wet snow and was held by it – when I came to rest I could see my right ski was pointing the wrong way with my boot still held firmly in the binding and it was obvious that I had broken my leg.'

The spectators quickly became Hull's rescuers, with one of them, Jack Bowen, persuading Hull to swallow a morphine tablet, which 'certainly calmed things.'

The ski patrol leads a chairlift evacuation after the Blue Bullet 2 lift broke down in its early days – the mid-1980s; 'It was probably with wind gusting around 120 kilometres an hour – they never happen on sunny days,' Terry Lyons said. BILL BACHMAN

Early evacuation involved stretchers (below) – among the carriers of this one in 1950 are Maurice Selle in the centre and Alan Carter at right. Later, akjas (above) were introduced. They were shipped out from Europe as additional cargo on BP oil tankers. Patrollers have always been innovators. EDWIN ADAMSON/MAX OTTER/NAMA

Evacuating a patient in the akja (below) down to the Federation chairlift in the early 1980s are pro-patroller Andy Laidlaw (at the front) and volunteer patroller Robin Peter. Robin's Run in the Wombat Bowl is named after Robin Peter in recognition of his service to the patrol and the mountain. BILL BACHMAN

In 2002, patrol director Speaky Lyons and Victoria Police Air Wing pilot Mike Tavcar work together in an evacuation exercise on the northern side of the summit, just below the fire tower.
TREVOR PINDER/*HERALD SUN*

They improvised a stretcher from snow gum branches, belts and straps. It was dark by the time they carried him out of Fanny's Finish and around midnight by the time they reached the original Mt Buller Chalet at Horse Hill.

'There Dr Jimmy Sewell and others had set up a first-aid post … his first job was to get the ski boot off my swollen leg.'

Sewell took to Hull's boots with a cutthroat razor. 'Oh my brand new Zug-leather ski boot from Uncle Ted Molony,' Hull exclaimed. But he was reassured by Tom Mitchell – '"Don't worry Mick, I'll get a new pair sent out for you from the best boot maker in Austria, Emil Walch of Bludenz".'

Hull's leg was set in plaster and he was carried on a stretcher to Dump Inn, the highest point cars could reach. 'I was then shot full of pain killers for the car-journey to Melbourne.'

He arrived at the Epworth Hospital in Richmond early in the afternoon of the day following his accident – almost 24 hours later. Hull's leg was set again and he spent three months in hospital recuperating.

It did nothing to set back one of the most adventurous skiers the country has known.

'In those days there was no ski patrol and no ambulance service, my leg was the first ever casualty of its kind and there was no special organisation to cope … just the commonsense and practical do-it-yourself attitude among skiers,' Hull wrote. (Hull, pp 243-46)

Compare the process in the 21st century. Fanny's Finish remains relatively remote but is within the resort boundaries. An accident there would be attended by a team from Mt Buller's 50-strong ski patrol, many of whom are accomplished in rope and ice-climbing techniques if they are required. They will have completed specialist first aid/paramedic training with the Australian Ski Patrol Association as well as joint training exercises, including helicopter evacuation, with the Victoria Police Air Wing and the Air Ambulance.

Depending on the circumstances, they could have a patient loaded into an akja (rescue sled) and into the care of a resident doctor at Mt Buller Medical Centre inside 20 minutes. If required, a doctor or ambulance officer from the medical centre could attend the accident scene with the patrol.

If time-critical, the Air Ambulance could evacuate a patient from the mountain and have them admitted to a Melbourne hospital within an hour, instead of hours by road.

The functions of the ski patrol are fundamentally unchanged – prevention, treatment and rescue – but the size, efficiency, equipment and skill-level of the patrol have grown enormously.

THE STARTING POINT was 1950 when Maurice Selle, the manager of the Ski Club of Victoria's (SCV) Ivor Whittaker Memorial Lodge, set up the Whitt's first aid room as a ski rescue base. He designed a badge for personnel, which incorporated the emblem of the Red Cross (Lloyd, p445), perhaps because the Red Cross was active in the foundation of ski patrols in North America and was a provider of first aid training in Australia. Using the emblem required the permission of the Red Cross.

Early in the 1950 winter, Selle asked SCV member Cyril Frost if he could arrange it.

Frost's contact with the Red Cross stirred their interest in ski rescue in general and led to the formation of the Victorian Red Cross Ski Patrol Corps, with patrols at Mt Buller, Mt Hotham and the Bogong High Plains, with a reserve group in Melbourne.

An SCV member, Derrick Stogdale, sourced an akja rescue sled from Europe and trialled it at Mt Buller in 1952.

Despite the initial enthusiasm, interest waned in the Red Cross Ski Patrol, dwindling to a low point after the 1953 winter.

> It is regretted that it was not possible in the time available to proceed with the meeting announced in last (May) issue for June 8 to reactivate the Victorian Ski Patrol. Organising work is however continuing, and the patrol will be operating this season. It would help a lot if skiers able to take part would give their names and phone numbers to the (SCV) Club office or contact Cyril Frost at JJ 2556 (evenings only). (*Schuss*, June 1954, p130)

In 1954, Roy Quilliam, who was with the Youth Hostel Association, led the revival, creating a patrol for that season which had less emphasis on its ties with the Red Cross and more emphasis on the skiers. (Lloyd, p452)

That patrol covered the mountain for the 1954 winter and then in the lead-up to the 1955 winter, the Red Cross Ski Rescue Service (as opposed to Ski Patrol Corps) was formed. It relocated the first aid station from the Whitt to the Bull Run Canteen.

This service endured until the end of the 1957 winter when the emerging and politically dynamic Victorian Ski Association (VSA) took over.

The VSA Ski Rescue Service was established in 1958 with Dr Howard Whitaker its chairman and Max Otter appointed Mt Buller area supervisor. (Lloyd, p453)

Under the VSA, the patrol's casualty room returned to the Whitt and remained there in one location or other until 1965, when the first medical centre opened in virtually the same location it is now to be found.

Robert Green, who went on to establish a ski-equipment importing business and had an early involvement with the VSA was one of the patrollers in those days.

'Because we had no radio communication, the first way to summon ski patrol was to use a battery-operated siren, an air-raid siren … you'd press this button, the siren would ring and you'd go out and find the body and bring it in.

'Then we got a bit more organised and finally got some radio communication,' Green said.

Andrea Broad first skied at Mt Buller in 1958 and first patrolled in 1966. She has put on the patroller's jacket every season since, typically volunteering for about 35 to 40 days each season. She recalls the advent of radio as the turning point in sophistication.

When the air-raid siren blew, 'you knew there was something going,' but it would be word of mouth after that to find out where the accident was.

'The Bull Run Canteen was a good spot for people to drop in and say, "Hey, there's someone hurt down in Bull Run or wherever," Broad said, 'but you couldn't even hear the siren if you were up around the summit.'

Radio made the operation much more efficient, but even so, early radio communications could be scratchy.

Kevin Ringrose recalled bouncing signals off a Douglas DC-3 aircraft flying above the mountain in extreme situations. Ringrose first skied Mt Buller with the Boy Scouts as a teenager in the 1940s; it was on the mountain that he met his wife, Mary Stokes, an outstanding skier who raced the international circuit with Judy Forras.

"*Now, how about splints and bandages?*"

A cartoon from the August/September 1970 edition of *Ski Australia*.
GLENN BERNHARDT/NAMA

An early ski patrol exercise in communication and evacuation. NAMA

By the time the VSA Ski Rescue Service was up and running, Ringrose was a qualified engineer working with BP. In the early 1950s, he worked in Britain and skied in Norway, Switzerland, Germany, Austria and France.

On his return he became more involved in ski rescue, joining the committee and eventually becoming its chairman.

'There wasn't much money floating around in those days for capital items. BP were great contributors to safety programs and, in a nutshell, they gave me some money and said, here you are, you can buy some equipment,' Ringrose said.

This was how Australia got a substantial shipment of akjas, colloquially known as banana boats or blood buckets.

'BP arranged to ship these things out on their tankers, which came into Westernport,' Ringrose said.

'They were for the whole skiing industry, everybody got akjas – Thredbo, Tasmania … in addition, they all got Oxy-Vivas [resuscitation and oxygen therapy equipment] and all the gear that goes with them.'

Ringrose and the committee started to improve the training for the patrollers, gaining access to the Mayfield Centre in East Malvern, the ambulance officers' and nurses' training school.

'That was quite a sophisticated course, to the level of licensed ambulance nurses. We were authorised to give intravenous morphine sul-

phate and administer Trilene inhalers and all that sort of stuff.'

Ringrose recalls a meeting with his father-in-law, Sir Harold Stokes, and a friend of Stokes, John Lindell, who was then chairman of the Victorian Hospitals and Charities Commission.

'They were talking about skiing and I said, "Well what these places need is a proper casualty reception centre which would almost have to be a mini-hospital."

'So they said, "You can get government funding, but Kevin, you'll have to sit on the ambulance board," that was the regional ambulance board based in Wangaratta, so I did that for 22 years.'

That was a foundation for medical centres above the snow line in Victoria.

Robert Green recalls the opening of the first Mt Buller Medical Centre clearly and with good reason. He was to present a plaque to the SCV to honour its hosting of the casualty room for so many years, but he and his then wife, the late Vivienne Green, had their first child due.

'To quote Macbeth, he "was from his mother's womb untimely ripped",' Green said, 'It was a social induction'.

Lloyd Green was born on April 20, 1965, so by Robert Green's calculations, Mt Buller's first medical centre opened on April 22, 1965. And the SCV got its plaque.

As much as they'd appreciated the SCV's support, the facilities were an improvement on the Whitt's woodshed where Green recalls 'literally passing the patient on the akja in through the back window.'

MT BULLER'S FIRST permanent patroller came on the scene in the early 1970s. Terry Donnell was recruited by the VSA's Ski Rescue Service to provide a patrol during the week. Then in March 1971, after receiving correspondence from the VSA indicating it was 'unwilling to carry out search work that was outside its scope of handling accident cases' the Forests Commission's Committee of Management decided to investigate having its own 'permanent paid patrol.' (minutes, March 1971).

At a later meeting, in June 1971, the committee resolved that 'John Steedman and Alfred Friedli be appointed to the positions of Ski Patrolmen for 1971.'

This was the point at which Buller effectively had two patrols – the VSA's Ski Rescue Service and the Forests Commission's paid ski patrol. In August that year, the area manager David Kirkham reported back to the committee that 'the Ski Patrol was working successfully and that both Lift Companies were pleased with the work being done.' (minutes, August 1971)

Also in 1971, the Hospitals and Charities Commission made contact with the committee urging some improvements to medical services on the mountain, with the committee hearing that 'Mt Buller, with a (winter) population of 4000 should have a qualified resident doctor.'

The meeting resolved to empower the chairman to 'discuss with the Hospitals and Charities Commission the possibility of calling tenders for a resident private medical practice at Mt Buller during the snow season.' (minutes, August 1971)

As a result, Dr Peter Graham was appointed to run a practice from the medical centre and it was made clear that 'North Eastern District Ambulance Service was the body responsible for the centre.'

When it came to patrolling the mountain however, competing interests were creating conflict. The Forests Commission, through its Committee of Management, wanted to be able to assert its pres-

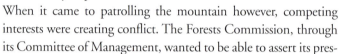

This memorial was erected in 2000 to acknowledge 50 years of ski patrolling on the mountain. Mt Buller's is Australia's longest serving continuous patrol. GLEN BAKER

Boys survived in snow cave

Fourteen-year-old Matthew Gray is helped from a snow vehicle after being rescued on Mount Buller yesterday.

SnowSafe

THE SNOWSAFE program was developed to help people understand the mountain environment. The driving force behind it was Ian Parfitt, a skier with a boundless interest and enthusiasm for the sport and the mountains.

It is difficult to measure the impact of a preventative program, but some incidents underscore the value of SnowSafe.

In 1990, a group of Melbourne school students became lost beyond McLaughlins Shoulder. They had seen the SnowSafe video on the trip up to Mt Buller and followed its instructions to the letter.

'They were found the next day at first light and they'd done everything right,' Terry Lyons said. 'They dug a snow cave, they huddled together for warmth. They did all the things the SnowSafe presentation had told them to do.'

A July 19, 1990 clipping from *The Age* newspaper showing ambulance officer Rod Polson (left), rescued skier Matthew Gray and the patrollers Andy Laidlaw and Ossi Ramp who found the four boys. *THE AGE*/NAMA

At a ski rescue launch in Melbourne in the mid-1980s are Alpine Resorts Commission chief executive Don Macallan (above, at left), SnowSafe pioneer Ian Parfitt and Victorian Ski Association president Alan Lipshut. PARFITT/NAMA

---

ence with its own ski patrol; after all, it was the landlord and it sought the appropriate control, respect and authority that status should provide.

The Victorian Ski Association, the representative body of the skiers, and its Ski Rescue Service wanted to control its own destiny; after all, it had run the show to that point and owned all the equipment. Ron Grose, as Committee of Management chairman, reported to the committee that it was 'impracticable for a patrolman to be employed by one organisation and supervised by another.'

At that June 1972 meeting, Grose said he could see 'tremendous value in retaining the dedicated and enthusiastic services of the Ski Rescue Service.'

However, here comes the catch.

'It was resolved that the action taken by the Committee to integrate the Ski Rescue Service ski patrolman's activities with those of the Committee's patrol men and area staff be endorsed.' (minutes, June 1972)

The 1970s was a decade where the patrollers lived 'in interesting times,' as the saying goes.

ROLF DENLER, A former Swiss ski racer was introduced to Mt Buller by some Latvian friends and stayed at their ski club, Firn. He worked on the mountain in 1972 for George Aivatoglou at Molony's and also managed the ski club. In 1973 he was interviewed by the VSA's Robert and Vivienne Green for a job as the Ski Rescue Service's paid patroller, Terry Donnell's replacement.

'The VSA was running the Ski Rescue Service, but the Forests Commission paid for the position,' Denler said.

The Forests Commission still had two paid patrollers of its own, Brahm Young and Ross Lloyd, wearing the brown jacket.

'Then in 1975 we got put together, we [all the paid patrollers] had all the same role, I was no longer working for the VSA but for the Forests Commission.

'It was a much better set-up, I used to be in the red parka and they were in the brown and yellow parka and it didn't work so well.' Even though the paid patrollers were united, the gulf remained between them and the Ski Rescue Service.

Reporting to the Committee of Management in June 1979, the district forester, Hugh Brown, outlined a discussion about an endless ski resort dilemma – lift queue priority – that summed up the schism.

'It was agreed that the [Forests Commission] ski patrol is to have priority on lifts until 10.30 and after 16.30.

'After 10.30, the ski patrol are expected to check safety straps etc along the queue and then to use the ski school entrance.

'The SRS [Ski Rescue Service] are not to receive priority on lifts except in emergency situations or when taking part in the sweep and in closing runs.' (minutes, June 1979)

Andrea Broad: 'Basically we got on with the job, but there were some difficult times. A little bit later on there was a perception … that the volunteers were trying to pinch the permanent patrollers' jobs.

'There was a sense of them and us and that was most unfortunate, but that was sorted out when we all started wearing the one uniform,' Broad said.

Michael Monester joined the Ski Rescue Service in 1974, aged 21. He had tried to join when he was 16 but 'Viv Green, who was pretty much running the patrol in those days, told me I was too young.'

One of the patrol bases in the 1970s was a portable hut (above) with volunteer patrol captain Michael Monester standing at the left. The hut that replaced it in the late 1970s (below) was known as the Chook Shed. After the construction of the existing patrol base, it was moved to a location near the resort entry at Mirimbah. MICHAEL MONESTER

Pro-patrollers in the Chook Shed in the 1970s. In the left window are Ray Rogers (left rear), Don Chamberlain, Brian Singer (front left) and Andy Laidlaw. In the right window are Brad Speller (rear), Paul Kirwin (front left) and Don Morgan. BILL BACHMAN

Even at 21, Monester said, some people still thought he was too young, 'so they tried to wear me out. In those days, they had this archaic system where patrollers were allocated a run for the day. 'Gerhard Kindler and myself were allocated Skyline … I was there every weekend, and all my university holidays … we patrolled Skyline for the entire season. We didn't complain.'

The strategy paid off. With a combination of drive, enthusiasm and hours on the mountain thanks to a flexible university law course, by 1976 he was the Ski Rescue Service captain and chief examiner for the Australian Ski Patrol Association.

Monester remained captain until 1981 and although the patrollers were united by their high standards, particularly as the Australian Ski Patrol Association (ASPA) developed and people like Dr John Zelcer and Rick Head improved its training programs, they were still divided by the groups they belonged to beneath that ASPA umbrella.

WHEN SANDIE JEFFCOAT arrived on the mountain as its area manager in 1982, he encountered one group, the Forests Commission's paid patrollers, wearing brown jackets with a yellow maltese cross and another group, the Ski Rescue Service, wearing red jackets with a white cross 'and never the twain would meet.' Jeffcoat said 'it was fairly controversial at the time, but I eventually

got them all into a blue jacket with a yellow maltese cross. I always felt from the public's point of view, if they were lying there with a broken leg they weren't going to care about the colour of the jacket that turned up.

'There was some controversy, but it all worked out. I think it works very well now, probably better on Buller than most mountains, the association between the volunteer and paid patrollers, and a lot of credit for that is due to Terry Lyons,' Jeffcoat said.

Terry 'Speaky' Lyons, from surf-central Torquay, was one of a group of Buller patrollers who made the transition from surf to snow. Another was Brian Singer, a founder of the Rip Curl surfing business. He has a crystal-clear recollection of the initial impact of the mountain.

'It would have been 1970. I'd been surfing with a friend at Winkipop, down near Bells Beach and he said he was going up to Buller so I scooted up there with him in his old grey panel van.

Ossi Ramp (above) and the signs of the times in 1990.
MARK ASHKANASY

Patrol director Speaky Lyons (left) uses the Ski Club of Victoria
building behind the patrol base to give a safety talk to Mt Buller
primary school students in 1986. BILL BACHMAN

'I vividly remember arriving in brilliant sunshine with fresh snow on the trees, fresh snow everywhere, it was just fantastic. I can even remember the music playing – it was *Sea of Joy* by Blind Faith.

'It was obviously a pretty social sort of a place, but for me the attraction was the mountain and the skiing – pretty similar to the feeling surfing gave me. I thought it was a pretty good game and I'd better learn it,' Singer said.

He found his feet as a skier and Singer joined the patrol as a professional in 1976.

'Ross Lloyd was the boss and Donny Morgan was on patrol.' Morgan, who started patrolling in 1974 and hasn't stopped yet, also had a Torquay connection.

Singer concedes the initial appeal was to be 'paid to go skiing, which counted for a fair bit. You got free stuff – skis and stuff or an allowance. It was also an enforced physical regime which was pretty good.'

But the fundamental appeal of the pursuit is something shared by virtually all patrollers who stick at it.

'There are some fantastic people at Buller. It's the people you work with, a great bunch of people to work with in a very close working arrangement,' Singer said.

Despite the success and demands of his surfing business (or maybe because of those factors), Singer patrolled for 25 years. All his children spent their winter primary school years on the mountain. Even though he has since given patrolling away, he still lives on the mountain in winter.

'I don't patrol any more but I keep my stuff there at the ski patrol base. The patrol heads off about 8.15 and I pretty much maintain the routine, wander over there 10 minutes later when it's quiet and put my boots on and have a wander around the mountain and have a coffee and a cookie at Koflers around 10am.'

The camaraderie Singer referred to also appealed to Cait Steiner, a nurse and full-time patroller at Mt Buller from 1987 to 2001. She knew the place by heart before she started on patrol – Steiner was born in the Mansfield Hospital in 1961 and grew up on Mt Buller with her parents Hans and Anne.

'Dad had the general store which was there prior to Molony's. I did my first couple of years [schooling] up there and then moved to Mansfield and I did most of my primary school down there.

'It was a great childhood with lots of freedom; the whole mountain was our playground. There were probably eight to 10 kids that lived on the mountain at that stage and we just used to go exploring … go for walks in the summer time and all our spare time in winter was spent skiing.'

Her parents separated just before she was in grade six and she moved to Melbourne with her mother. Her father remained in the area though and 'I ended up going up there quite regularly from about the age of 15, each winter.

'I did my nursing in Melbourne at the Royal Children's Hospital and decided I wanted to work in the snow.

'I went up in 1984 or 85 and worked at the Whitt and did a few jobs over the next couple of years. I got to know the patrollers and ended up applying for a job in 1987.

'Buller was particularly great in the team of patrollers, the way they worked together and their professionalism. I'm not saying other areas aren't as good, just that from my point of view, they were a group of people who had worked together for years and years.

'They all knew each other's skills and what we were best at and everyone had their own qualities … we worked so well together as a team,' Steiner said.

As Sandie Jeffcoat indicated, the unity of that team, particularly after the division of the 1970s, owed a lot to its leaders and in particular Terry 'Speaky' Lyons.

LYONS HAD A surf retailing business around Geelong and Torquay and he started to become a Mt Buller regular in the 1970s, first working as a fill-in lift operator for his tickets and then as a part-time ski instructor.

'Both Donny Morgan and Brian Singer from Torquay were on the ski patrol with the Forests Commission. 'I always thought that looked like the job for me and I approached [the Forests Commission's] Dave Kirkham at the end of one of the seasons and he said, "There's a job for you next year if you want it" so I started in 1978 or 79.'

Don Chamberlain was the ski patrol director at the time. Lyons took the reins from Chamberlain in 1983. The patrol had been operating out of a portable work shed up until this point and in 1984 it moved into its new home – the current patrol base on the northern side of Bourke Street. It may be coincidence, but that patrol base does bear a striking resemblance to a surf club building. 'I really do see those similarities, we've even got the garage where we can roll the skidoos out instead of the rubber ducks or the surf boat,' Mt Buller's current patrol manager, Sam McDougall, said. 'It really is a good vantage point and our radio operator sits up

there in the fish bowl and she has a really good vision of what's happening on Bourke Street – we often see incidents on Bourke Street before they're called in.

'We're right next to the medical centre and we work closely with the ambulance officers,' he said.

'If we need to take one of the doctors out with us, we can give them a quick buzz on the internal phone and they'll jump on the back of the skidoo and off we go,' McDougall said.

The ambulance service is provided by Rural Ambulance Victoria with a rotating roster from Mansfield.

Dr Tim Houghton ran the medical centre until the early 1980s when Dr Craig McCauley took over. It is now run by a health contractor with some doctors from Mansfield. 'You'll find these doctors and nurses in rural or regional areas have fantastic experience in accident and emergency treatment. They deal with a wide range of incidents and have a real strength for this,' Sam McDougall said.

'They can anaesthetise people and take x-rays, the level of service is extremely high.'

Cait Steiner agreed with the quality of the location.

'It is just the most fantastic place to have it [the patrol headquarters] because you can get anywhere from that point so quickly on a snowmobile.

'Another great thing about that building is the history that Speaky has created in there with the photo albums, the photos on the wall, it's just a fascinating place to walk into and walk around.

Treating an injury on Burnt Hut Spur in 1988 are Mt Buller's first exchange patroller from Squaw Valley Bill Nicholson (left), Speaky Lyons and Don Chamberlain. BILL BACHMAN

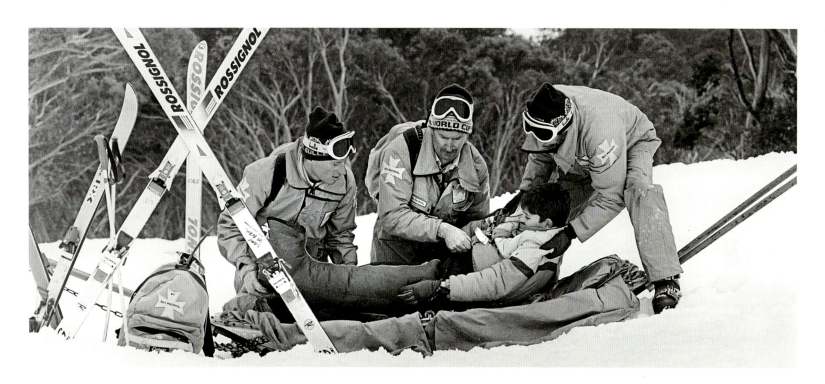

'That's something Speaky concentrated on and no other patrol that I have seen has that, it's all thanks to Speak who had that foresight and vision,' she said.

Another of Lyons' achievements was to build closer relationships with other agencies, such as the police. Mt Buller patrollers now conduct joint exercises with patrollers from other Victorian resorts and the Victoria Police Search and Rescue Squad and the Police Air Wing. There are many good reasons for this but a key one is the nature of Mt Buller's terrain and the occasional need for helicopter extraction as part of a rescue.

'We have ski patrol exchanges with Squaw Valley in the States and Tignes in France, but I think anyone who comes out to Buller will tell you that parts of Buller are just as demanding as anywhere in the world,' Lyons said.

'Very few mountains in Australia have got the steep terrain that we have and that calls for a particular type of rescue … you need more technical skills and climbing skills.

'In areas like Fanny's Finish and the [Summit] chutes we've done a lot of training and cross training including the police search and rescue squad. It doesn't happen very often, but when people do get into trouble out there, it's critical we get there quickly and save them from further injuries.

The three tiny dots towards the centre of the photograph in a climbing exercise in the Buller Chutes below the summit in 1991 are Brian Singer, Ed Mahon and Chris Fogg. MARK ASHKANASY

'ASPA has always been very good at the first aid side of training, but the technical rescue side of it has been left to the mountains to develop. Obviously some mountains don't need the technical skills that perhaps some of the rescues that we've done at Buller have required,' Lyons said.

Although most Victorian ski patrols come under the control of the Resort Management Board (RMB), in NSW and elsewhere in the skiing world the service is generally provided by the lift companies. The transition of the patrol from the RMB to Buller Ski Lifts occurred in the 1990s in a rationalisation of RMB functions.

Lyons saw it this way: 'When I started, we had three sorts of bosses in Blue Lifts and Orange Lifts and we worked for the Forests Commission.

Climbing the northern face of the summit (left) are Ossi Ramp (at rear) and Andy Laidlaw in 1990. MARK ASHKANASY

'But the way I always looked at it was I worked for ski patrol and ski patrol's job is to look after the skiers and that's the way I've always approached it.

'When we became part of the lift company I didn't see our role changing one bit. Our job was still to look after the safety of skiers,' he said. Cait Steiner has worked recently in patrols with both models. 'When we were separate bodies we tended to make our own decisions about how things would happen and then talk to the lift company about what we were doing.

'As a combined entity the communications channels were a bit freer, there was more getting together and discussing what was going on.

'When we worked together we were still left to do the job we'd always done and always had the final say in our own area,' she said.

SAM McDOUGALL, MT Buller's current patrol manager, joined the patrol in 1997 just after the transition had been completed. McDougall grew up in inner Melbourne Carlton and went to the local school, Princes Hill Secondary College, which has a camp at Sawmill Settlement.

'So we went on school camps and I fell in love with the whole skiing idea.

The 2007 ski patrol, photographed at the top of the Abom lift in its last season as a triple chairlift.
From left, standing in the back, are Don Morgan, Mel Tyrrell, Bryan Matthews, Brad Carter, Rob Sparrow, Nathan Lyons, Cam Gordon, Ossi Ramp, Ed Mahon and Bob Bateup.
Kneeling and at the front are Terry Lyons (left), Andy Laidlaw, Tim Byrne (standing), Brad Carter, Squaw Valley exchange patroller Nick Frey, Steve Sparks, Tignes exchange patroller Christophe Estebe with his son Jimy, Marshall Yencken, patrol director Sam McDougall and his daughter Mille and Laurie Blampied. FUN PHOTOS

Koflers (below) is a regular ski patrol destination. If patrollers are asked for their whereabouts, 'Code 5600' means Koflers (it is at 5600 feet), similarly a 'Code 5400' means Tyrol Restaurant. In this 2002 photograph are Don Morgan (left), Ed Mahon, Ossi Ramp, Squaw Valley exchange patroller Wes Schimmelpfennig and Terry Lyons. TREVOR PINDER/*HERALD SUN*

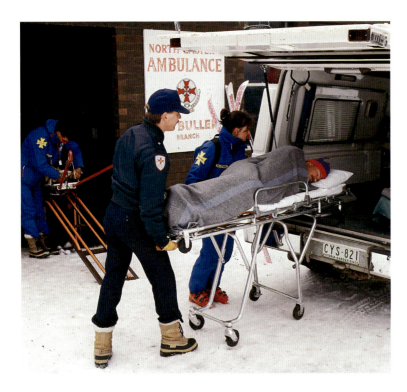

Outside the old medical centre in 1990 (patients are now transferred indoors). The ambulance officer is Steve Hollowood and the patrollers are Chris Fogg (left) and Cait Steiner. MARK ASHKANASY

John Winters from Victoria Police (left), Ossi Ramp and Andy Laidlaw discuss a training exercise in 1990 at the top of the summit chairlift. MARK ASHKANASY

'When I was about 19, I came up and did a bit of work at the camp and before I knew it I got a job on the lifts as a lift operator.'

He became a lift supervisor, then when there was a vacancy on the ski patrol, he applied for the job, got it and started with the ski patrol in 1997, taking over the patrol manager's job when Speaky stood down in 2004.

While the basic functions of the patrol are unchanged – mountain safety, first aid and rescue – a significant change in the last decade has been in the demands of documentation.

'That's the stuff that forced me away,' Lyons said, 'I've got enough of that with my own [surf retail] business, let alone going back up to Buller and doing more paper work.

'I went up there to be a ski patroller, not a lawyer. I guess that's where society has gone, I think I liked it better in the old days when you just went out there and did your job.'

Brian Singer agreed: 'Towards the end of my 25 years there, one of the main changes was the increase in litigation, it was a bad state of affairs in our community, where somebody has a legitimate accident but they have to blame somebody else.

'That became an intrusion, not just into skiing but throughout our society. It had an impact on patrolling – you had to spend much more time with documentation, photographing, witness reports. It increases the extent of documentation and decreases to a degree the experience of adventure by people in the mountains,' Singer said.

Sam McDougall recognised the problem but believes we've turned a corner.

'That has definitely changed the face of all adventure sports, there's more of a magnifying glass on who is responsible and the duty of care and all that.

'However, along the line, there was a recognition that some of the legislation was actually putting adventure sports or inherently risky sports out of business, things like horse riding and rafting, where some of the smaller companies couldn't carry the insurance burden.

'As a result of changes in legislation, people taking part in adventure sports take on a lot more of the responsibility, a lot more than they used to, rather than just the people providing the service.

'So it [litigation and the related insurance crisis] went through a peak period and in 2003 it started to die down. At the moment it's a good reality for both the user and the provider,' McDougall said.

Another progression has been in the nature of equipment available to the patrol.

In 2002, a skier suffered a heart attack getting off the chairlift on Bourke Street but was successfully saved, simply because defibrillation equipment was close at hand.

'He probably had more chance of survival up here on Bourke Street Mt Buller than in Bourke Street Melbourne – we have three defibrillators located around the mountain,' McDougall said.

'Vacuum mattresses are another thing that have really changed the face of first aid response, being able to immobilise someone out in the field – hip injuries, back injuries, we can conform what is essentially a bean-bag bed to the shape of the person or the limbs and depending on the scenario it can set rock-hard.'

Equipment is always improving and while most of it and the patrol budget comes from Buller Ski Lifts, there is a component

SKI PATROL

that the mountain's volunteer patrollers generate through different forms of fund raising.

'We've got 14 paid people within the patrol – 13 pro-patrollers and one radio operator – and we have 35 volunteers, they've got a minimum requirement of 12 days on-snow and that's what they have to fulfil to keep on coming back,' McDougall said.

'Training is exactly the same as the paid patrol, it's all done through ASPA, it's a three-yearly update but every year we have minimum skills we have to update, with things like CPR, administering Pentane – a pain relief drug – oxygen use. It's more related to our equipment and CPR.

'The volunteers also come up and help out with mountain biking during the summer and we had a few of them up helping out when the bushfires were on; they're not just active in the winter months, they help out whenever needed, they're fantastic.'

As Mt Buller's summer trade grows, particularly with pursuits such as mountain biking, there is also a necessary safety and first aid function there that McDougall fulfils.

'So part of my summer role is to manage activities like mountain biking, not just first aid but also organising events and track maintenance.

'The other part of my role is occupational health and safety, working with height training for chair evacuation and in doing risk assessment for the company.'

Ski patrol is one link in a major chain involved with mountain safety. Lyons put it this way: 'Our relationship with other emergency services like the police, ambulance, CFA, medical centre and other bodies like the Resort Management Board, the lift company and people on the snow like lift operators, snow groomers, snowmakers and instructors has grown through all the changes over the years.

'Getting the right mix of paid and volunteer patrollers has also been an important factor in maintaining a strong patrol.

'Allan Terrens and Tony Sullivan are great examples of just that. For over 30 years, Allan has contributed enormously to our first aid training and training manuals and, like Tony, patrols for nearly as many days as our paid patrollers.'

Search and rescue

NOT EVERY SEARCH at Mt Buller has a happy ending. Some have ended in tragedy, some have extended so far, they have called on resources as broad as the local cattlemen and women for their horse skills and local knowledge.

Some have had a lighter side though. One in particular gave strength to all the clichés about alpine resorts.

'A girl came and saw us about 5 or 5.30pm one evening, just as it was starting to get dark, and said, "My friend's missing",' Speaky Lyons recalled.

'So we implemented a search and the police became involved and the search started to escalate, but we couldn't really find anything.

'It was dark and we were re-sweeping the area around McLaughlins Shoulder and we brought in the ski instructors, we got some of the lifts restarted, some of the cats going.

'Around about 8.30, the local sergeant said to this young lady, we're going to have to ring this guy's parents in Melbourne just to let them know what's going on.

'So the police officer has rung the people in Melbourne and said, "Look, its sergeant so-and-so here from the Mt Buller police, I'm just letting you know your son's been reported missing by his girlfriend up here and we're doing everything we possibly can to find him."

'And there was silence on the other end of the phone for a while until the person said, "My son's married and he's at work at Melbourne."

'And the sergeant then said, "Well, I'm not sure whether he's married or not but the fact is, he's lost on Mt Buller."

'So the following morning the Police Air Wing was called in and Police Search and Rescue were there and this bloke's mum and dad and his wife … and his girlfriend.

'We'd found some tracks late in the night so we had a rough idea of where he was, out on McLaughlins Shoulder, and the Police Air Wing went out and winched him back and they landed back on Baldy.

Mansfield cattleman and state parliamentarian Graeme Stoney finds a path for the Hagglunds oversnow vehicle in a search and rescue exercise near his family's Bluff Hut. SANDIE JEFFCOAT

'Donny Morgan went up to get him on the snowmobile and as he was getting out of the helicopter, he asked Donny who was on the mountain.

'Donny told him and he said he'd like to get back in the helicopter and go back out there and get lost again!

'One of the police women from Mansfield finished up having to separate the wife and the girlfriend … his nice little trip to the snow turned pretty ugly.'

MOUNTAIN SPORTS

Richard 'RJMC' McGechie takes the
Federation Bluff. First tracks on a powder
morning in 2005. KIT RUNDLE

8

Ski schools

Good technique is crucial in snow sports, but obtaining it isn't always simple. In the early years, those who could teach it were rare and, above the snow line at least, were close to nobility.

TECHNIQUE WAS FIRST learned from observation, from books, from the advice and tips of fellow skiers, from the occasional expert such as Helmut Kofler and from the experts' better apprentices.

Around Kofler's time, Gerald Rush was a regular technical correspondent to the Ski Club of Victoria's (SCV) *Schuss* magazine, explaining arts such as the 'body lift in turning' and the 'classification and progression of ski turns'.

The SCV ran indoor tuition classes for members at Melbourne's Railways Institute. The classes were organised by the Technical and Tuition Committee, which included Rush. (Lloyd, p555)

Post-war, as Australia's migration program gathered pace, more people with some background in the European Alps were making their way to the mountain. Some had training as instructors or had an understanding of the art and also an understanding of the business opportunity in ski schools, given the demand from potential pupils.

One of the instructors was the British-born and Arlberg-trained Maurice Selle who recruited a local, Les Ramsay, to help him. 'According to Les, Maurice Selle went to the SCV hut at Boggy Creek in 1947, where he accommodated guests and taught skiing. Les was a 17-year-old who had skied for three years. Maurice was impressed and suggested to Les that he should concentrate on technique and become his junior instructor. They worked together for the 1949 and 1950 seasons and Les was therefore the first Australian ski instructor on Buller.' (Hume, p7)

In a 1949 advertisement, Selle invited skiers to join the Mt Buller Ski School for 'expert tuition at standard prices either in class groups or by personal tutoring (with) special classes for beginners by assistant instructor Les Ramsay'. (*Schuss*, February 1949, p46)

Technique was recognised formally through the certification of standards by the likes of the SCV and the Victorian Ski Association (VSA) and informally, through the admiration of achievements among fellow skiers. Nothing has changed in the latter part.

A full cover, a sunny day and the ski school has left for the mountain from its home in the heart of Bourke Street, 2007. MARK ASHKANASY

Instructors in the 1950s, Alan Richards (left), Max Otter and Aurel Forras. SANDRA BARDAS

Walter Frois, 1984. BILL BACHMAN

The French Ski School instructors with their signature caps. NAMA

Ludwig Sorger (left) and Max Otter in 1958, then instructing for the Arlberg Ski School. SORGER/NAMA

United Ski School instructors in 1960. Ludwig Sorger (left) Fritz Halbwidl, Eddy Hausegger and Theo Gurtner. SORGER

Almost united. Mt Buller ski instructors in 1981. BILL BACHMAN

Instructor Tony Aslangul riding the Bourke Street rope tow in 1953. *SCHUSS*

David Kirkham (left) Walter Frois, Bob Fleming and Don Chamberlain at the party to mark Frois' retirement in 1984. BILL BACHMAN

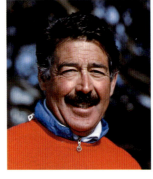

Alexi Sudan, 1983. BILL BACHMAN

The Mt Buller Ski School, 1994. BSL

Brian Maguire, 1985.
BILL BACHMAN

The French Ski School in 1979. CHRIS HILTON-WOOD

The International Ski School in 1986. BILL BACHMAN

Paul Romagna, 2006.
MATT DARBY

Mt Buller's snowboard instructors, 2007. FUN PHOTOS

The Ski School is on the map, 2001. MARK W ASHBY

Egon Hierzegger, 2006.
CHRISTOPH MAIER/BSL

Susie Rogers (left), Bernd Greber and Helen Leaney in 1986.
MARK ASHKANASY

Ross Taylor, 2006.
MARK ASHKANASY

A mutli-tiered operation. The Mt Buller Ski School on the summit in 1984.
BILL BACHMAN

105

In a 1953 article titled 'Parallel Versus Stemming', Tom Fisher discussed the nature of technique and confessed to a sense of guilt in absorbing technique through observation, presumably rather than paid participation:

> Mount Buller skiers this year are very fortunate in having a choice of several very keen and competent instructors to choose from, offering a diversity of techniques also … Although one feels a cad in closely observing these instructors at work with their classes, one must, nevertheless, be impressed by their demonstrations to their pupils of their respective techniques, whether they be stemming or parallel. A new angle to the case was recently expressed to me, with regard to the age of a beginner having a bearing on the technique to be adopted.
>
> A child taught skiing should be started on parallel only, but an adult commence with stem turns, stem christies and then parallels.
>
> In conclusion, whether it be stem or parallel, "lead your skis, don't chase them," to quote American star, Dick Durrance. (*Schuss*, Sept-Oct 1953)

The following year, Leopold Parker responded to Tom Fisher, with another perspective on technique.

> The fighting and the shouting of the past season's skiing have died down, and we who have survived so many a battle, notice that friend and enemy alike do not prepare for the next struggle of French versus Arlberg (technique). No, we all just prepare for another season of skiing.
>
> Some of the French advocates believe that they must be right, because their technique was built up after years of practice and progress with and of the old (Arlberg) method … All skiing schools show a common tendency to proselytize. The innovator, who kept his methods secret, would win all races if his technique was so superior.
>
> But most people do not start skiing in order to start in races … Today's happy youngsters begin skiing often as an additional thrill ... and it is more or less chance which brings them to the Arlberg or French School.
>
> In *Schuss*, Mr Fisher asked us to forgo the emotional and suggested one reasonable distinction: Young beginners should learn French – not so young the Arlberg-stem.
>
> I would like to add another one: As we all have to learn so much in a very short time, if you want to wander on snow after two to three days tuition, choose Arlberg.
>
> With mastery of snow-plow turn and kick-turn, every mountain is then accessible to you. (*Schuss*, March-April, 1954, p62)

Later in the decade, in a 1957 'World Ski News' column, Geoff Henke wrote of the 'wedeln ... a series of racing turns executed on the fall-line of a slope without a static intermediate phase of tra-

Ludwig Sorger (above left) has the undivided attention of his pupil in the mid-1950s. SORGER/NAMA

Instructors like French champion Charles Bozon (below), pictured here in 1956, had all the tips for a skiing public eager to learn. FORRAS

versing between turns. Linked turns in the fall-line have formed part of many ski-ing techniques, but only in the past few years has this manoeuvre developed into the clearly defined … wedeln – the running style which skiers all over the world now either use or aspire to.' (*Schuss*, Nov-Dec 1957, p294)

Whichever technique they chose or had chosen for them, the way skiers applied it across the mountain owed something to teaching and a lot to imitation, the copying of manoeuvres and style outside ski lessons.

The instructors were nevertheless the trendsetters, the holders of the flame, and the keepers of the knowledge.

IN AUSTRALIAN MOUNTAIN resorts, snow sports schools are typically associated with the lift company. In Mt Buller's early years however, they followed the European model (if they were following any model at all), with numerous schools emerging, often associated with an accommodation venue.

'Ski schools came and went at Buller in the 1950s. Paul Heikkila started the short-lived Canadian Ski School at Buller in 1951 and Max Otter (ex Innsbruck, Austria) took over the school headquartered at the Whitt.

'The following season, 1952, Karel Nekvapil and Ernest Forras opened the Alpine Ski School at the Bull Run Canteen and they concentrated on teaching the modern method.' (Lloyd, p559)

Max Otter ran the Mt Buller Ski School from the SCV's Ivor Whittaker Lodge in 1953 and then, in 1954, a magazine advertisement announced the opening of 'The Modern Arlberg Ski School Mount Buller.'

The instructors, Max Otter, Andre Papp, Karel Nekvapil and Max Magreiter described themselves as 'highly experienced overseas instructors who will operate the school throughout the season. Lessons daily … meeting point at the top of Bourke Street.'

The Arlberg Ski School also offered ski-hire and ski-repair services. (*Schuss*, June 1954)

Karel Nekvapil and his wife Sasha were running the Australian Postal Institute Lodge at Mt Buller before they established themselves at Thredbo.

Max Otter was the manager of the Whitt for the SCV and Mick Hull described him as an outstanding instructor, particularly of children. 'He was hero-worshipped by the young for his understanding of the kind of things that at their age they related to and enjoyed most.

'Max knew well that, for the very young, skiing had to be presented as just another happy form of play, another game.

'It was an attitude that transformed the learning stage for the children, far away from the concentration expected of adult beginners.

'For instance, to encourage them to use their new-found turns, Max would set an easy slalom … down one side of Bourke Street

'Modern' technique was pioneered in Austria's Arlberg region – it was natural to name a ski school after it. This advertisement was in *Schuss* magazine in 1957. NAMA

– the difference was that at each gate, instead of flags, there would be toffee-apples or other goodies tied to the poles which the kids would have to bite off as they turned through them. In later years, Ernest Forras did this also.' (Hull, p261)

Ed Adamson, who was a student of Selle, Otter and Forras through his childhood remembers the differences: 'Maurice Selle gave formal instruction, Max Otter demonstrated, encouraged and coached. If you did particularly well he might give you an Arlberg cloth badge to sew on your parka.

In the early 2000s (above), an instructor takes the class through the steps. Even if the profile of the typical instructor has changed, snow sports are still among the sports best suited to instruction. MARK W ASHBY

In the early 1950s (below), Ernest Forras teaches technique to his class. The interested onlookers were typical of the time, picking up whatever understanding they could, even at a distance. JOHN HIRAMS/FORRAS

'Ernest Forras on the other hand was a show to ogle at. Ernest was also careful to explain, demonstrate and then wave you to follow, and I'll never forget him doing ballet on skis down the top part of Bull Run, pirouetting around and around, then skating and whirling again. It was marvellous to watch,' Adamson said. During the 1940s and 50s another ski instructor taught and tested skiers for their VSA test levels. Standard one was for beginners and included coping in the snow, walking out on skis using herring-bone or side step and doing kick turns. Level two was more advanced and level three quite accomplished. There were skiing tests as well as ski jumping tests one could try out for. The instructor and tester was Flight Lieutenant Ted Tyler. 'He was a kindly man,' Adamson recalled, 'but a stickler for the rules.'

BY 1960, THE VSA was expressing concern to the Committee of Management over the conduct of ski classes by unqualified instructors.

'Mr Burt [Eric Burt, a committee member representing the VSA] stressed the danger of allowing non-qualified persons to act as instructors on a professional basis and stated that the Victorian Ski

Association was concerned with the problem and would like to see the Committee call tenders for the establishment of a recognised ski school.' (minutes, October 1960)

The committee stalled, requesting that the VSA supply 'further information concerning proposals for controlling ski instructors and to indicate the policy operating in other well-known ski resorts.' (minutes, October 1960)

The teaching momentum built regardless.

The name might have been a run-of-the-mill political ploy to bring all Mt Buller's instructors together, but in 1961, the Arlberg Ski School became the United Ski School.

Its chief instructor was Fritz Halbwidl and its instructors included Aurel Forras, Max Otter, Eddy Hausegger, Ludwig Sorger and Theo Gurtner. (Lloyd, p560)

Even the United Ski School couldn't unite all the instructors. The next year, 1962, the SCV sought the franchise for the mountain's sole ski school, but Max Otter and Aurel Forras wouldn't join in, so they continued to operate as the United Ski School.

The Committee of Management resolved that 'two franchises for ski schools be granted for the 1962 snow season at a rate of £150 per school, payable in advance. These franchises be given to the following: Ski Club of Victoria; M. Otter and A. Forras (in partnership).' (minutes, March 1962)

As the lift operators continued their transformation from cooperative ventures to businesses, they saw the scope in including ski schools in their enterprise.

For Orange Lifts, in 1962, 'the United Ski School became the focal point, with Max Otter and Aurel Forras sharing 50 per cent, Orange Lifts 33.4 per cent and Blue Lifts 16.6 per cent. This company was taken over about a year later by Orange Lifts.' (Hume, p7)

Leading in to the 1962 season, the Whitt's manager, George Hicks, recruited some instructors from St Christoph in Austria's Arlberg. Something went wrong however, 'and the misconduct of the instructors forced George Hicks, with SCV board backing, to terminate their employment prior to the end of the season.

'It is minuted that they were "dismissed and returned forthwith to Zurich by plane on 9 September, 1962".' (Lloyd, p560)

Their transgression has become hazy in the dust of the years, but there is a suggestion there may have been some female fraternisation that went beyond club principles. Fancy that, among young ski instructors. That was enough for the SCV – it advised the Committee of Management in October 1962 that it would not be seeking a ski school franchise for season 1963.

Orange Lifts took over the United Ski School and used Max Otter's connections with the Austrian ski instructor institute, the Bundessportheim and its legendary director, Professor Franz Hoppichler, to create a link for their ski school.

'Correspondence was entered into with the professor and this formalised the influx of Austrian instructors.' (Hume, p7)

Instructors in the midst of the children are Kathy Cumming (left), John Whitehouse and Ian Browning in the late 1970s. BILL BACHMAN

Walter Frois was appointed director of what became known as the Austrian Ski School in 1967 and held the post until the end of the 1984 snow season. Frois was succeeded by Paul Romagna (1985-1997 – he also ran the merged International Ski School), Brian Maguire (1997-99), Bernd Greber (1999-2001), Egon Hierzegger (2002-06) and Paul Romagna once again (2007-).

Orange Lifts' 1963 takeover of the United Ski School marginalised Blue Lifts in the ski teaching business, so John Hilton-Wood responded.

'We persuaded the Forests Commission that we should have our own ski school,' he said. Thus began the French Ski School. If Orange Lifts had a connection to the cream of Austria's instructors, Hilton-Wood established a similar connection with the French, tapping into the Ecole du Ski Francais at its headquarters in Chamonix.

He did this through instructors like Alexi Sudan who led Mt Buller's French Ski School until 1984 and held the same status in France as Hoppichler held in Austria.

The rivalry of the era cannot be underestimated. The Austrians held themselves as the creators and guardians of modern ski technique, on the back of Hannes Schneider and his creation of the Arlberg teaching method in the early 1900s.

There was also fierce competition with the French in the sport that mattered most to the Austrians – ski racing.

The French approach was seen as less structured, more flamboyant, an embodiment of the French attitude to life. It was a system that created the great Jean-Claude Killy, the triple alpine gold medallist (slalom, giant slalom and downhill) at the 1968 Grenoble Winter Olympics. The Austrian style was more disciplined, more formal, more rigid and from it emerged the first skier to accomplish the Winter Olympic skiing trifecta, Austrian Toni Sailer, at Cortina d'Ampezzo in 1956.

One Austrian and one Frenchman.

BRIAN MAGUIRE WAS 18 when he joined the French Ski School in 1978; he had been an instructor at a small ski school in Michigan and, through a family connection, was offered a job at Mt Buller. Maguire is now director of the Jackson Hole Mountain Sports School in Wyoming where he lives with his wife (Elizabeth Powell – originally a Mt Buller skier) and their three children. He remembers his Mt Buller years very fondly.

Lukey Robbo leads a group of snowboarding pupils down the summit in 2007. MARK ASHKANASY

'The ski school director [in 1978], Alexi Sudan, was a professor of the national school in Chamonix, so he would be doing his exams over the course of the year in Chamonix where all these Frenchmen would go to get qualified.

'He'd always siphon off some of the best instructors that were interested in teaching skiing over summer and bring them to Australia. '[In 1978], there would have been about 12 or so Frenchmen from all over France and we lived right above the Bourke Street chair. 'They had folks there that cooked for you … you had big spaghetti dinners and red wine for lunch and you could look out the window to see who was lining up for your class.

'It was definitely one of the most cultured sort of ski teaching experiences you could have. We used to stay open all night long. There was just too much temptation for a youngster,' Maguire said.

He clearly recalled the rivalry between the lift companies and, related to this, between their ski schools.

'There was a certain amount of pride involved between the Austrians and the Frenchmen, you know. There were some quite big name instructors both from the Austrian and the French side who came to Buller over the years. That included the Strolz boys from Langen on the Austrian side and several World Cup racers, with names like Duvillard in the French Ski School.

Inner skiing

New age started to come of age in the 1970s, when the hippie era grew up. An American author, Tim Gallwey wrote *Inner Tennis* (1972) and it was a watershed in the way people approached sport. It took off, dealing as it did with the mind of the sportsperson, going beyond the physical and into the psychological aspects of sports performance. Gallwey applied the ideas to skiing with *Inner Skiing* (1982 and revised in 1997).

At Mt Buller in 1985, Peter Forras, who had retired as a ski racer, and John Falkiner, an Australian instructor and freestyle skier who now lives in Switzerland and works as a mountain guide, created a program loosely based on *Inner Skiing*. A sports psychologist helped develop the program and Forras and Falkiner delivered it.

'We had a ball. We probably only did half a dozen courses but anyone that did them will still talk about them,' Forras said.

'We used a lot of video loops and imagery, combined with the inner game concepts,' Falkiner said.

With the mountain's ski school hierarchy concentrating on bringing their ski schools together, Forras and Falkiner may have been ahead of their time.

'It was driven mainly by Pete and myself and received well by the customer, however we did not receive much support from the ski school,' Falkiner recalled. He was also a clinician and examiner for the ski instructors' association at the time and gave lectures on the

John Falkiner (above) skiing the Summit Chutes with Fanny's Finish above in 1984. BILL BACHMAN

psychological side of sport for the Australian Professional Ski Instructors during the ski instructor courses.

'That was also a little bit outside of the box for the curriculum and was received well by the students but not really supported by the powers that were in place at the time,' he said.

Instructor Susie Petty talks her charge through the slalom course on Bourke Street in 1985. BILL BACHMAN

'[Jean-Claude] Killy even visited Mount Buller a couple of times in the early 60s and used to ride his bike up and down the hill training for ski races.'

The Whitt's management always recognised the drawcard ski instructors could be. 'It was definitely one of the classier clubs you could go to back in the day,' Maguire said. Instructors from both ski schools would find themselves socialising there, but it was a loose kind of camaraderie, more 'like two footy teams socialising,' Maguire said.

Ed Adamson recalled skiers taking French Ski School lessons 'from a tall larrikin whose name was supposedly Henri Mason.

'Henri's French accent invariably gave way to a certain brand of English – he was, in fact, a New Zealander whose enthusiasm was as contagious as his high energy levels.

'Another French Ski School instructor for many years was Mansfield-bred Peter Reynolds, a gun skier,' Adamson said.

PAUL ROMAGNA RECALLED 'quite a bit of animosity, between the companies more than the instructors – we were quite good friends even if we were in heavy competition.'

Romagna joined the Austrian Ski School in 1973 – he had trained as a car mechanic but taught skiing in the Austrian winters and sought to do the same during the summers. He had a friend who was teaching at Mt Buller who gave him the contact details for the ski school director so he wrote to him. 'I thought I'd have no hope but a few weeks later I got a job offer.'

Romagna has only missed one season at Mt Buller since 1973, the 1978 winter when he got married, but his wife saw him pining for the Australian winter, so they worked out a way to travel together and spend the winters at Mt Buller.

He said the situation with an Austrian and a French ski school was 'absolutely hilarious'. From the perspective of attracting business, the main difference was in the location of the two ski schools.

'The French Ski School had by far the better location – where the clock tower now is. We were up at Helicopter Flat, so everybody who came into the village joined the French Ski School.

'We were highly qualified but we were not very busy. However, it turned around fairly quickly. The French had fantastic skiers as ski instructors, ex-World Cup racers who were brilliant skiers.

'Some of the Buller people used to say "ski French, drink Austrian", meaning if you wanted to have a good party, go with the Austrians and if you wanted to have good skiing, go with the French.'

Despite their skiing skills, Romagna believes language skills let the French down. 'Their English was quite poor and our English was quite good then. People realised that and slowly, slowly the change started and we had more and more pupils,' Romagna said.

Another advantage was in terrain. The association with Orange Lifts gave the Austrian Ski School access to Mt Buller's summit, so in marginal snow years, they had access to snow-covered slopes that the French instructors could not get to – Baldy was as high as they could go.

Apart from the cultural differences, there were distinct differences in technique. To initiate a skiing turn, the French used rotation, whereas the fundamental element in the Austrian style was upper-body/lower-body separation.

Romagna said the French technique would get a skier moving faster, but they'd hit a wall when they had to tackle steeper slopes.

A day in the forest – the Buller Kids Centre in the area off Bourke Street known as the Black Forest. KEREN FREEMAN

'The people at the French Ski School learnt to turn quite quickly. On the first day, the beginners' classes would be up at Baldy.

'But to master the steeper terrain, you had to change the technique and they were not able to.

'Then they [the skiers] would come to us, change the technique and by the end of the week they would be skiing the summit,' Romagna said.

When the lift companies became one in 1985, so did the ski schools. Paul Romagna was appointed director of the International Ski School, with Brian Maguire his deputy.

'Not only were the ski-teaching fundamentals different, but also the philosophy, the work ethic, the etiquette, the strategies. It was a huge challenge,' Romagna said.

'Our [Austrian] ski school had quite a structure, they were working eight hours a day, were hard workers. The French had morning coffee at 10 o'clock and they couldn't be bothered to go out when the weather was bad.

Inside the Kids Centre – the largest licensed childcare facility in Victoria – Jacqui Tsamakis keeps the children occupied in 2006. KIT RUNDLE

'All of a sudden they came into our system and it was a culture shock for them, a real culture shock.' Maguire remembered the merger of ski schools as an education in conflict resolution.

'We just had two completely different cultures and methods of what ski teaching should be, living in very close proximity it was very interesting.'

In the management-obsessed 21st century, experts would have come in and run courses and workshops and laid down workplace rules and guidelines.

Not so in the mid-1980s.

'I think we almost resolved them [the conflicts] through not resolving them,' Maguire said.

'It was probably at a time when worldwide a lot of the unique aspects of different countries' techniques were starting to blend together anyway, so you had some technical issues that were coming closer together.

'But nobody would admit to it, [even] these senior guys who actually skied very similarly. It just came down to more interpersonal relationships in the end. Ski schools are all about priority and seniority,' Maguire said.

WHEN PAUL ROMAGNA started with the Austrian Ski School in 1973, there were 16 overseas instructors and one Australian.

In 2006, Mt Buller had instructors from Australia, Austria, Italy, France, Switzerland, Germany, Britain, the Netherlands, Russia, the Czech Republic, Slovakia, Slovenia, Canada, the United States, Japan, South Korea and New Zealand – virtually all the world's nations where there is snow.

Despite the mix of nationalities, the ratio in a group that grows to about 300 instructors in peak season, is now about two thirds Australian and one third international.

The emergence of Australian instructors was not without some pain. In the mid-1970s, some Australian instructors were agitating for a better share of the business and, according to Orange Lifts chairman David Hume, called on the government to 'halt the importation of overseas instructors, on the basis that they were taking the jobs of Australians'. (Hume, p7)

The conflict developed between the fledgling Australian Professional Ski Instructors (APSI) group and the politically powerful Australian Ski Areas Association – the body representing Australia's lift companies.

What emerged was a vastly improved system of training and accreditation within Australian ski schools.

'The examiners were mainly ski school directors, assisted by senior instructors,' Hume wrote.

'The exams were of the same standard as those overseas and while the failure rate was high, those who passed could be employed anywhere.' (Hume, p8)

The Buller ski schools were brought together, in a sense, over the need to improve the lot of the locals.

Paul Romagna recalled working with the director of the French Ski School, Alexi Sudan ('he was an absolute professional, a very, very nice gentleman and very experienced with a high profile in

France') and Mike Porter, an American, to help introduce accreditation and exams in Australia.

It was not until the merger of the ski schools though, coinciding with the evolution of the profession in Australia, that an Australian technique or teaching method started to develop, introduced by the APSI.

'Nowadays technique is pretty uniform throughout those nations [represented by Buller instructors],' Egon Hierzegger, Mt Buller Ski and Snowboard School manager from 2002 to 2006, said.

However, in the training of Buller's instructors, they 'strongly follow the APSI – the Australian Professional Snowsports Instructors – manual,' he said.

Hierzegger has a fine alpine heritage; he came from Tauplitz, an Austrian village with a small ski area and a background in salt mining – stretching back to the days of the Roman Empire – and farming. His grandfather built Austria's first ski lift at Tauplitz, in 1933.

Egon Hierzegger beat a typical path for an instructor. He was keen to travel and first worked at Falls Creek in 1987, moving to Mt Buller for the winter of 1988, becoming the Ski and Snowboard School manager in 2002.

Jorg Dutschke in the Summit Chutes in 1984. Then, as in any other year, the uniform has always been the mark of a solid skier. Tradition demands instructors live up to the standard. BILL BACHMAN

The combination of new equipment and improved grooming has changed the way people ski and changed the way the sport is taught. Instructor Ross Taylor skis the summit in 2007. KEREN FREEMAN

The visual impact of the Australian mountains must have been as dramatic for a young Austrian in the 1980s as it was in the 1930s. 'Back home, all the leaf trees lose their leaves in autumn. Here in Australia, you've got the eucalyptus trees and they're always green, even when it snows. I found it pretty amazing. I think it gives it a bit of an exotic touch.'

In his years as manager, while Mt Buller may have followed an international trend of smaller numbers of adults seeking tuition, there was enormous growth in children's programs.

'For example, here [at Mt Buller] we built the new kids centre. We're the biggest registered childcare centre in Victoria.

'That's a huge investment … that's not a money maker [in itself], it's simply an investment so people can enjoy themselves; the family can enjoy it and can go skiing.

'We have some well-developed seasonal programs. In 2006 we had about 500 kids signed up for those programs when the kids ski with the same instructor, with the same coach during school holidays and also each Saturday and Sunday.'

Another major growth area has been snowboarding. 'It has really grown and it's really important for the ski school, although only about one quarter or one third of our business is snowboarding and the rest is alpine with a small amount of cross-country.'

While instructors are still crucial in the modern resort, their status has changed over the years.

'In the old days, instructing was a job for a lifetime,' Hierzegger said. 'It is still in certain areas but even in Austria, we see the change coming through.

'A lot of people use it as a job in holidays, like for university students or when people just finish their school, they do one or two years instructing to move around a bit and maybe go from Austria to Australia. It's a bit of a lifestyle thing, but then they start to get serious and people are not following that [long-term career] path anymore.'

As well as the younger participants, snow sports schools are recruiting people at the other end of the age scale.

'A lot of people do it for a lifestyle change,' Hierzegger said.

'They have been busy, they come up here and love to be up here. They love to teach and they don't actually need that income anymore.

'They have made their money already. They just do it for a lifestyle.'

Bernd Greber

The Snowsports School building at Helicopter Flat is named after him, as is the cup for the best boy and girl skiers at secondary level in the Interschools competition.

The sculpture, *The Spirit of the Skier* is dedicated to him at Mt Buller.

Bernd Greber was a brilliant skier, but it was his understanding of ski instructing as a profession, the breadth of its appeal and his ability to engage all those involved in it – teachers and pupils, parents and children, that gained him respect in the mountains.

Born in Mellau, Austria, on August 26, 1965, Bernd Greber died in an avalanche in his home country on December 27, 2001.

He was the director of the Mt Buller Ski and Snowboard School at the time of his death.

Paul Romagna first noticed Greber as a young ski instructor and admired his ability and ambition. Greber attended Austria's Bundessportheim and achieved the senior level, the Staatliche.

'I was convinced that Bernd had not only the makings of an excellent skier, but also those of an exceptional leader,' Romagna said. 'I was delighted when Bernd expressed his wish to join my team of instructors in Australia.'

'Over the years he was to become my most valued team member and one to who I owe a great deal.' (Oshika, p9)

Romagna said Greber quickly recognised the competitive spirit in young Australians and within that recognised the opportunity for the ski school.

'He really got Mt Buller on the map in regards to ski racing, the logistics of races and the training.'

From that nucleus, he drew in a segment of Melbourne's population that made the Mt Buller Race Club so popular. It translated to new business for Mt Buller, more visitors and a greater commitment from existing visitors.

In driving the race programs 'he [Greber] really was responsible for the real estate boom Mt Buller has had over the last 10 or 12 years,' Romagna said.

Greber was also a frequent action model for ski photographers and won the World Powder 8s in Canada alongside Richi Berger in 1993.

Bernd Greber was survived by his wife Birgit and their son Tim.

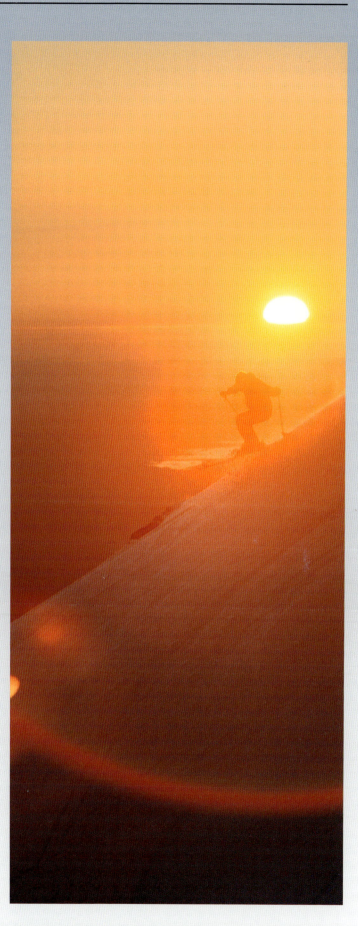

Bernd Greber through the gates (above) and into a Mt Buller sunset (right). MARK ASHKANASY/MARK W ASHBY

9 Evolution

Gravity is seductive. Some defy it on horseback or freeheeling uphill on skis or snowshoes, but most of Mt Buller's riders work with it on bikes and boards, on toboggans and skis. Ironically for the skiers, it took snowboarding – a movement that many on the mountain resisted – to prompt a dramatic improvement in the equipment for their chosen sport.

WHO WAS MT Buller's first snowboarder? It's hard to say. With the primitive equipment snowboarders used in the early days, it could theoretically have been somebody with exceptional balance riding a cafeteria tray from the Arlberg to Kooroora.

Part of the evolution was the mono-ski that emerged from Europe towards the end of the 1970s; a wider ski with traditional ski bindings mounted on it – both feet on a single platform, but with the skier facing forward. Did it work? They aren't widespread today.

Surfers with a taste for the snow were inventing and adapting equipment that could accommodate the surf or skateboard stance for a long time before they struck the right formula. The Snurfer

went into production as early as 1965 and the Winterstick in 1970. In 1977, Americans Jake Burton and Tom Sims started to produce snowboards. (skiclub.co.uk)

Some of the very early boards were available from Kooroora's ski hire. Peter Forras recalled Wally Morrell, who ran the ski hire at the time, giving him a board to try in 1979 or 1980.

Hans Muhlgraber jumps the Fanny's Finish cornice on his 210cm skis in the early 1970s. This shot was a magazine cover at the time. ERIC BURT

'We used to use it out the back of home (the family lodge at Horse Hill) or we'd hike and ride the Tyrol run after the lifts had closed,' Forras said.

Morrell recalled them as 'nothing like the boards we have now.' They had a rope at the front for balance and to keep the tip up and water-ski style bindings.

'Another who got into them early was Mark Adams,' Morrell said. (Mark Adams now has a real estate business on the mountain and is the son of Twin Towers apartments developer Adam Adams). 'I remember him coming up to me and asking if I was going to get into these boards. "It's gunna catch on," he said and I thought, "Oh bullshit, it'll never catch on." Bad mistake.'

Another to try those early Kooroora boards was Thor Prohaska, a surfer from Queensland who developed a taste for the snow and a distaste for ski boots.

'I snowboarded at Buller for three years before I met another snowboarder – I think the first year would have been 1981.

'The first board I ever rode I got from the Kooroora ski hire, they had these chopped-down water skis with some rubber decking on the back [rather than a binding], an aluminium fin and a rope on the front.

'I took that to the top of Chamois and got on it, slid about a quarter of the length, came unstuck and the board went all the way to the bottom of Chamois. That was my first experience.'

The mountain authorities initially took no notice. 'I really went under the radar,' Prohaska said.

In the early 1980s, one of Mt Buller's first snowboarders, Thor Prohaska (above), explores the combination of new equipment and new technique on Skyline. His board, like most of the early models, includes a rope and handle for balance and to keep the tip up. The Burton Backhill snowboard from 1982 (below) was built along the same lines. PROHASKA/MORDY

Regis Emery (below left) and Lionel Adam about to launch down the mountain on their 1988 mono skis. BILL BACHMAN

As the 1980s unfolded and the sport grew, albeit at a snail's pace, he found that 'Blue Lifts were friendly and Orange Lifts were unfriendly.'

'My first exposure to snowboarding was in the 1970s when *Tracks* surfing magazine featured a couple of stories about people using Wintersticks in Europe.

'They were a deep snowboard with a deep keel that wouldn't work on anything but deep snow,' Prohaska said.

Snowboarder Dave Pavlich owned one of those early Wintersticks when he worked at Bill Duff's ski hire.

'I used to ride my Winterstick at night and out the back, as it was outlawed at Mt Buller. Thor Prohaska was the first serious snowboarder in Victoria. He was making boards in the early 1980s. They were the first snowboards in Victoria, I reckon.

'He used them at Buller and Falls, but Buller was very anti-snowboarding for years, that was the reason for me migrating to Hotham,' Pavlich said.

The equipment Prohaska made included a prototype

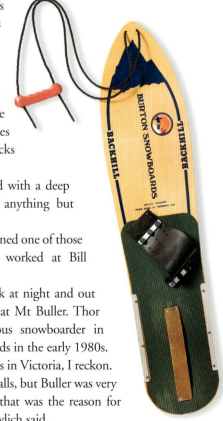

boarding system similar to a skateboard, with the board on top and skis underneath which he tried at Mt Baw Baw in 1981 ('They kicked me off the mountain').

It didn't work too well, so he tried building a board that would run flat to the snow. It gave some basic performance, but it wasn't until 1984, when he had some skiing lessons at Mt Buller, that Prohaska became aware of the role sidecut played in the turning equation.

'So I went and built a snowboard with sidecut and steel edges and a P-tex base. That worked, but it didn't have the flex in it to get the sidecut working properly.'

He wore cross-country ski boots and used short skis with cross-country bindings to ride the drag lifts, with his snowboard strapped on his back. Then he would swap equipment for the ride down.

Ed Mahon, later a patroller, was a lift operator in 1985. 'I was working on Enzian and I can remember seeing this guy riding Chamois on short cross-country skis and this type of snowboard on his back.

'At the top, he would take off the cross-country skis and ride the board down, I remember going back to Fawlty Towers [the staff accommodation] and telling them all about it.'

That person was Thor Prohaska.

Prohaska recalled some growing momentum in the snowboarding fraternity around 1986, when Peter Hill, who had a business called Hardcore Industries that went on to become the Globe board sports business, started importing Sims snowboards.

Prohaska and Hill got in touch with the Victorian Ski Association (VSA) to get some support for their sport – they wanted it to succeed but they also had a commercial incentive; they wanted to sell boards.

'The VSA were pretty good, they were not of the same mind-set as the Forests Commission, who at one point told me boards were banned,' Prohaska said.

'So I started to get involved in the political side of things. Buller was the last resort [in Victoria] to allow snowboarding, they were the last one to come along.'

TO BE FAIR, lack of riding skills among the early boarders and the poor quality of their equipment made the resort's reluctance understandable. Moreover, being outlawed is not entirely a negative for a youth sport.

Terry 'Speaky' Lyons who was patrol director at the time recalled a formal ban in some form being put in place around 1985.

'I think it was a general decision of lift companies and resort management. They were just a bit unsure about it. The main issue was – would they be able to stop themselves on the steep slopes? Would they be safe?

'No one really knew a lot about snowboarding and a few of the lifties started coming back from Canada and North America with snowboards.'

Michael Monester, head of the lift company in 1987, was in favour of the ban – 'I saw it as incompatible [with skiing],' he said.

The ban was eased towards the end of the 1980s, when resort

In 2004, Team Buller coach Jarrod Wouters rides Mt Buller's permanent halfpipe located near the top of the Bull Run chair. MARK ASHKANASY

In the late 1980s, Rolf Denler (below) with a sign that said it all as far as the mountain's view towards snowboarders was at the time. MHS

management introduced a structure where the boarders could ride areas such as Standard and Skyline but not the steeper southern slopes, Bull Run and Federation.

'In 1990, there were no restrictions, they could go wherever they liked,' Mahon said.

Lyons saw it this way: 'We soon realised we were wrong, that the learning curve was much quicker [on a board] than it was for a skier and that they could actually handle the steeper stuff and icy stuff.'

Peter Lynn (above, in red) and Peter Forras take flight on their short Figl skis in 1990. The skis were developed for mountaineering, but later used as a balance and technique-refining tool. MARK ASHKANASY

Mt Buller snowmaker and snowboarder Greg Sheppard takes a drop below the summit in 2007. It's still all about balance. KIT RUNDLE

Mahon recalled snowboarding really taking off around 1992. 'We first noticed a change in the accident statistics in 1994.

'The 1993 season was so bad [for snow cover], we didn't notice anything then, but in 1994 we noticed a real spike in the statistics. 'That matched up with what I saw overseas – it was growing when I worked at Squaw Valley in 1992-93 and really went off when I worked at Blackcomb in 1994-95,' Mahon said.

Thor Prohaska always believed it would take off, but was surprised at the speed of snowboarding's growth when the critical mass eventually accumulated.

He had a rally-driving friend who put it to him this way. 'He said, "Look, Thor, I've studied the way motion affects the pleasure centres of the body and snowboarding affects those pleasure centres like nothing else".'

A strong correlation was identified between snowboarding, surfing and skateboarding, but that may have owed more to fashion and the peer-appeal of the sports than a crossover in technique. 'When you're surfing, you're driving off your back foot,' Prohaska said, 'and when you're snowboarding off anything with any firmness about it, you're off your front foot.'

REBECCA PICKETT-HEAPS came from Colorado to Australia in 1990 and headed straight for the hills, joining Team Buller and helping develop its snowboarding program. Although the mountain was open to snowboarders when she arrived, she recalled an enduring gulf in attitude. 'There was a lot of angst; people letting us know we weren't really welcome. I think they saw the grunge attitude as a problem,' she said.

'We also stood out – people learning to ski don't really tend to stand out, but grungy snowboarders with long hair and badly fitting jeans really do tend to stand out.

'I can honestly say a lot of the snowboarders didn't help – there was plenty of attitude going on. The same thing happened overseas,' Pickett-Heaps said.

'There was definitely an element of apprehension from people with an alpine skiing background.'

Snowboarding brought a lot of people into snow sports that wouldn't otherwise have been involved and, more recently, a bridge has been created by skiers trying snowboarding.

In Pickett-Heaps' observation, 'when we have a bad season, a lot of people get on a snowboard and try it – they don't want to go skiing in such nasty conditions, so they try snowboarding and love it.

'Also, all of a sudden, skiers are getting on twin tips skis and doing the things snowboarders are doing, skiing backwards and doing the same flips and tricks snowboarders are doing.

'That's done a lot to bring the sports together, it killed a lot of the attitude.'

Better snowboarders like Mt Buller for the same reasons better skiers do – steeper terrain such as the Summit Chutes. 'That was what I loved about Australian snowboarding, having the gum trees and these steep drops. I found it really peaceful back there,' Pickett-Heaps said.

Christine Hughes skiing Federation Bluff in 1994. MARK ASHKANASY

Cutting edge Henke ski boots (right) in a 1959 advertisement from *Schuss* magazine. NAMA

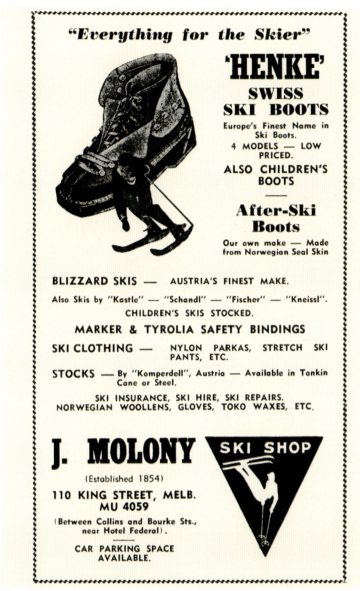

A downside is traversing, which affects some snowboarders more than others. 'Because of the way the slopes tend to lean, Buller seems to be a better mountain for a natural foot (a natural footer on a board leads with the left foot and a goofy footer leads with the right foot).

'I hadn't really noticed it, but quite a few snowboarders said that to me – if you're traversing on your heel-side edge, that can really fry your calves, you're much better off on your toe-side, leaning into the hill.'

AT MT BULLER and elsewhere in the world above the snow line, snowboarding sparked a revolution in skiing. There are all sorts of style guides for skiers and other mountain sports people – new ways of learning and new techniques for turning. But these are generally refinements to established arts. The phenomenon that always sparks a revolution in mountain sports is a revolution in equipment. Technique pushes equipment to its limits. The demand for better performance drives the development of better equipment, but it is the breakthrough in equipment that reveals new horizons in technique. In hindsight, it took ski manufacturers an excruciatingly long time

to produce skis of the quality and versatility of the current crop. In 1947, an American, Howard Head created the first metal ski, but according to US historians, his early attempts were failures. Head was an aircraft engineer who skied a little and thought the equipment could be improved. His first effort, a combination of aluminium and plastic 'broke in the hands of Stowe ski instructors who were testing its flexibility.' (www.aspenhistory.org)

He persevered and eventually encountered success with a wood core ski with steel edges and plastics in addition to aluminium; this evolved to include fibreglass for strength and durability and neoprene to reduce vibration.

Towards the end of the 1950s, skis for sale to Mt Buller skiers were still being made from local and imported timbers. The Tasmanian Timber Bending Works in Northcote offered skis made from spotted gum,

OVERLEAF: A lone skier rides the bumps on Federation in 1985, typical terrain of the time. New skis, new turn types and better grooming have munched the moguls. At left is a collection of skis from the 1930s to 2007. BILL BACHMAN/NAMA/TSM

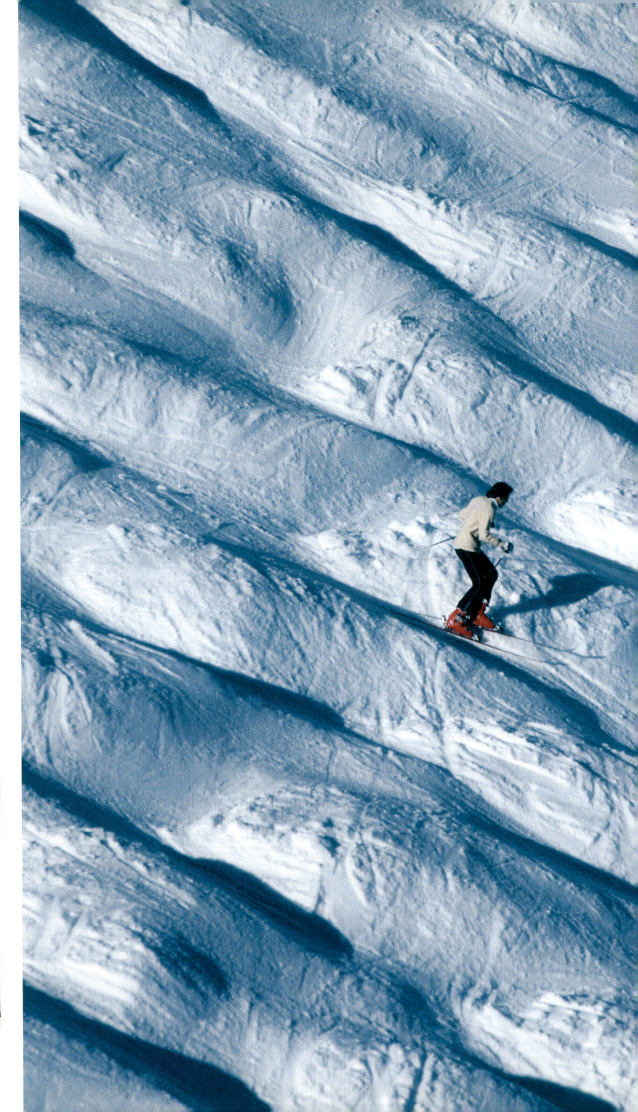

1940s 1950s 1960s

1970s 1980s 1990s

2002 2004 2007

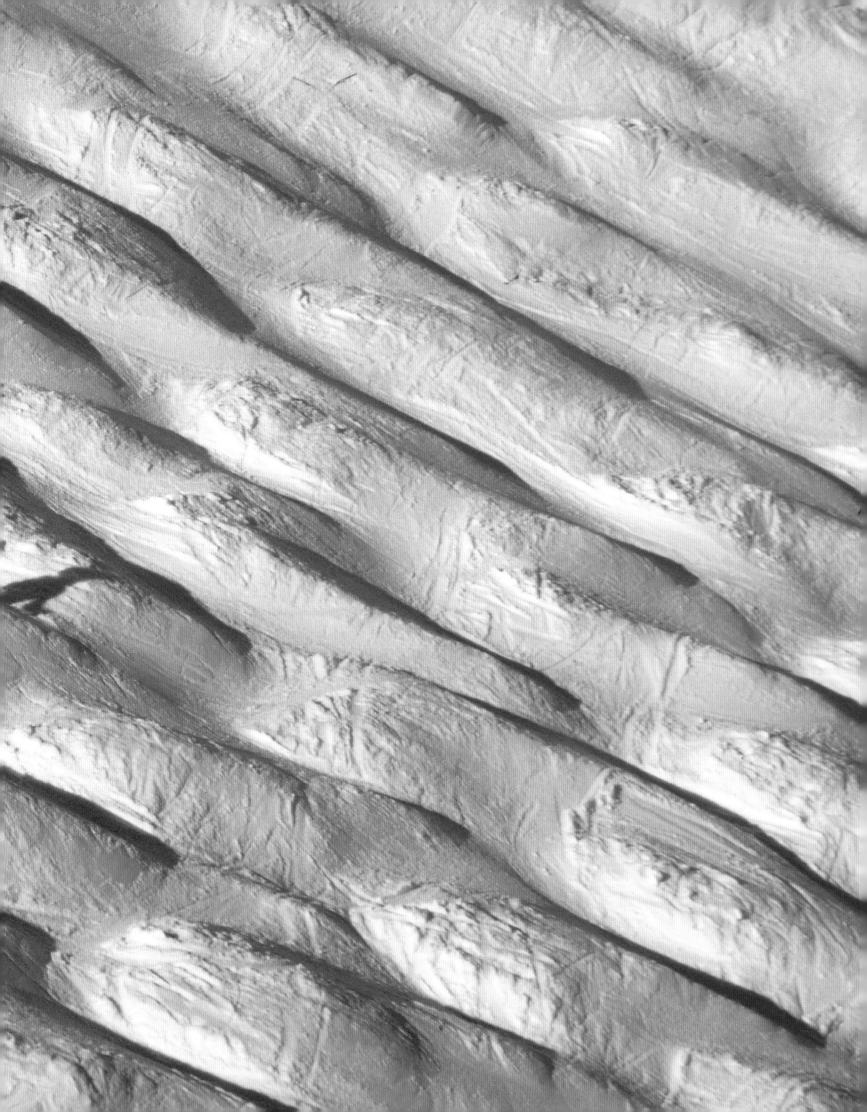

tulip oak and blackwood. (*Schuss*, January-February 1959, p30)

An important safety breakthrough came with automatic-release bindings, as opposed to the traditional lock-in cable or Kandahar-style binding.

In 1959, Melbourne ski retailers J Molony and Auski were both offering standard Kandahar or Marker and Tyrolia safety release bindings from their city stores, while DJ Smart of Malvern was offering safety bindings or standard Kandahar types to mount on solid hickory skis 'with edges and plastic running surfaces for £14 a pair.' (*Schuss*, May 1959, p82)

Around this time, Henke plastic 'speed fit' buckle-up boots started to appear (Geoff Henke, the Australian winter sports pioneer and for a time a ski retailer, is a relative of the Swiss Henke bootmakers and recalled their catch phrase – 'are you still lacing whilst I'm out racing?').

Despite the introduction of new materials and welcome refinements such as better edges and hardier construction, skis really remained fundamentally the same until snowboarding came to town.

Mike Balfe, a former Mt Buller racer and instructor, is the distributor of K2 skis in Australia and also operates the Black Mountain Equipment rental and demo centre at Mt Buller.

'Skis hadn't changed forever, other than maybe in materials. You can get one of those old wooden skis that everybody has above their fireplace and they're fundamentally the same shape as the skis I was using in the early 1990s,' Balfe said.

'Snowboarding was the catalyst for shaped skis. Snowboarders started doing amazing things and ski engineers took that as a sign or a direction to move.

'It was the same with bikes – road bikes were always the same until mountain bikes came in and suddenly they were putting gear shifts up on the handle bars. It's a different way of looking at things, it's like putting wheels on a suitcase.'

The revolution started in the mid-1990s and took hold towards the end of that decade. It all revolved around the shape and torsional rigidity of skis. Making skis shorter and with more sidecut encouraged turning and more reliable strength along the length of the ski held the turn in place. It has also created a very different turning style – the carve turn.

'It changed everything,' Balfe said. 'Skiing became more achievable for more people. Because the skis are quite a bit shorter, that makes the mogul terrain easier for most people and there's quite a bit less mogulled terrain.'

Snowboarders and skiers gather in the twilight on the summit, 2006.
TONY HARRINGTON

EVERY MOUNTAIN HAS regulars who are biased about the standard of athlete on their home mountain and Mt Buller is no exception, its people are passionate admirers of their own. For a time, it possibly held an edge.

Laurie Blampied, Buller Ski Lifts' general manager, noticed it when he moved over from Falls Creek in the 1990s.

'If you saw a strong skier or a very good skier at Falls Creek, you inevitably knew who they were, they really stood out from the crowd, whereas at Buller, there were too many good skiers to recognise them all individually. There were a lot of very good skiers,' Blampied said.

Dominic Zimmerman (above left) and Jacqui Whitby carving the Summit run 2007-style. KIT RUNDLE

Richard McGechie feels the powder like a surfer feels the wave in August 2006. KIT RUNDLE

Mike Balfe puts it down to the terrain. 'Buller skiers were better than other resorts in Australia and it was because we had extremely difficult terrain to ski – predominantly steep and icy and often bumpy. 'To ski even a Boggy Creek, it was predominantly a bump field. Buller didn't have any really easy terrain, especially if you were an Orange [Lifts] skier.

'The easiest terrain was probably Shaky Knees and it was a mogul field, the summit was a mogul field, so you had to have certain skills,' Balfe said.

Aurel Forras agreed. 'If you can ski on Buller, you can ski anywhere in the world. Because you've got the steeps, you've got everything. If you can handle Buller, you can handle any slope anywhere,' Forras said.

However, the combination of snowmaking for better snow cover, better snow grooming and better equipment is perhaps bringing Mt Buller back to the field.

Mike Balfe: 'I don't think Buller skiers are necessarily better than other areas now, simply because skiing is different now.'

Former Mt Buller ski school director, Egon Hierzegger, had a suspicion that skis became so good in the early part of the 21st century, it led to a decline in adult participation in snow sports schools.

'That's an international trend, that the adult classes are getting a bit smaller … my understanding is one of the main reasons is the development of the equipment.

'The skis became a lot shorter and the sidecut became stronger. These things made turning a lot easier so people picked it up a lot faster. I think that's one of the main drivers why adult lessons are getting smaller.

'These are relatively recent developments though,' Hierzegger said. Ski manufacturers have taken the sidecut story a step further, developing new skis to lure younger people away from snowboarding and back to skiing.

Twin tip skis, according to Balfe, is the snow industry's biggest growth category.

'That's because of who it targets [youth]. It's exciting and it appeals to those sort of big air, upside down, going fast, going backwards, anti-establishment people.'

New skis and better snow grooming have also extended the appeal of the sport at the other end of the age spectrum.

Now in his 70s, Aurel Forras still likes to ski as often as possible and still likes going fast. He rides a Fischer RC4 racing ski. 'They're 170cm, when I first got to Buller, I would have been teaching on a pair of 215cm skis.'

BMW Ski Club veteran Merrick Summers is another who found new passion through new equipment. His daughter told him his old skis were no good and got him on a pair of 170cm Head Monster skis. 'I couldn't believe there could be such a difference. I went out on them and we went straight up the summit and I never skied like it before,' Summers said.

Rip Curl founder Brian Singer, who came from a surfing background, conceded he probably would have taken up snowboarding had it been available when he first started going to Mt Buller in the 1970s.

'It has changed the way people get around on the mountain, how they have fun on the mountain, but it really hasn't changed the mountain at all,' Singer said.

'You find overseas that people who have been avid skiers take up snowboarding but come back to skiing on certain days. It's horses for courses.

'When you look at some of the French resorts and some of the American resorts, as people spend more time in the mountains, they stick various different things on their feet to help them get around.

'Today I think you'll find the avante garde on the mountain has gravitated back towards skiing, but that's really only incidental to the real issue which is the mountain itself,' Singer said.

American Glen Plake (left) skis the Summit Chutes during a promotional tour for K2 skis, Rip Curl skiwear and Oakley eyewear in 1992. MARK ASHKANASY

Australian Rob Moore (right) skis into Federation on the skier's left of the old T-bar line, in the deep 1981 season. The passion remains for powder snow. BILL BACHMAN

10 Competition

Competition has been a part of snow sports virtually since their creation, certainly since their introduction to Australia. In the 1870s, the miners of Kiandra in the Snowy Mountains were racing each other the instant they could get the fence palings bent at the tip and strapped to their feet. At Mt Buller, competition has come in many forms.

THERE IS NO better road map for the way freestyle skiing got a haircut and got a job than the metamorphosis of Tribe Gonzo into Team Buller.

Geoff Lipshut had an ambition. He wanted to be a mogul skier. He wanted to be the best around. In a sense, he became the mogul of freestyle skiing, but not as a competitor.

Lipshut had a destiny for Mt Buller and snow sports. He was born on opening weekend in 1960 and visited the mountain with his family as far back as his earliest memories. His father Maurice was a pioneering skier, making the walk as they did from White Bridge, which was as far as the road went in those days.

As a teenager, Geoff Lipshut was a ski racing fan. 'I used to follow it and loved watching the Olympics and knew all the big ski racing stars by reading magazines,' he said.

In 1975, aged 14, he went on a family skiing holiday to the United States and encountered the short-ski movement of the era, something that took another 20 years to take hold globally, but something that was moving with a new form of the sport in the US. It was hot dogging, the long-haired, free-wheeling, freestyling break from the formal structure of ski racing.

Lipshut liked it and, back at home, he skied in the Peter Stuyvesant professional freestyle tour making the final of the tour's first visit to Mt Buller in 1978. That tour was run by Randy Wieman who wrote the original manual for freestyle competition, transforming

Australian women's Olympic and World Cup aerialist Lydia Ierodiaconou, then ranked third in the world, on her way to winning one of the two Mt Buller World Cup Aerials events in 2003. MARK ASHKANASY

hot dogging into freestyle skiing and Walt Hiltner, a US freestyle pioneer who moved to Australia and ran the Volvo tour.

Then along came Gonzo. In 1983, with Ted Nugent's heavy metal album *Double Live Gonzo* for inspiration, Lipshut, Peter Braun, David Frydman, Eyal Talmor and Tim Skate became a band of Mt Buller freestyle skiers.

They were mostly from Melbourne, apart from Skate, whose family had a property in the Yarra Valley with a dam that later hosted a ramp for aerials training.

Despite Tribe Gonzo's name and appearance, they were taken seriously on the mountain. It was still a relatively small community. Having worked there on the lifts and in the restaurants, Lipshut and Talmor 'always knew more people than we didn't know'.

The tribe approached Orange Lifts and sought sponsorship. The company took some persuading, but eventually agreed to get involved and in 1984 helped Tribe Gonzo build its jump on Federation Bluff.

Tribe Gonzo's role on the mountain evolved and with the encouragement of the merged lift companies' general manager, Michael Monester, the tribe played more of a part in promoting Mt Buller. This included trampoline shows in Melbourne and more sophisticated aerial displays at Mt Buller.

The tribe was growing up. In 1986 the name change came, but Melbourne solicitor Leon Zwier, who skied with Lipshut, suggested they honour their origins, so it became Team Buller, The Spirit of Gonzo.

Tribe Gonzo dressed to make an impression outside the Melbourne Arts Centre in 1983. BILL BACHMAN

Tribe Gonzo's first promotional photo shoot (below) in 1985 included Eyal Talmor doing a flip, David 'Worm' Frydman doing a spread and Peter 'Doc' Braun (standing at left) and Tim Skate urging them on. MARK ASHKANASY

Tribe Gonzo, transformed into Team Buller (above), perform on Bourke Street in 1987. Andrew Cozma (left), Chris Larner and Kirstie Marshall. MARK ASHKANASY

At the 1992 Australian Ski Awards in Melbourne are Ian Johnson, the Nine Network's head of sport (left), Nick Cleaver (Special Achievement Award), Kirstie Marshall (Skier of the Year), Geoff Lipshut (Coach of the Year) and Mt Buller marketing manager Clive Dwyer. MARK ASHKANASY

By 1987, the team was a force; its numbers had swelled to over 20, including team photographer Mark Ashkanasy; video cameraman Anthony Hampel; team spruiker and entertainer Andrew Dwyer; athlete, shows and merchandise manager Eyal Talmor; and team doctor Peter Braun.

In its last year as Tribe Gonzo, Lipshut had recruited some other Buller skiers who were contemplating starting a freestyle team of their own. They included brothers Phil and Chris Schwarz. Lipshut described Phil Schwarz as one of the best athletes he'd ever seen. 'He was a gymnast and an incredible skier; he could have been close to winning a World Cup straight away.'

In the Team Buller aerial displays, Phil Schwarz wouldn't just do somersaults, which were impressive enough for the time, 'he would do front pikes or full twists and double somersaults, he was unbelievable.'

Schwarz knew some other talented athletes, including a 16-year-old named Kirstie Marshall. He approached Lipshut and said he knew someone who could be good for the team. 'Can she jump?'

Lipshut asked. 'I think she'll be OK to jump,' Schwarz replied. So Lipshut, who was by then Team Buller manager, met Kirstie Marshall and the next day, the then gymnast lined up for the Tyrol jump and did some somersaults.

Geoff Henke, who would play an important role in the growth and structure of freestyle skiing, described her as 'probably one of the most talented girls I've ever seen, a natural talent; she could have been a great alpine skier.'

He also admired her for her pioneering work, particularly in women's aerial skiing, which eventually delivered Australia its first Olympic gold medal on skis.

THE SUPPORT NETWORK at the time was basic. Marshall's first, and for a time only, sponsor was Felicity Moss through a travel business Philomena's/Myriad Holidays. She was then supported by Michael Vickers-Willis and the Techne Group who, according to Lipshut 'gave her the first real opportunity for success', funding her program for two years, including her coach Marcus Lovett, a former World Cup freestyle skier. There was also a growing list of personal sponsors.

In her first year, Marshall travelled with the bare necessities. A helmet was compulsory so she wore a bike helmet. 'It didn't even fit me properly – it looked like a mushroom; it was just the funniest thing,' Marshall said.

She finished that first year ranked tenth in the world and in her second year of World Cup competition Marshall was third.

By 1992, she was ranked number one in the world and it was at this point, coinciding with freestyle aerials' acceptance as a demonstration sport at the Lillehammer Winter Olympics that a support structure started to emerge.

'I was already ranked number one in the world in 1992 so it was obvious that there were great possibilities there … I think people like Geoff [Lipshut] probably knew that I was good but not great and by providing the right support to an athlete who is great, you're more or less guaranteed success.

'Jacqui [Cooper] did a very hard slog. I started in 1989; she actually started in 1990 so she was with me for years and 1997 I think was her first World Cup podium, that was just years of slogging it out and she did it when it was probably a lot harder,' Marshall said.

Cooper has done it tough, with injury as much as infrastructure, but perseverance has paid for the athlete who once funded her time on the mountain working in the Mt Buller supermarket. She has four overall World Cup titles, including 2006-07.

Nick Place (above) sets the pace on Wood Run in the 1994 Abom Mogul Challenge, the world's longest continually running event of its kind. MARK ASHKANASY

Team Buller skiers and World Cup competitors in their own disciplines, Kirstie Marshall (left – aerials) and Andrew Evans (moguls) explode for the camera in 1991. MARK ASHKANASY

'When you look at Alisa [Camplin] and when you look at Lydia [Ierodiaconou] and when you look at Liz [Gardner] you can see that structure in place and the results that come from it,' Marshall said.

Alisa Camplin, deservedly, took the headlines for her Olympic gold in Salt Lake City but it was the Spirit of Gonzo that drew her in.

'In May 1994, I attended a ski show with my ex-boyfriend … When we arrived, my eyes fell upon a trampoline that had been set up by Team Buller for an aerial skiing display,' Camplin wrote.

She had a try on the trampoline, complete with a harness for the athlete, and as a gymnast performed well and was encouraged to become an aerial skier.

'As I turned to leave, the man handed me a form and the bubbly girl gave me her number and insisted I call her. As I walked away she called after me, "We can teach you to ski you know".' (Camplin, p41) The 'bubbly girl' was Jacqui Cooper and the man was Geoff Lipshut.

TIMING IS EVERYTHING and, while Kirstie Marshall is right in pointing to freestyle's Olympic acceptance as a turning point in the support of winter athletes, it was a funding initiative at Mt Buller in the 1990s that drove snow sports around that corner.

In line with his growing involvement with Mt Buller, Rino Grollo proposed some support for alpine sports. He saw the benefits success in snow sports could bring to the mountain in particular and the snow industry in general.

Geoff Henke was a vice president of the Australian Olympic Committee (AOC) and Grollo contacted him to offer some financial support.

Henke recalled being direct in his response, 'I said "Rino, you've got to put in a million dollars or forget it," and he asked, "Well, what do we get for that?" and I told him I would get back to him. Henke was chairman of the AOC's marketing committee at the time and he knew the value of the Olympic rings.

'So I came back to Rino and said "I've been talking with Craig McClutchy [the AOC secretary general] and what we would do is give Mt Buller the rights to have the rings with the AOC crest, the coat of arms, and it would be known as the official Olympic winter training institute," so Rino said, "You've got a deal".'

Thus in 1995, the Australian Ski Institute (ASI) was born with Mt Buller as its host; Rino and Diana Grollo committed $2 million over four years for the ASI.

Zali Steggall won bronze in slalom at the 1998 Nagano Winter Olympics while skiing for the ASI. It was Australia's first Olympic medal on skis and this was the catalyst for the Australian Olympic Committee to form the Australian Institute of Winter Sports (AIWS). In 2001, this was renamed the Olympic Winter Institute of Australia (OWI).

Its chief executive is Geoff Lipshut.

Abom Mogul Challenge

It first ran in 1989 and has run every season since, making the Abom Mogul Challenge Australia's longest running bump-skiing event.

Its male winners are a who's who of Australian freestyle skiing, including Martin Rowley, Nick Cleaver, Adrian Costa, Tom Costa, Nick Fisher and the 2006 Olympic gold medallist, Dale Begg-Smith.

Women's winners have included Maria Despas, Jane Sexton, Manuela Berchtold, Allie Blackwell and, in 1992, Kirstie Marshall who fell across the line with an injured knee. 'I decided to get into mogul skiing in 1992 so I competed and won all the mogul competitions in Australia with the aim of representing Australia in mogul skiing and aerial skiing, which is something that Nick Cleaver, who was also of my era, was looking to do – he was an exceptional talent in both,' Marshall said.

'Unfortunately for me, in the last competition of the season, the Abom, I fell, blew my knee out and crossed the finish line without my skis but actually won the competition. I was out of the sport for 18 months and never entertained the thought of going back to mogul skiing.'

Despite those setbacks, the Abom has been a trail blazer for international freestyle competition. In 1998, a poor snow year, Michael Kennedy, then the head Team Buller coach and Australian mogul and aerial team manager, came up with the idea of running a dual mogul short course competition.

The snow they used was almost all that was left on the mountain, including some leftovers from road clearing which they used to build a kicker, or jump, at the top of the in-run to the World Cup aerials jump. The short course moguls then ran down the in-run.

'It was amazing,' Geoff Lipshut said. 'They raced to the jump and then they could do whatever they liked – inverts, flips, whatever [these manoeuvres were banned at the time in World Cup and Olympic mogul events].

'He was just so far ahead of his time; if you look at a moguls event today, it's exactly what Kenno created in 1998,' Lipshut said.

Dale Begg-Smith, the World No. 1 and 2006 Olympic gold medalist, in the 2002 Abom Mogul Challenge. MARK ASHKANASY

World Cup aerials

World Cup-level events have been limited in Australia; on snow, the only events outside Mt Buller's World Cup aerials were alpine slalom and giant slalom World Cup events in Thredbo in 1989.

Mt Buller's first World Cup aerials was run in 1997. It has been a festival for the mountain and the region and a stage for Australian aerials athletes. The slopes of Chamois have been transformed for the event, with a permanent judge's facility installed, along with snow-making infrastructure.

The location is stunning, particularly for photographers and for the Seven Network's television coverage, with skiers jumping in the foreground and the peaks of Little Buller and beyond it the Bluff in the background.

To gain approval to host a World Cup, Mt Buller had to present its credentials at an international level; the lead-up was the 1995 International Youth Freestyle Championships, which included moguls, aerials and ballet events.

The aerials were held on Tyrol but the site wasn't ideal. In 1996, Hanno Trendl [then the International Ski Federation/FIS freestyle coordinator] inspected a site on Chamois and agreed it would suit.

'In 1996, Bruce Dowding [then general manager of Buller Ski lifts] and Rino Grollo made the commitment,' Geoff Lipshut said. 'There was a calendar meeting at the FIS conference and the decision was made.'

In their first year, 1997, Mt Buller's World Cup aerials were described by Trendl as the best events of the season and second only to the Olympics in the quality of the organisation and infrastructure.

The World Cup trophy (above) was designed by Mark Ashkanasy. NAMA

Jacqui Cooper (at left) celebrates her victory in both World Cup events at Mt Buller in1999. Alongside her is teammate Alisa Camplin. MARK ASHKANASY

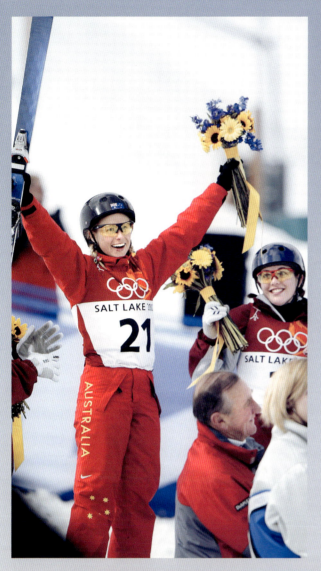

Team Buller

The Spirit of Gonzo lives on as a commercial success for Mt Buller as a program and has been a remarkable success story in snow sports. In its 20 years, Team Buller athletes have accumulated 124 medals in World Cup, World Championships and Olympic Games competitions from a total of 192 won by Australia.

Olympics: Australia's first ever snow sports Olympic gold, Alisa Camplin, 2002; and Olympic bronze, Alisa Camplin, 2006; seven Australian Olympians in all, Kirstie Marshall, Nick Cleaver, Jacqui Cooper, Jono Sweet, Alisa Camplin, Lydia Ierodiaconou and Liz Gardner.

World Championships: The first Australian to win a World Championship, Kirstie Marshall and two other world champions, Jacqui Cooper and Alisa Camplin.

World Cup: The first Australian to win an overall World Cup title, Kirstie Marshall, and seven overall World Cup aerials titles in total, Jacqui Cooper (four times), Alisa Camplin (twice), Kirstie Marshall (once). In total, team athletes have recorded 53 World Cup victories and accumulated 117 World Cup medals.

Where next: Team Buller's Anna Segal won gold in slopestyle at the 2007 US Freesking Open and Jacqui Cooper, in 2007, broke the record for the most World Cup victories by a female aerial skier.

Three Team Buller/Buller Riders athletes, Robert Lovick, Hugh Norton and Kate Blamey are members of the National Development Mogul team, operated by the New South Wales Institute of Sport.

Robert Lovick, from Merrijig, made his World Cup mogul debut in February 2006, finishing in the top half of the field. He joined Buller Riders in 2000.

Team Buller skier Alisa Camplin (left) celebrates her gold medal performance at the 2002 Salt Lake City Winter Olympics and Australia's first freestyle skiing Olympic medal. At right is silver medalist, Canadian Veronica Brenner, and below them is Geoff Henke. SANDRA TEDDY/STL

Kirstie Marshall (below) in her Techne Team hat, sizes up the course in the 1992 Abom Mogul Challenge. MARK ASHKANASY

MT BULLER HAS nurtured some outstanding alpine competitors, people who have gone through the gates in intra-club and inter-club races; in school competitions and at state, national and international level.

The Ski Club of Victoria (SCV) was the initial keeper of the competition keys, governing its own club competitions and Victoria's state competitions in the post-war years.

In 1949, the SCV competition program for the week of July 23 to July 30 included jumping, langlauf and men's and women's slalom and downhill.

In reviewing the events, the club referee, TD Fisher, noted that the downhill, on a 'new run starting near the top of the [Bourke Street] ski tow and extending down … below Postal Institute Lodge was limiting good skiers because of the narrowness of the trail.'

With regret, the review also noted that 'the langlaufs didn't create as much interest as the other events either amongst starters or spectators … waxing is, I fear, becoming a lost art in this branch of the sport, in which it is so important.' (*Schuss*, September 1949)

The enthusiasm for competition carried some ambition with it. Dr RG Orr, the secretary of the Australian National Ski Federation posed this query in 1949, when Melbourne was bidding for the 1956 summer Olympics: 'Could she [Melbourne] ask for the winter events including skiing? As I see it, there is no real reason why the skiing Olympics could not be organised here … though provision of the essential facilities would be a huge and costly task.' (*Schuss*, May 1949)

Melbourne stuck with the summer sports, but the mountain has nevertheless nurtured some outstanding Olympic alpine competitors.

The teams for Oslo in 1952 and Cortina in 1956 were managed by SCV member George Chisholm. In Cortina, Mt Buller skiers Tony Aslangul and Frank Prihoda skied for Australia (Prihoda later moved to live in Thredbo).

In 1964, SCV members Simon Brown, Peter Brockhoff, Judy Forras and Peter Wenzel were among the team. (Lloyd, pp647-51) Falls Creek skier Malcolm Milne was the strongest alpine competitor in 1968 at Grenoble and 1972 in Sapporo, but Mt Buller's representative strength was renewed in 1976 at Innsbruck.

Jill McDonald (left) and Elyne Mitchell, with eye shields as big as windscreens, prepare themselves for the 1939 National Championships at Mt Buller. BROCKHOFF

THE 1976 TEAM included Mt Buller skiers Robert McIntyre and Sally Rodd, both natural talents who had the advantage of being able to do the skiing miles.

Sally Rodd's early memories of Mt Buller are of playing in the snow outside the Whitt, 'under the giant icicles that used to form outside the restaurant windows. They were huge, three or four feet long. They used to terrify my parents,' she said.

Like so many their age, she and her brother (John) took to skiing 'like ducks to water' and their parents 'used to buy us about 10 little rope tow tickets but we'd be back at the house with no tickets left before Dad had actually got out.'

Walter Frois was in charge of the Austrian ski school and, as was the way, would be invited to the Rodds' apartment for dinner. 'We used to peer over the edge of the cupboard where our bunks were set in-behind and listen to the adult conversation.'

Alistair Guss (right) racing a championship slalom event on the Summit Slide in 1985, in the gear he wore at the 1985 World Championships in Bormio, Italy. BILL BACHMAN

Mt Buller instructor and international racer Ludwig Sorger (left) competes in the 1960 Australian National Championships on Federation. SORGER/NAMA

To improve her skiing, Sally Rodd shadowed Frois. 'Walter taught us how to ski, then I used to trail around behind his classes until I crashed into someone at the back of the class. Then I was banned from trailing them around.'

Her first racing memory is a respectable one – she won the Buller Cup aged 12. At that time her family skied with Orange Lifts but she turned to Blue when that company started a racing program. 'We got lift tickets, accommodation at Candoux Lodge up the Chamois Road and food at the Abom. I think that they [her parents] stuck us in because it was this great package, it didn't cost them a lot and it got us out of their hair.

'We were just terrorising the mountain; Mum said we were appalling – we used to fill up the sugar shakers with salt at the Abom, you know the sort of thing.'

She stayed with the race squad and her performances improved to the point where she achieved selection in the national and then Olympic teams. It wasn't always an easy road and was occasionally potholed with athlete/coach type conflicts, particularly leading in to the 1976 Olympics.

'It was a poor season [1975] and we were skiing on Chamois and it was just dangerous; we were skiing slalom in the untrimmed trees of Chamois with shocking snow and bad ruts and I said to Robert

Boarding the Qantas V-Jet for the 1964 Innsbruck Winter Olympics. From the top down are Ross Milne, Simon Brown, Peter Brockhoff, Christine Smith, John Wagner (team manager), Peter Wenzel (team doctor), Ivor Roberts and Judy Forras. NAMA

Back to Innsbruck, this time for the 1976 games in their Prue Acton-designed, Louis Preiss-made uniforms are Antony Guss (left), Robbie McIntyre, Joanne Henke, Doug McConville, Sally Rodd and Kim Clifford. BILL BACHMAN

Sally Rodd thinking through the downhill in front of her at the 1976 Innsbruck Olympics. BILL BACHMAN

[Tessa, her coach] "I'm not going to ski this", you know, it was 12 months out from the Olympics, I said, "If you shoot out of a rut here, you'll be straight into a tree, and he effectively said something like, "Well girlie, if you can't take the heat …" – in more colourful French language – "… why don't you piss off and come back when you can."

'So I did. I rang up my friends in New South Wales and … I just said "Could I come and stay up there and maybe ski with the New South Wales team?" which was being coached by Martin [Kerscher, the coach of the 1976 Olympic team].'

The people she was staying with had some other guests for the week, including Bill Bachman, now Sally Rodd's partner who has been a Mt Buller photographer and was also a Mt Buller ski instructor.

'If I hadn't had a fight with Robert Tessa, I wouldn't have met Bill.' There was an enthusiastic base supporting the young Olympians, chiefly comprised of parents who volunteered their time, including Rodd's own parents and others such as the Forras, Guss, Gadsden, Pilkington and Green families.

Innsbruck in 1976 was a turning point for Australian participation. Sally Rodd puts that down to Dick Watson and Geoff Henke pushing it through at a competitive level and securing funding for the team.

Her preferred disciplines were slalom and giant slalom, but she recorded her best finish – thirty-first – in the downhill. Rodd was disqualified in the slalom and was thirty-third in the giant slalom. Robert McIntyre fell in the downhill, injuring his ankle and putting him out of any further events in Innsbruck (Lloyd, p652), although he went on to carry the flag for Australia in 1980 at Lake Placid.

Looking back, Rodd appreciates the phenomenal parental input, particularly from her mother, as her father had work commitments. 'She used to drive us all over the place, up to the different resorts with a whole car load of kids and ski bags streaming out the back. You'd ski the whole weekend and come home exhausted. 'The parents did the most phenomenal job to actually make racing possible. Us kids just sort of, you know, scooted along as you do, oblivious I guess of the machinations and the politics going on in the background.'

A YOUNG PETER Forras fell to the spell of competitive skiing when he saw the team including Sally Rodd and Robert McIntyre introduced. 'I was in Kooroora watching them announce the 1976 Olympic Team. It blew me away. I was sitting there and they were announcing the team and I knew that was what I wanted to do.' Peter Forras grew up on the mountain, and was the first child christened there. His father Aurel was, and still is, a handy skier and his late mother, Georgina Forras, raced as Georgina Watson, skiing for Australia in inter-dominion competition against New Zealand.

He had it in his blood and remembered escaping from the family apartment beneath the Bull Run Canteen to ski Bourke Street and beyond, wearing gumboots and riding some wooden skis made by his father the builder.

'I think I must have started harassing them [his parents] when I was 12 or 13 and then by 14 they let me go. And that was it.

Disabled skier, the late Michael Norton (above) represented Australia at Albertville in 1992 for a bronze in slalom and at Lillehammer in 1994 for gold in slalom and giant slalom. MARK ASHKANASY

I think I won the Buller Cup the first year and with this little junior team I got to America and that was it – I was gone,' Forras said. His Olympic opportunity eventually arrived at Calgary in 1988, but not without the volatility that can surround Olympic selection. 'I had a big crash in Europe leading up to the Olympics, I was a little bit injured, my confidence was down a bit and I was getting messed with by the selectors and coach.

'They actually didn't confirm that I was in the team even while I was there, doing the opening [ceremony].

'I enjoyed the experience, it was tough, I crashed [in the downhill] but it was a fantastic experience,' Forras said.

Another bitten by the racing bug was Lorenz Grollo. His family's first lodge on the mountain was Ullr, so they raced for their own Ullr Cup.

'I was always the youngest of the four Grollo boys [including his brother Mark and cousins Adam and Daniel] and I was always wanting to compete with those guys.

'I guess I started to get very competitive in our club races, particularly with those four and then as time moved on, I started to get more and more competitive.

'One year I beat my brother and one of my cousins and then the following year I came back and I beat them all. So I guess it took off from there,' Lorenz Grollo said.

He raced in Interschools competition for his school, Parade College, and for a few years the school was finishing in the top three in state and national Interschools skiing.

As a tertiary student at La Trobe University, he started to take his racing more seriously and together with a friend, Andrew Rocco, hired a coach and raced nationally and internationally.

'We were a self-made team, myself and Andrew Rocco and our coach Patrick Schmidt.'

He's long since left racing to work in the family business and raise a family of his own, but the feeling for speed that seduces racers hasn't left him.

'My favourite run at Buller? Oh, it would have to be Little Buller

Mt Buller Ski Racing Club members in Courcheval, December 1996. Alisa Curinier (above, at left), Holly Green, Tori Greer, Georgina Rogers and Lara Grollo. GROLLO

Peter Forras (below) on his way to winning the Victorian championships on a course at Boggy Creek in 1987. 'It was one of my sweetest victories,' Forras said. 'I won it at my home mountain, knocked off Steve [Lee] and the rest of the national team and got pre-selected for the 88 Olympics.' MARK ASHKANASY/BILL BACHMAN

Spur early in the morning. I haven't got over the speed thing I guess, but I'm more passionate about having the right sensation, the right feeling, knowing that your skis are the right angle and they do what they're meant to do.'

Lorenz Grollo's sister, Monica Grollo, a director of the Olympic Winter Institute, also raced, first for her school and then at university and eventually state level, with her best performance the Victorian title in slalom and giant slalom in 1993, making her the overall Victorian champion for that year.

MT. BULLER SKI RACING CLUB

ski Mt.Buller

1995

BUNDESSPORTHEIM ST. CHRISTOPH

Race Club

Spending the entire winter above the snow line was once the exclusive privilege of mountain staff and business owners. The expansion of educational facilities on the mountain and particularly the building of the La Trobe University campus created a small revolution in the winter population, an idea pushed by Dino Ruzzene and his sister, Diana Grollo.

It has meant secondary school programs can be transferred from Melbourne-based or other schools and taught on the mountain for winter. In turn, the Mt Buller Race Club (MBRC) has boomed. The club was formed in 1989 to offer racing and training for school-age skiers and snowboarders. Full-time athletes live at Mt Buller during term three and train during the July school holidays and for six days a week during term three, skiing in the morning and attending school at the Australian Alpine Institute in the former La Trobe University building in the afternoon.

The flow-on is that parents can also spend the winter on the mountain – they eat there, sleep there, buy property there and ski there. Many attribute the Mt Buller property boom of the 1990s and first half of the 2000s to race club participation.

The children's racing circuit feeds into the junior Topolino event in Italy and the Whistler Cup in Canada, while senior racers compete in state and national championships and Continental Cup events.

The Mt Buller Ski Racing Club team in training at Austria's prestigious Bundessportheim in 1995.

In the back row are Geoff Stone (left), Nerida Lardner, Suzie Whan, Nerida Blanch, Melanie Hayden, Alister Coleman, Chester Cunningham, Martin Ansell, Tully Hatswell, Fred Goetz, Jacques Reid, Jamie Dunlop, Bernd Greber, Jurgen Graller, Thomas Rimmel and Pascale Hasler.

In the front are Anthony Lardner (left), Hanness Zirknitzer, Nick Paton, James Greer, Tori Greer, Amanda Greer and Sam Speed.

Participants gain in many ways, not least through time on snow, the wonder of a winter on the mountain and improved skiing or boarding technique. 'Many of these kids aren't wanting for much; what the race club gives them is organisational skills,' Jon Hutchins, MBRC general manager said. 'They have to get up at 6.30am, get the first lift and have the first run and if they've forgotten their gloves, they're stuffed.'

Travel is also a broadening experience for the young racers; snow sports expose participants to a unique mix of cultures and experiences.

The MBRC contracts the ski school's race department to provide coaches and run their race and training program. Ross Taylor, a former program director of the MBRC is now head of the ski school race department.

To everyone at the ABOM!!
Thank you from the 1994 National Alpine Ski Team.

The 1994 Australian national alpine team. Nils Coberger (above left, coach) Zali Steggall, Brett Vale, Anthony Huguet and Marty Hanson (coach). GROLLO

MBRC skier Tom Mathias (right) in the 2006 Intervarsity Championships on Little Buller Spur. FUN PHOTOS

'I loved the discipline of racing and the speed. I did a downhill at the University games in Spain and reached 96 km/h, I was on a high, it was the biggest buzz ever … I still keep my 210cm racing skis in the bedroom.

'I always believed ski racing should be for everyone. I started the Victorian University Championships in 1996 with Joanne Stepp. That was an opportunity for anyone at university to join their ski team and race,' Monica Grollo said.

In addition to Australia's freestyle success, she believes the competitive future for the nation still lies in alpine racing and also in emerging disciplines like skiercross and boardercross – exciting, televisual events that pit racers against one another on the same course.

'They're the sports that people want to see and with our terrain parks and with the popularity of in-line skating and skateboarding, there's a lot of potential in those sports.'

To the Grollo family,
your support of Aussie
winter sport is coool!

1st Gold

Australia had an outstanding Winter Olympics in Salt Lake City, affirming the value of the Olympic Winter Institute (OWI) and the Australian Olympic Committee's (AOC) support of it. Connected to that were AOC chairman John Coates (left) former International Olympic Committee (IOC) president Juan Antonio Samaranch (below left) IOC vice president Kevan Gosper and Rino Grollo. JEFF CROW/STL/GROLLO

Steven Bradbury (above) was Australia's first Winter Olympics gold medallist, in the 1000m short track speed skating event in Salt Lake City, 2002. Bradbury was supported by Mt Buller's Olympic Winter Institute (OWI). DAVID GRAY/REUTERS

With the *Spirit of the Skier* donated to Nagano in 1998. Rino Grollo (below left) Zali Steggall, Lorenz Grollo and Geoff Henke. BILL BACHMAN/STL

OWI athlete Dale Begg-Smith (above left) won gold in the freestyle moguls at Torino in 2006. He is pictured here with the Torino team's chef de mission, Ian Chesterman (centre) and OWI media manager Barry White. WHITE

Zali Steggall (right) on course in the 1998 Nagano slalom for third place. Her bronze medal was Australia's first Olympic alpine skiing medal. MARK ASHKANASY/STL

Australia's first Olympic gold medallist wearing skis, Alisa Camplin (left), Salt Lake City, 2002. She is pictured with OWI chief executive Geoff Lipshut. CAMPLIN

THE VICTORIAN INTERSCHOOLS Championships at Mt Buller is probably the largest multi-discipline snow sports event in the world, but it had humble beginnings.

It started with eight competitors from two schools racing a giant slalom in 1957. By 2006, the Victorian Interschools Championships grew to include 3500 participants from 150 schools making 6000 entries in 64 events.

In 1957, the first races were over in about 30 minutes; by 2006, the championships, including alpine giant slalom, snowboard giant slalom, boardercross, skiercross, moguls, cross-country classical, and cross-country freestyle relay competition covered six days.

The 1957 event was informal, with eight starters from Scotch College and Melbourne Grammar, the two schools that played one of the first games of Australian football, albeit a century earlier.

Michael David, a Mt Buller skier since 1953 who went on to establish a real estate business on the mountain, was in that first event.

'In those days, Ernest Forras used to encourage our parents to go down to the old Kooroora for a few tipples in the evening –

there was a very small skiing community – maybe a couple of hundred families if that,' David said.

On one of those après evenings, his father, Lance David, and a friend, Bruce Wenzel 'between them said, "we're all up here during the holidays, why don't we get the kids to race off against each other," and Bruce Wenzel donated the trophy which is still awarded to division one boys' alpine skiers,' David said.

Following that informal beginning, the next year, 1958, it became an official event between Melbourne Grammar and Scotch College, the third school to join was Geelong Grammar

'in 1959 or 1960,' David said, but they were one skier short of a four-person team so 'they actually had to rope in a skier from Wesley College to make up the numbers.'

In 1998, the School Snowsports Development Foundation held a fortieth anniversary for the event, because, David claims, 'no one believed me about the 1957 event.'

But then, 'we found an *Old Melburnian* [the Melbourne Grammar school magazine] where the team captain, Roger Richards, acknowledged the 1957 event,' Michael David said. Hence the celebration of 50 years in 2007.

Michael David in the 1961 Interschools competition, complete with leather racing helmet. DAVID/NAMA

The Mansfield Secondary College (MSC) Snowsports Team photographed in 2004 when it was awarded School Club of the Year (jointly with Sydney's Scots College). In 2003 it won the Victorian Interschools Mars Co-Ed Cup for the first time, beating Victoria's major private schools and other strong mountain colleges like Bright. In the back row are Rob Lovick (left), Tom Lovick, Kate Blampied, Courtney Wareham, Taylor Chapman, Alex Pullin, and Geoff Walker (snow sports coordinator). In the front row are Hannah Dolling (left), Elle Raidal, Lainie Plummer, Bill Reynolds, Kane Reid and Emma Pullin. MARK ASHKANASY

THE TEACHERS AT Scotch College took on the organisation of Interschools for a decade and in 1968, according to Mike Tinsley, an Interschools coordinator and former secretary of the Victorian Ski Association's alpine committee, it was handed to the VSA.

In the 1970s, with the three-term school year, Interschools was held on the second Tuesday in August with teams consisting of four racers, with the three fastest counting for the result.

Tinsley's involvement started in the early 1980s, when 'my children liked to race and I liked to help. My mother [Kathleen Moore] was a great racer in the 1930s and I raced in the 50s and 60s.'

The event was supported by the VSA and some Mt Buller businesses, but it was mainly the parents who took the workload.

'The teams were submitted on the Monday night at the Whitt and the draw done shortly afterwards for about 100 competitors and the individual racer bibs handed out the next morning,' Tinsley said.

'David Hosking and I would start the race around 9am and it was all over by lunchtime. The VSA would supply the poles and the timing equipment and the ski school supplied an instructor to set the course.'

The races were held on the Village run, below the Whitt and at the back of the Abom. That meant the courses were close to the container that housed the VSA's slalom poles and other equipment. As the numbers grew, they transferred to Shaky Knees, which provided a slightly longer course, with good skiing nearby and good viewing areas for parents.

With a small field and few different races or categories, calculating the results was relatively simple; they'd be announced after lunch at the Whitt with the presentation held in the Dump Inn Bar. After one of the events, Tinsley recalled discussing the future of Interschools with fellow skiers and Mt Buller regulars, Nick Regos from University High and Rod Hill from Melbourne High.

'We all agreed that the event could definitely grow and that we could get other high schools involved,' Tinsley said.

The winning Xavier College team in 1981, including brothers Philip (above left) and Christopher Schwarz and Dominic Coleman. In the background are Peter Dunlop and Darryl Gallagher (at right).
SCHWARZ

In 2007 on Burnt Hut Spur, Grace Woodsford (right) is riding for Merrijig Primary School. She came second in the division 4 girls snowboarding and Merrijig came second of the teams.
FUN PHOTOS

Alicia Racovolis on course on Little Buller Spur, 2002.
LUCIA MEDZIHRADSKA

A barrier was the elitist perception of the sport, a barrier that remains for some unfamiliar with snow sports. The perception is given strength because skiing, and particularly ski racing, is pursued by some very wealthy people. But wealthy people also go fishing. Interschools was an opportunity to broaden the base of snow sports.

Tinsley encountered resistance even from some of Melbourne's private schools, such as the original participant Melbourne Grammar and the girls' school, St Catherine's.

'I always maintained that skiing was not elitist, only very expensive,' Tinsley said.

He produced a flyer to that effect, pointing out that Scotch College teachers started the event, that skiing had been an Olympic sport since 1924 with Australia first competing in the Winter Olympics in 1936.

'I argued that surely a multi-million dollar school oval on St Kilda Road for 11 or 18 boys to play their sport was even more elitist.'

Tinsley recalled forwarding his arguments to Rino and Diana Grollo as their children reached the age when they wanted to compete and they were encountering similar resistance at Parade College.

'We spent a lot of time trying to legitimise the sport in schools,' former Interschools chief Debbie Bennett said. 'When the principals [of the schools] got up there, they realised it was a lot of hard work, the kids weren't cavorting around in the snow, they put a lot of effort into it.'

IT WAS IN the 1990s that Interschools really started to hit its straps. Debbie Bennett took a break from teaching to become executive director of the Victorian Ski Association (VSA) in 1989. She ran Interschools in one way or another from 1989 to 1994, missing 1995 and taking it on again in 1996 and 1997.

'Mike Tinsley came to me at the VSA one day, when I was pretty green, and he said, "You're a teacher, you know about school kids and we've got this school race and I want you to help me run it."

'And I said, "Oh yeah, I'll help you with that".'

At that stage Bennett estimates there would have been about 250 competitors in junior and senior divisions skiing in alpine

Interschools competition now includes cross-country skiing (above), snowboarding and alpine skiing events. FUN PHOTOS

events alone, with girls only recently introduced as competitors. By the time she left, there were around 3400 entries.

'Mike [Tinsley] was always getting me to get more people involved so I started marketing it, because I knew schools, and we got into the Education Department and got their support,' Bennett said.

'Then we went into the different disciplines and introduced snowboarding and then cross-country and moguls; we got [former freestyle competitor and FIS official] Ian Pidgeon involved to run the moguls,' Bennett said.

The involvement of the Education Department provided impetus for growth in participation among government schools. Those close to the snowfields – Bright, Mt Beauty and Mansfield in particular – have had outstanding success in Interschools events.

DEMAND FOR LABOUR has always been strong. The technical delegates for the courses have been provided by the Mt Buller Race Club, with parents volunteering as gate keepers.

One year the Army Reserve was recruited to help, indeed recruiting was their excuse. The Reserve set up a tent at Helicopter Flat as a temporary recruiting office and 40 of their members helped man the Interschools courses.

'They all turned up in the back of canvas covered vehicles wearing their camouflage gear. By the time they got to the course, they were frozen,' Debbie Bennett recalled.

During this era, an on-course timing mechanism was used to record racers' times and when 20 or 30 racers had been through a course, runners on skis and snowmobiles would progressively run rolls of tape back to event administration.

'We'd have banks of computers there and people entering the data into the computers and then we'd tabulate the results,' Debbie Bennett said. 'But that was fraught with danger because there were so many errors transcribing the results.

'It was just shocking … so many times I had to go around and get trophies back from schools and go to assemblies so they could be awarded again to the right school.'

Technology eventually intervened, but before it could, some capable people emerged to improve the system.

Mei-Larn Whan was an interested parent when her daughter was competing for Melbourne Girls Grammar.

'I'm fairly mathematical and so being a mum at the bottom of the course, I worked out that in her division, Melbourne Girls Grammar had come second or third,' Whan said.

'So I just made a very quiet enquiry as to where they came and I got told, "Oh thirteenth or fourteenth and I said, "Well, I don't think that's right, can we have another look at these results?"'

'I knew my maths wasn't that bad … they had a look at it and worked out that they had come second or third … I opened a whole can of worms; half the presentations they had done were wrong.'

'So I said, "Look, don't worry about being in a tizz, just give me the raw data and I'll sit down with a pen, paper and a calculator and I'll give you the right results," and they did and I got it all perfect.'

As so often happens in voluntary organisations, proof of capability can lead to immediate responsibility.

Mei-Larn Whan initially resisted, but was eventually recruited and spent 10 years as a volunteer supporting Interschools' administration and growth; by 1991 she had the title chief administrator, she was by 1993 chief of race operations and by 1995, the Interschools chairman.

Whan and Debbie Bennett eventually found a solution to the complexity in event timing and results calculation with the help of the then director of the Mt Buller Ski School race department, Bernd Greber.

'Bernd came back [after a winter in Austria] with a computer program which married the timing device with the algorithm to do the tabulation of the team scores automatically; from then on it was fantastic,' Bennett said.

'Bernd really understood the significance of the event, he understood what we were trying to create, he was just fabulous to work with – Mt Buller's race department is second to none really,' she said.

MT BULLER'S BUSINESSES have always recognised the value of the competition, to underpin growth in the sport overall, but also as an important source of activity on the mountain – there are estimates that up to a third of ski school business is Interschools-related.

Leading up to the major event, schools hold training and selection trials on the mountain. Similarly, for each of the entrants, there are probably two or three others who attend; meaning Interschools draws somewhere between 9000 and 12,000 people to the mountain and the region.

Debbie Bennett would approach Rino and Diana Grollo for support annually and in addition to financial support, they also

Nick Blampied on course on Little Buller Spur in 2006.
LUCIA MEDZIHRADSKA

'gave cow bells [for participants and spectators to ring courseside in the European tradition] and he gave every competitor a medallion for a number of years,' she said.

It went beyond the gift of the medals – Roger Kemelfield, Interschools chairman from 1991 to 1994, recalled Rino and Diana Grollo working together all night long to get the medals and their ribbons ready for presentation.

John Perks and Hans Grimus were others who gave their support, along with the Mt Buller Chamber of Commerce 'who I would harangue and harass every year for some help with accommodation for sponsors and things like that,' Debbie Bennett said.

Mei-Larn Whan recalled going to see John Perks each year – Perks owned both the Arlberg and the Mt Buller transport business at the time – and he would see her coming.

'He told me, "Every year you'd come to me and you'd ask me for something more and I'd already know that I'd have to give it to you".'

While support from Mt Buller has endured, the remaining sponsorship and support for Interschools have changed.

'If you look back say 10 years ago,' said Interschools' current general manager, Rob Osborne, who works for the School Snowsports Development Foundation (SSDF), 'it was predominantly government sponsored through Vic Health in particular and through programs such as the Life Be in It campaign and then Sunsmart and the anti-smoking campaigns.

'We also had good support from Sport and Recreation Victoria and the Department of Education, but that level of support has dissipated. Now, roughly 75 per cent of funding comes through corporate sponsorship from businesses like Subaru, Mt Buller, Mt Hotham, Falls Creek, Dynastar and Travelplan. The remaining 25 per cent comes through entry fees,' Osborne said.

In the late 1980s and 1990s, with the support they were getting from the Victorian Education department and other State Government authorities, the Interschools organisers saw the wisdom in getting politicians involved.

Graeme Fenton, a chairman of the VSA's Interschools sub-committee, had the foresight to try to engage them and in this way secure government funding.

In 1988, the then premier of Victoria, John Cain donated the cup for the fastest individual, the Premier's Cup. This created an opportunity for the premier of the day or their representative to present the cup at Mt Buller.

There was the occasional problem on either side of the political divide. Steve Crabb, the minister for tourism in the Cain Labor government arrived at the event one year 'and his driver got out of the car, slipped over in his town shoes and broke his arm,' Debbie Bennett recalled.

When Jeff Kennett was Victorian premier he didn't carry a

SPONSORED BY Life. Be in it. WITH FUNDING FROM VIC. HEALTH FOUNDATION. INFORMATION SERVICE 823 6288

Interschools timing

1957	Event run informally between students of Melbourne Grammar School and Scotch College.
1958	Formal competition commences with Scotch College teachers as event organisers.
1968	Victorian Ski Association takes over the organisation, event run under the VSA's alpine committee.
1977–1991	Key VSA Interschools personnel include Graeme Fenton, Darryl Gallagher, David Hosking, Mike Tinsley.
1991	VSA establishes a dedicated Interschools committee, first chairman is Roger Kemelfield (to 1994).
1995	Mei-Larn Whan chairman.
1996	Michael David chairman.
1997	Snow Sports Victoria, formerly the VSA, merges with Skiing Australia; Interschools Committee becomes the Schools Development Committee.
1997–2000	David Perkins chairman.
1999	School Snowsports Development Foundation established, taking over from the Schools Development Committee. The SSDF is affiliated with Ski and Snowboard Australia, the peak body for Australian snow sports which took over from Skiing Australia in 2002. SSDF has two full-time staff members – general manager Rob Osborne and event manager Steve Nelson who are supported by volunteers and tertiary students.
2000	Tom Swan chairman.

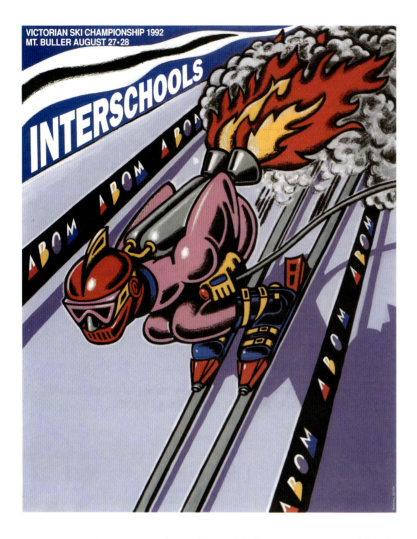

VICTORIAN SKI CHAMPIONSHIP 1992
MT. BULLER AUGUST 27•28

INTERSCHOOLS

Interschools posters for 1991 and 1992 by Alan Marshall, who was also a driving force behind the Abom Mogul Challenge, designing much of the promotional material and the visual identity of that event in its early years. NAMA

JUST WHAT DO the participants get out of it? Debbie Bennett has gone from running the event with the VSA and Skiing Australia to managing the ski team for the Melbourne girls' school, MLC, and is a member of the Interschools committee.

'Ski racing is a pretty exciting sport and it gives a real sense of unity,' she said.

'We've got one of the biggest teams, we've got about 100 girls in our team. It's just such an exciting event for the kids to do, to be a part of.

'I started a cross-country team four years ago and within three years we had a national champion, Juliette Booth, who started with us at MLC and had never been a cross-country skier before.

'But it's also an opportunity a lot of kids wouldn't get unless they did it through their school,' Bennett said.

Many of Australia's national team alpine racers have gone through the Interschools program, as have champion snowboarders Torah Bright and Alex 'Chumpy' Pullin.

For Rob Osborne, it was summed up when he and his chairman Tom Swan were watching an event on Little Buller Spur.

'We were at the finish area, it was a division two boys alpine event and we were watching one young guy come down and he obviously wasn't going to win it. He came over the finish line, turned around, looked at his time on the clock and had the biggest smile on his face and he started punching the air and yelling.

'I looked at Tom and said, "This kid obviously thinks he's won it but he's way off the pace," the best time was a minute thirty and he'd clocked over two minutes.

'Tom looked at me and said, "Well, I'm the chairman and you're the general manager, you get paid so you'd better go over and break the news to him that he hasn't won."

'I was getting ready to go and unfortunately burst this kid's bubble, and he came out through the finish gate and said to his mates, "Did you see that? I beat my time last year by 15 seconds!"

'Then it hit me,' Osborne said, 'the sense of achievement the event can bring to its participants.

'That's the whole thing. I mean the focus is entirely on participation, it's not an elite championship, 95 per cent do it just for the fun of it, of being part of it and part of a team.'

Mt Buller continues its unbroken run as host of the Victorian Interschools Championships. It and the New South Wales Interschools serve as selection events for the National Interschools, which rotates between the major five Australian mountain resorts – Mt Buller, Mt Hotham and Falls Creek in Victoria and Thredbo and Perisher Blue in New South Wales.

Rino and Diana Grollo see school students as the most important people for the future of the mountain. 'You've got to have these kids up there having fun – they're the future,' Rino Grollo said.

reputation as a good traveller and helicopters were possibly his least preferred form of transport. He made the trip to the mountain by helicopter and landed in the Horse Hill car park.

'Kennett walked into the Abom and was white, and he saw me and asked if I was the one running the event, I said yes, so he said, "Get me a whisky and make it a big one," so I did and then he said "Now get me another",' Debbie Bennett recalled.

The following year was an election year and with the premier tied up in that battle, the governor of Victoria, Richard McGarvie, was the VIP for the event.

A vice-regal visit carries with it all sorts of complexities however; Bennett and her chairman Roger Kemelfield made numerous trips to Government House to work through the protocol (and share the advice that the vice-regal Rolls Royce was possibly not the ideal car for the mountain drive).

The visit went smoothly and following a final luncheon, the governor's party left the Abom in two Kassbohrer snow grooming machines displaying his ensign. The Kassbohrers had a police escort on snowmobiles up Bourke Street and over to the Horse Hill chairlift, where the governor left the mountain by gondola.

The social satisfaction in a trip to the mountains lures dignitaries, politicians, parents and teachers, but the participation and achievement of school children remain the basis for Interschools.

2003
JEAN-MARC LAROQUE

THE VILLAGE

1961
OLOS SKI CLUB

1975
CHRIS HILTON-WOOD

1992
BILL BACHMAN

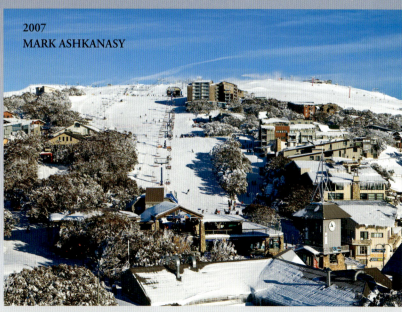

2007
MARK ASHKANASY

11 Getting there

In the mountains access is often the triumph of will and technology over terrain and weather but at peak times even the strongest will and smartest technology can fail in the face of overwhelming demand.

ACCESS IS AN invitation for invention. The solutions for Mt Buller have varied from cable cars running from Mirimbah or Sawmill Settlement to the mountain village, to track railways or trams modelled on those of the timber gatherers, which were always precarious and, in the case of Helmut and Peggy Kofler, proved lethal.

Despite the visions, since white settlement access to Mt Buller has really only followed two paths.

The first was the Klingsporn Bridle Path, a track blazed for cattle and horses and used by the first adventurous skiers and bushwalkers. It heads east from Mirimbah, turns south at the relief-point – Thank Christ Corner – and then pushes up the mountain in the lee of McLaughlins Shoulder to Boggy Creek and the Burnt Hut Spur, where some of the earliest accommodation was to be found. The alternative, which is the route the Mount Buller Tourist Road now follows, was cleared by or on behalf of the developers and oper-

ators of the first Mt Buller Chalet at Horse Hill and eventually pushed through to the village by the irrepressible local timber miller and Ski Club of Victoria (SCV) member, Harold Doughty.

Recognition that access was vital for an emerging resort came early in the piece. Canadian ski instructor Herbert Hall, in making a comparison between his home resorts and Australia's noted in 1949 that:

Many of you hardened skiers will say that if a person wants to ski badly enough, he won't mind walking anywhere up to seven or eight miles to ski … maybe I am lazy, but it is my opinion based on past experience that the resort with the good road leading to it gets the most skiers … more skiers is what Australia needs [for] bigger and better ski lodges and more ski lifts. (*Schuss*, January 1949, p25)

A group of skiers makes the transition from bus to horseback for the final stage of the journey to the mountain in 1926. They are at Klingsporns' property near Sawmill Settlement. EDWIN ADAMSON

He and fellow BMW Ski Club members 'used to maintain the road, we used to drain it, make sure it was clear. We used to run ahead of the vehicle to throw off the boulders to save the tyres.' Parking wasn't nearly as organised as it now is – there wasn't the demand to have it nor to justify managing it, but this didn't prevent some anarchic behaviour among the mountain's visitors. And some stern words to the SCV:

> I take this opportunity of bringing to your notice the fact that some persons visiting and taking part in the Snow Sports on Mount Buller have during past seasons caused considerable annoyance and danger to others by leaving cars parked in such a manner that the road to the mount was seriously obstructed.
> This lack of normal road courtesy has caused several nasty accidents with the result that the police will take a more active interest in traffic there and will be instructed to prosecute all drivers who are so inconsiderate as to offend.
> I would be pleased if you would advise your members that in future they should avoid any obstruction of the narrow road. T Morris, Superintendent, Victoria Police. (*Schuss*, November 1949, p455)

And there were further complaints, this one in 1957:

> Skiers at Mt Buller recently saw a rather unusual vehicle on the mountain. It was a Vice-Regal Humber station wagon,

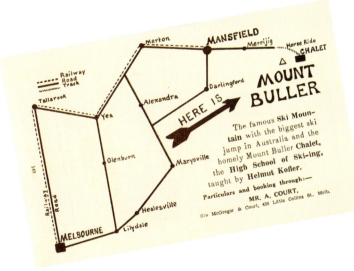

That same year, the editors of *Schuss* had some advice for skiers approaching the mountain.

> As with all senior mountain areas, access at Mt Buller is not open by road all the way to your place of accommodation. A walk in of a mile or more in the depth of winter is unavoidable, consequently a matter of utmost importance is your mobility. A skier loaded to the plimsol line with unnecessary gear will not arrive at the lodge in such a good frame of mind as one who has given forethought to preparations for the days ahead. (*Schuss*, July 1949, p276)

After Doughty's efforts in clearing the way to the SCV's Ivor Whittaker Memorial Lodge, Merrick Summers recalled the clubs taking responsibility for sections of the mountain road.

complete with the gold crown in place of number plates. Unfortunately, the reason that the car was so outstanding was due to the fact that it was parked at Hell's Corner, across the road, in such a manner as to deny access to the village to all but Land Rovers. We look forward to further visits from the same party, but we hope that the next time the vehicle will be more unselfishly parked. [The Victorian Governor from 1949 to 1963 was General Sir Reginald Alexander Dallas Brooks.] (*Schuss*, **August 1957, p216**)

During the 1950s, as the village grew and the skiing population expanded alongside, the quality of the road, the availability of parking and transport services grew in response.

In 1956, the Forests Commission (FCV) improved the road with a 35 feet (10.6 metre) wide extension from the site of the original chalet to the Skating Rink 'to meet the present requirement for parking on the mountain.' (minutes, May 1956)

The road still had to be cleared though, and the commercial operators were keen for it to be cleared all the way to their premises.

Kooroora's Ernest Forras: 'The road had to be cleared to make access easier for the winter season, so I asked Jimmy Betts from the Grey Rocks Ski Club to design and make a V-shaped snow blade at his South Melbourne engineering shop.'

The Forras brothers had some limited success mounting the blade onto a truck and mid-season were upbraided by Country Roads Board officials for 'messing around with snow clearing.'

Their response was to tell the CRB to go and clear the roads. The CRB in turn advised them that if they could raise £200, they would do it. Ernest Forras passed the hat around, raised £180 and, thanks to a 'big bulldozer from Benalla and a driver who had never seen snow', the snow clearing was under way. (Forras, pp104-105)

The first parking attendant had deep connections with the mountains. Alfred 'Dick' Klingsporn was appointed in June 1961 and his duties included the collection 'of parking fees as prescribed and

The journey: a family takes the 4WD taxi in 1985. BILL BACHMAN

The Land Rovers line up outside Kooroora in 1965. The improvement in 4WD transport revolutionised access. ERNEST FORRAS

Skiers came by the busload in the boom years of the 1980s. This photograph was taken mid-winter 1987 in the Skating Rink Car Park. MICHAEL MONESTER

the issue of parking tickets and to regulate the orderly parking of all vehicles.' The hours of duty were 6pm Friday to 2am Saturday, 10am to 4pm Saturday and 9am to 4pm Sunday. For these 21 hours, the remuneration was £15-10/- per week. Klingsporn was issued with a 'distinguishing armband' and it was suggested he should wear an 'easily identifiable coat.' (minutes, July 1961). He was reappointed in 1962 and given an assistant. By way of contrast, in the 2007 winter, the Resort Management Board employed 26 people on car parking and resort entry.

ALWAYS WILLING TO provide a horse for hire, the Lovicks and Klingsporns were among the earliest providers of commercial transport, but this was a sideline.

One of the first to dedicate himself to the task was Eric Johnson who Ernest Forras described as a 'tough Norwegian horseman and cross-country skier, a handyman who never seemed to sleep … For several days our trailer could only get as far as White Bridge. Eric's horse and sledge then took over…' (Forras, p84)

The inventive Bill Heathcote (below left) ran the transport service from the 1950s to 1977. John Perks (at left in the centre photo) with Fred Johnson. Perks turned the transport service into Mansfield Mt Buller Bus Lines and ran it until 1994, building up to a fleet of 75 vehicles. The current manager of the transport service is John Christopher (below right). FCV/MHS/BSL

Another of the early transport operators was Frank Blackmore. Ed Adamson recalled him as 'a mill and road worker who sought to make his fortune. He started a passenger service from Mansfield and from Melbourne using a multi-door black bus, but a combination of difficulty getting the bus far enough up the mountain and inconsistent business sent him away with just the pioneer tag to his memory.'

In 1954, the SCV was pleased to announce that 'bus transport up the mountain to the snow line will be run by Harold Rachor, linking with the regular rail and bus services through Mansfield to Mirimbah. Timetables are at the club office.' (Schuss, May1954, p91)

'Harold Rachor was a tough, small-statured outdoors man,' Ed Adamson said. 'He worked as a contractor and mill worker, living at Sawmill Settlement and Mansfield. He did clearing and dam building for farmers using a little British Bulldog bulldozer and was one of those people who knew how to fix old equipment. 'Rachor, always industrious, used a Second World War Chev Blitz 4X4 truck with a canvas canopy to carry up to 22 passengers with their luggage and skis up the mountain and down again until the truck ran off the road and down the steep hillside in heavy snow conditions at White Bridge (so-named, it is said, because as an early wooden bridge it would be so heavily covered in frost it turned white).

The horse and cart were introduced for romance but also as part of a strategy to create an intra-village transport service. BILL BACHMAN

The strategy worked; in the mid-1990s a free shuttle service was introduced to move skiers around the village. MARK ASHKANASY

'The canopy fell off the truck as it rolled over and all the passengers were tipped out with it at the top of the slope, uninjured; but not Harold, who remained in the cab all the way until it stopped at the bottom of the creek valley. Nobody thought that Harold could have survived, but he emerged from the crushed cab with only a broken wrist,' Adamson said.

In 1956, Bill Heathcote bought the old bus from Frank Blackmore and developed regular and more reliable transport, including sturdy buses for mass transport and 4WDs for better accessibility. Heathcote's timing coincided with the improvement in the early model Land Rover 4WD vehicles. In hindsight, they were outrageously idiosyncratic, but they gave unprecedented access over rough or snow-covered roads in their day.

In the early 1970s, Bill Heathcote's fleet of vehicles included an oversnow track machine. FCV

Neville Kay bought Heathcote out in 1977 and John Perks bought a half share with Kay in 1979, creating Mansfield Mt Buller Bus Lines. At that time, the fleet included six Land Rovers, three buses and an oversnow vehicle.

'In the second year we built it up to 20 and then we had 30; we just kept building it up. We ran all Land Rovers until about 1983,' John Perks said.

'In 1984, Toyota gave us a loan of four Troop Carriers, and they were like chalk and cheese, they were like a Rolls Royce compared to the Land Rover and by about 1986 or 1987, we went all Toyota. 'I've been all over the world and every time I travel I look to see if there's a better vehicle, one that's better value-for-money and there just isn't.'

Perks bought Neville Kay out in 1983. Kay died in a helicopter accident on the Mornington Peninsula in 1985.

'The numbers in the 1980s were terrific,' Perks said. 'We had day trippers down to the [White] Bridge and there were just as many car parks then as there are now.'

Perks ran the business until 1994, when the Pullitano family bought it; at that time, the bus line had a fleet of 75 vehicles.

After his time running the business, Perks has nothing but respect for Mt Buller's transport operators.

'It's probably the hardest business on Mt Buller to run – and I've run a fair share of them – you're relying on road conditions, other vehicles and other people – on peak days it can be like a flood and drains just can't cope with floods.'

Perks doesn't see an alternative for Mt Buller other than the evolution of the current transport model, and that includes 4WD access to the village for those that are willing or able to pay.

When he started, he estimates there would have been permits for around 300 vehicles – 'now there's about 1200 and they're letting more and more in and there's been a push for lodges to be able to pick up their own guests. I don't want to pick up my own guests, but they're going through a heap of debate on it.'

Buller Ski Lifts' Laurie Blampied isn't in complete agreement with Perks: 'I would go with an airport bus style of option with some sort of covered-in transport hub; the concept of parking the cars and standing out in the weather is outdated,' he said.

The worst weather creates the worst situations on the road. Victorian coach drivers are now specially trained and licensed to drive in the mountains. SANDIE JEFFCOAT

Snow clearing, now the RMB's responsibility was previously handled by the state government road authority. MARK ASHKANASY

On track

Mt BULLER'S PROXIMITY to Melbourne has always given it an edge over its rivals. While this is now best reflected in road access, it was once the iron horse that led the way.

When the railway connection that branched off the main Melbourne/Sydney line at Tallarook came through to Mansfield on October 6, 1891 it was a transformation for the town, clearing the path for commerce in the form of tourism and freight.

'When a plume of smoke was seen rising above the railway cutting half a mile from the town, the cheering began and almost drowned the long-sustained whistling of the finally triumphant iron horse.' (*Newsrail*)

Mansfield was at last connected, a connection that was well used by the early skiers and tourism promoters and remained in force, with winter specials timetabled well into the 1960s.

The flexibility of road transport led to the demise of railway services and the line was closed on November 8, 1978.

The Mountaineer special crosses the rail bridge near Bonnie Doon on Saturday August 25, 1962. LINDSAY CROW/*NEWSRAIL*

THIS *SNOW SEASON*

☀ SPECIAL TRAIN SERVICE
WITH CO-ORDINATED BUS FOR

WEEK-END SKIERS AT MT. BULLER

Leaves Spencer St. 6.30 p.m. Fridays, on return leaves Mansfield 6 p.m. Sundays, to reach Spencer St. at 10.7 p.m. (Flinders St. 10.3 p.m.)

COMBINED RAIL-BUS FARE ONLY 75/-

BOOK AT SPENCER ST. OR FLINDERS ST. STATIONS OR VICTOUR

☀ TRAVEL SAFE BY TRAIN WITHOUT DRIVING STRAIN

GETTING PEOPLE INTO the village is one challenge; moving them around within the village is another and it came to a head in the early 1990s.

'At one point, in order to keep it as a ski village and hinder people wanting to get 4WD permits, the roads were not cleared within the village,' former ski patroller and lift company general manager Michael Monester recalled.

'So you then needed 4WDs with chains and it was horrendous, you'd get deep ruts or polished hard pack – it was a total mess.

'The next evolution was clearing roads, but this disrupted skiers who were used to skiing on the roads.'

In 1993, Rino and Diana Grollo introduced a horse and cart – it was partly romantic, to add some character to the village, but also partly strategic, the thin end of the wedge for free transport within the village.

'It was to create a bit of character on the mountain,' Grollo said, 'but also to bring in public transport and make it easier for people to get around. You have horses in places like Vail and St Moritz and Courcheval and so on, you create a bit of atmosphere.'

It worked. Safety issues – particularly traction on ice for the horses – saw the demise of the horse and cart, but there is now a free shuttle service within the village and linking the main car parking area and the Skating Rink Bus Park with the village.

The older photograph (below) shows road construction work at White Bridge around 1936. The timber bridge was built to cross Boggy Creek prior to that, this was the farthest vehicles could go on the trip to the mountain. One Sunday in winter 1986 a landslide just above White Bridge (right) closed the mountain road for several days, trapping people in the village and forcing back those trying to reach it for their holiday. Extensive retaining work has been undertaken in this area. There is a certain irony in the sign at bottom right in the photograph. COURT/NAMA

Having descended by horseback, a party of skiers is forced to retrieve their car from a snow drift after the 1939 Australian National Championships at Mt Buller. BROCKHOFF

Access is substantially simpler in the 21st century, with 4WD vehicles able to easily navigate the village roads. Helicopters are another option; here pilot Mark Grollo touches down in the alps. GROLLO

The gnome home

ONE AUTUMN AFTERNOON in 2000 or 2001, Anne Walters who works for the Mt Buller Resort Management Board, recalls going down the mountain on a staff bus. 'Someone said, "Hey, I just saw a tree with a red door in it."

'We imagined all sorts of things and the next morning we drove up again and, sure enough, the red door was there,' Walters said.

Mt Buller had a Gnome Tree.

'Over the next couple of months more things were added to it, like the letterbox and the chimney and the window. The road signs went up about a year later.'

'People put their own gnomes there or flowers; often children stop and write letters to the gnomes and pop them in the letterbox. Our postie, the mail contractor who brings the mail up to Mt Buller from Monday to Friday, stops there and collects the mail.'

How the Gnome Tree came to be and how the gnomes come and go remains one the mountain's mysteries, but all letters to the gnomes receive a reply. It is also well protected; the Gnome Tree survived the devastating 2006-07 fires, despite the surrounding bush being almost entirely burnt. Such is its popularity, it has inspired a gnome-walk in the village area.

The gnomes have a home at Mt Buller. MARK ASHKANASY

12

Landlords & boards

Mountain resorts come with a certain glamour but beneath that, their managers have to deal with day-to-day fundamentals like roads, rates and rubbish, although they'll be pushed and pulled by numerous passionate interest groups.

TIMBER HAS BEEN a buzzing regional enterprise virtually since Victoria was settled. The state government body controlling the industry from 1918 to 1983, the Forests Commission of Victoria (FCV) was a leader in forest management and related research. It was also ambitious and assertive, ensuring timber country remained under its control.

The harvesting of the stringybark, box and, to a lesser extent, ash forests in the upper reaches of the Delatite Valley, gave the FCV control over the area and, by default, peaks like Mt Buller and Mt Stirling. Such an inheritance wasn't unusual. Until the creation of the Alpine Resorts Commission in 1985, the FCV controlled Mt Buller, Mt Stirling, Lake Mountain, Mt Baw Baw and Mt Donna Buang; the Department of Crown Lands and Survey was responsible for Mt Hotham because the area had a mining background; and the State Electricity Commission controlled Falls Creek as a result of the Kiewa hydro-electric scheme.

Despite the austerity of the post-war years – and perhaps in part as a release from it – tourism was growing. Alongside that, there was pressure on the land managers to nurture that growth, even if the demands of tourists were going to be quite different from those of trees or mines or power generation.

As the parliamentarian and skier Tom Mitchell pointed out (see chapter 4), in the late 1940s, the management of Mt Buller was so loose, it bordered on anarchy with the original chalets burnt and skiers creating a shanty town of caravans and other camps. Something had to be done.

The first meeting of the FCV's Mt Buller Recreational Reserve Committee was held at the Mansfield Shire Office on December 17, 1948. Its chairman was Andrew Benallack of the FCV and other committee members represented the Public Works Department (PWD), the Country Roads Board (CRB), the Mansfield Shire, the Upper Goulburn Regional Committee, the Ski Club of Victoria (SCV) and the Federation of Victorian Ski Clubs (FVSC).

The committee's objective was to guide the development of a mountain village. It only controlled 20 acres (eight hectares) around the Cow Camp site, the present village square, and excluded the SCV's Ivor Whittaker Memorial Lodge. At that initial meeting, it agreed to assert its influence over broader issues such as road access and water supply.

The CRB representative, Mr Gibbs, was cautious – he feared 'insurmountable difficulties in providing an all-weather road to the Cow Camp area' and thought the area near Horse Hill/Skating Rink could be a more suitable site for a village.

The SCV's Arthur Shands and the FVSC's Vern Corr both stated that 'naturally they would like a good road to the building site, but they felt sure that their members would still prefer the Cow Camp area, even if it meant a good road only to the old Youth Hostel site and a more or less passable road on the last section.'

With foresight, and surrounded by pressure from prospective clubs, Benallack suggested 'the Committee proceed as far as possible with the 20 acres under its control and that the Forests Commission be notified that it may need to extend its area of operation to prevent crowding of Cow Camp Site.' (minutes, December 1948)

Apart from access, the committee went on to discuss water supply, sanitation, site allocation and building and finally allocated sites to seven clubs (see chapter 16).

At later meetings in 1949, the committee sought to increase its span of control, recognising that the sites available for allocation to clubs would soon be exhausted.

The FCSV's Vern Corr also recommended that 'some control over ski-tow sites in regard to tree cutting and general planning might be beneficial.' (minutes, September 1949)

In March 1950, the committee had an overnight stay at the SCV lodge. During their meeting the following day, they agreed to contact the FCV and encourage them to survey and subdivide two additional areas – an area 'westerly of the existing subdivision along the Howqua escarpment [along what is now known as The Avenue]' and 'an area in the Horse Hill area.' (minutes, March 1950) The first proposal took off, but the idea of a 'lower village' fizzled.

Later in 1950, it was time to name the village – the suggestions included 'Kofler' for its pioneering Austrian, 'Cow Camp' because it was 'typically Australian', 'Marrang', an Aboriginal name for the mountain, or 'Coonmah' an Aboriginal word for snow. The committee contemplated those options and narrowed it to a further two – 'Mt Buller Snow Village' and 'Mt Buller Alpine Village'. They unanimously chose the latter because it was 'expressive and definitive.' (minutes, June 1950).

By the mid-1950s, the steady growth in club lodges was absorbing the available land and putting pressure on the committee to provide infrastructure.

The Mt Buller Alpine Village with a full cover in 2003. MARK ASHKANASY

IN 1954, THE Public Works Department's representative, CF Fitzsimon pointed out that the 'problem confronting the committee was one of managing an area that could become a small township and that funds were not available to carry out the necessary works involved, such as water supply, sanitation, rubbish disposal and drainage.

'Water supply had been promised six years ago and provisionally clubs had been permitted to install individual septic tanks.' (minutes, November 1954).

Here was the key challenge, the hygiene standard that divided civilised and uncivilised communities and put a ceiling on population size: water in and water out.

In November 1955, the chairman of the FCV, Fenton George Gerraty, wrote to the committee explaining that he and the minister for forests were aware of the committee's need to be able to raise rates for maintenance and development works and that the minister would legislate to give them that ability.

A barrier to progress was the proposed Tourist Resorts and National Parks Bill – it was constantly referred to by committee chairman Benallack as holding the answers for Mt Buller, but it was dawdling through the political processes.

If enacted, it was likely the 'whole snowfield would be vested in the committee,' Benallack said. (minutes, November 1955)

To this point, it had under its responsibility the original 20 acres and the added 10 or so acres in the extension along The Avenue.

ple were rarely, if ever, mentioned in the early years. The quality of ski club buildings and the provision of municipal services completely absorbed it.

In December 1956, the committee allocated sites from a further subdivision, the land now bordered by Stirling and Chamois Roads. This slightly increased its area of control, but in March 1957, it agreed to recommend to the FCV that the committee extend its reach to 'cover all operations above the 4500' [1370m] level,' and that it be able to 'levy charges on the following basis:

a) 20/- per bed accommodation to be levied as a site rental charge in respect to all private lodges;

b) 40/- per bed accommodation per annum in respect to any commercial enterprise; and

c) an annual fee of £15 per annum in respect of any other tariff enterprise.' (minutes, March 1957)

This extended area would give it control over the skifields and related facilities such as the SCV lodge and canteens run by Maurice Selle and the Forras brothers and services such as ski school franchises.

In 1958, Victoria's Tourist Bill passed through Parliament and things started to move. Andrew Benallack informed his committee that the FCV had decided to extend the area the committee controlled 'to include the whole snowfield and would give the committee power to raise levies and fees in order to finance urgent works.' (minutes, June 1958)

Quarrying in 1984 at a site since decommissioned on the Corn Hill Road. SANDIE JEFFCOAT.

Concreting the realigned Summit Road in 1998. Work to upgrade all the village roads went from 1994 to 2002. RMB

To meet visitor requirements, 'public conveniences' were urgently required, but their construction was initially linked to the provision of an overall water supply.

Harold Doughty, who had become an SCV representative on the committee, helped the cause when he and a Mansfield Water Supply surveyor, Mr Finlason, 'inspected the location between Boggy Creek and the village,' and Finlason found 'sufficient quantities of water for fire protection and use in the village.' (minutes, February 1956).

The issues the committee didn't discuss are as revealing as those they did. Because their span of control was within the village area, the demands and requirements of skiing and snow sports for exam-

THIS WAS A dramatic change to the committee's capability and responsibility and with it came a name change – from June 1958, at the FCV's suggestion, it became known as the Mt Buller Committee of Management.

In May 1958, it defined its terrain as a rectangular-shaped area bordered by Caravan Corner, Corn Hill, Mirimbah Spur and Little Buller.

In addition to the bed rates, it also introduced parking fees of 1/- per day or 5/- per week for a car or trailer (double that for cars carrying six or more passengers) and fees of £2-10/- per week of operation for a fixed tow and £1 per week for a mobile tow. (minutes, May 1958)

Mt Buller's long-awaited water supply, as it appeared in autumn 2007 (above) and under construction in the summer of 1964-65 (right). Luigi Grollo is in the white shirt at right. MARK ASHKANASY/GROLLO

But they continued to struggle. In 1960, Harold Doughty stressed his concern that the committee had still been unable to overcome the village water supply problem and they agreed to ask the FCV to approach the State Rivers and Water Supply Commission regarding the formation of a water trust at Mt Buller and to raise fees on the mountain to finance its projects. (minutes, January 1960)

A year later, Andrew Benallack reported that 'a Public Works Department survey team had been on Mt Buller gathering information to effectively plan a reticulated water supply system. It was estimated that the proposed plan would take two months to prepare.' (minutes, February 1961)

The PWD's scheme was presented to the committee two years later, in February 1963, with plans for a three-stage water supply project with storage of 1.9 million gallons (8.6 million litres) and reticulation throughout the village. The total cost was estimated at £60,000. (minutes, February 1963)

Dr Frank Moulds, who had become chairman in 1961, advised the committee in July 1963 that the FCV had received an allocation of £24,000 for stage one of the water supply project.

The water supply works became the Grollo family's first commercial connection with the mountain, when their company Conpor won the contract to build the dam.

'We built the dam there, the million gallon dam,' Rino Grollo said. 'My dad [Luigi Grollo] and my brother [Bruno Grollo] built that, I was 16 at the time, didn't have a licence but I went up there with my dad a few times.'

With the water supply in place in 1965, the emphasis swung to some form of reticulated sewerage system for the mountain, replacing the grubby collection of septic tanks that were doing the job to varying levels of success.

It was a significant barrier to growth – the number of beds in the village and the overall visitor numbers the mountain could accommodate were governed by this kind of infrastructure, or the lack of it.

When Dr Ron Grose became committee chairman in 1968, there were around 1200 beds in the village. When he left, in 1981, the village had grown to around 6500 beds.

'Sewering the joint was the biggest project I managed,' he said, 'it was done by Gutteridge, Haskins & Davies, Ben Fink was the GHD chairman at the time and he and I did the job I suppose.'

Grose recalled having 'a hell of a lot of trouble with the shit-stirrers, as we called them.'

By this he was being more technical than colloquial. Mt Buller has always had its share of stirrers in the colloquial sense, but here he was talking about the mechanism used to stir the waste in the tanks.

'It took a long time to get them used to the climate, to get them tuned up to deal with the climate,' Grose said.

Sandie Jeffcoat, the area manager from 1982 and the resort management board's chief executive from 1997 to 2005, described the reticulated sewerage system as a 'huge undertaking and way ahead of its time.'

The Resort Management Board office as it appeared in 2007. The RMB has since moved to the university campus building, centre right in this photograph. MARK ASHKANASY

JEFFCOAT WAS THE constant through a period of enormous change and growth on the mountain and in the industry and politics surrounding it.

A forester by profession, he took the job as area manager 'on a two year secondment'. His first winter, 1982, was one of the worst seasons for years. 'I wondered what had hit me. We had no facilities, no facilities at all.' He and his wife Rae and their then three-month-old daughter had a single bedroom in a staff lodge and shared everything else with the staff.

'But we stuck with it,' Jeffcoat said, 'it was a great life. I guess with a bad winter you learn a lot. You learn about the relationships with commercial operators.'

Among the many achievements during those years were the construction of the snowmaking dam and the gas reticulation system, the sealing of all the village roads, substantial landscaping, the chapel and the village centre, bridge and clock tower.

Jeffcoat came into the job working for the FCV, but he soon found himself with a new employer.

On March 1, 1983, the Victorian government's minister for economic development, Ian Cathie, called a press conference to announce the government's intention to establish 'an Alpine Resorts Commission [ARC] to co-ordinate control and management of all Victorian snow resorts except Mt Buffalo.'

Mt Buffalo's exclusion was on the basis that it was a national park with 'no room for more ski slopes or accommodation,' Cathie said. The minister made a few remarks, including the point that, as the

Victorian resorts were run by three different government departments, it was 'impossible for government authorities with very different main objectives to the management and development of ski resorts, to raise enough capital to ensure the resorts were adequately serviced.'

Cathie was slightly overshadowed at the event by his director of tourism, the flamboyant former South Australian premier Don Dunstan, who said that 'by international standards the services and general infrastructure of our ski areas must be regarded as poor, but it is estimated that our existing resorts have potential for a 50 per cent growth in their capacity.'

Some Labor governments have had difficulty with mountain resorts – falling for the perception that they are the domain of the idle rich, the crowd from Barry Humphries' *Snow Complications* who 'belted up to Buller with a couple of great old mates of mine from school.' (*Moonee Ponds Muse*, Vol 1)

But even they see the significance in the resorts' economic contribution and their role as a regional employer.

That dichotomy may have been behind Cathie's statement that 'one of the main aims of the commission would be to make skiing cheaper and more readily available to a wider range of people.' (Victorian government media release, 1983)

Resort entry on a busy morning in 1981 (above) as Robyn Hughes takes the toll. The entry now has three lanes and covers visitors to both Mt Buller and Mt Stirling. NAMA

The village's reticulated gas system was installed in 1992. This second tank had an interesting journey up the mountain road in autumn, 1997. SANDIE JEFFCOAT

The ARC had numerous achievements, but it has never been accused of making the sport cheaper.

The resorts were gazetted by the government, with boundaries that were either historic or redefined in conjunction with the Land Conservation Council. Over the next few years, the three major resorts – Mt Buller, Falls Creek and Mt Hotham – found themselves neighbours with the newly created Alpine National Park. Mt Stirling was also defined as an alpine resort, separate to Mt Buller and earmarked for development (see chapter 19).

The ARC was established in 1984 and at Mt Buller, the transition from the FCV to the ARC occurred before the 1985 winter.

Philip Bentley was the chief executive of the ARC from April 1990

to September 1994. He wasn't a skier, he 'took on the ARC as a management challenge.'

He joined the ARC at a volatile time: 'the ARC was losing money, about $2 million a year, and the government objective was for it to be self-funding by 1992.

'I also discovered the ARC had about $6.5 million in debt owed to it and I had to go and collect that. I collected about $5.5 million,' Bentley said.

Some of that debt was in unpaid rates and that was surrounded by a ratepayers' strike as a reaction to the ARC's escalating charges (see chapter 16). The strike was at its strongest at Mt Buller.

'I knew about the ratepayers' strike, at ratepayer meetings I thought, "What have I walked into?" but I negotiated a deal with Daryl Gallagher and Peter Dyson to get rid of the ratepayers' dispute,' Bentley said.

'Six months later I started to think we'd been too generous, but at least we got peace. Rate concessions were introduced and they at least had a time limit.'

Green snow

MT BULLER HAS been a global pioneer in water recycling. Its $3.43 million water reuse project has been coordinated by the Resort Management Board and supported by Buller Ski Lifts and the Victorian Water Trust.

Recycled water is carried along a 2.5-kilometre pipeline from the sewerage treatment plant to the snowmaking dam, providing up to a 30 per cent increase in snowmaking capacity.

The project actually improves the quality and reduces the volume of the treated effluent that is discharged into the Howqua River and reduces the demand on local water courses for snowmaking.

It also ensures that up to 80 per cent of the village's waste water is recycled, using a disinfection system of UV irradiation, chlorination and ultrafiltration to purify the waste water and recycle up to 2 million litres of Class A water daily.

The disinfection process that forms a part of the new water recycling infrastructure is similar to that currently being used for the resort's drinking water, ensuring it ranks alongside the cleanest water in the region.

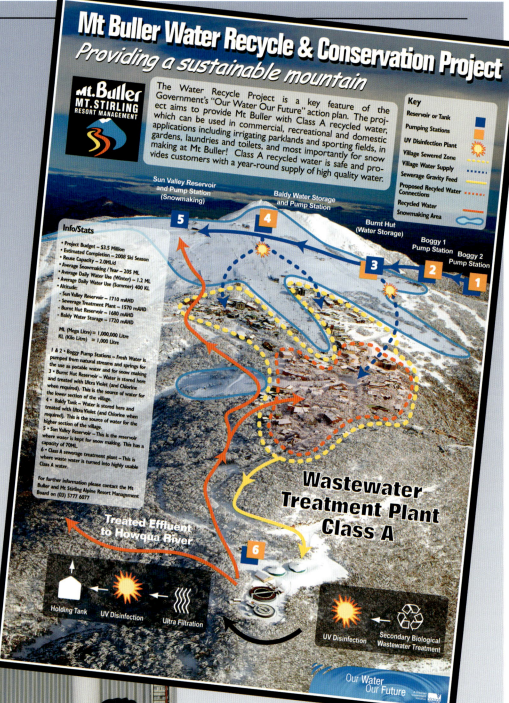

Mt Buller Water Recycle & Conservation Project
Providing a sustainable mountain

The Water Recycle Project is a key feature of the Government's "Our Water Our Future" action plan. The project aims to provide Mt Buller with Class A recycled water, which can be used in commercial, recreational and domestic applications including irrigating parklands and sporting fields, in gardens, laundries and toilets, and most importantly for snow making at Mt Buller! Class A recycled water is safe and provides customers with a year-round supply of high quality water.

Key
- Reservoir or Tank
- Pumping Stations
- UV Disinfection Plant
- Village Sewered Zone
- Village Water Supply
- Sewerage Gravity Feed
- Proposed Recyled Water Connections
- Recycled Water
- Snowmaking Area

Info/Stats
- Project Budget – $3.5 Million
- Estimated Completion – 2008 Ski Season
- Reuse Capacity – 2.0ML/d
- Average Snowmaking / Year – 205 ML
- Average Daily Water Use (Winter) – 1.2 ML
- Average Daily Water Use (Summer) 400 KL
- Altitude:
  - Sun Valley Reservoir – 1710 mAHD
  - Sewerage Treatment Plant – 1570 mAHD
  - Burnt Hut Reservoir – 1680 mAHD
  - Baldy Water Storage – 1720 mAHD

ML (Mega Litre)= 1,000,000 Litre
KL (Kilo Litre) = 1,000 Litre

1 & 2 - Boggy Pump Stations – Fresh Water is pumped from natural streams and springs for the use as potable water and for snow making
3 - Burnt Hut Reservoir – Water is stored here and treated with Ultra Violet (and Chlorine when required). This is the source of water for the lower section of the village.
4 - Baldy Tank – Water is stored here and treated with Ultra Violet (and Chlorine when required). This is the source of water for the higher section of the village.
5 - Sun Valley Reservoir –This is the reservoir where water is kept for snow making. This has a capacity of 70ML.
6 - Class A sewerage treatment plant – This is where waste water is turned into highly usable Class A water.

For further information please contact the Mt Buller and Mt Stirling Alpine Resort Management Board on (03) 5777 6077

Sun Valley Reservoir and Pump Station (Snowmaking)

Baldy Water Storage and Pump Station

Burnt Hut (Water Storage)

Boggy 1 Pump Station
Boggy 2 Pump Station

Wastewater Treatment Plant Class A

Treated Effluent to Howqua River

Holding Tank → UV Disinfection → Ultra Filtration

UV Disinfection ← Secondary Biological Wastewater Treatment

Our Water Our Future

The then conservation minister, John Thwaites (left) and Resort Management Board chairman John Dyson at the opening of Mt Buller's water recycle and conservation project in June 2007.
KEREN FREEMAN/RMB

Not all of Mt Buller's ratepayers agreed to the settlement however, with a couple refusing to pay, 'so we evicted them,' Bentley said, 'we put the place up for auction and put the money back into infrastructure.

'It put a message into the industry that there was new management around; there were no further problems with ratepayers.'

A change in government eventually saw a change in approach; in 1994, the Kennett government announced a review of the ARC, with natural resources minister Geoff Coleman pointing out that 'in 1988 a reform process was commenced by the ARC to secure its financial viability. Substantial reductions in operating expenses have been achieved in a time when successive poor seasons have impacted on the growth of participation in the sport.

'However, growth in visitor days has not met Government expectations and a greater emphasis on out-of-winter tourism may be able to achieve this,' Coleman said. (Victorian government media release, 1994)

In 1997, the *Alpine Resorts Act 1983* was amended by the *Alpine Resorts (Management) Act 1997*.

'The Liberals wanted to get rid of the ARC', Bentley said, 'and they set up resort management boards to run each resort – there's good and bad things about that, but I suspect the percentage of rates and rents that goes back into administration and marketing has gone up considerably.'

The ARC had served a valuable purpose, in that it removed the resorts from landlords like the FCV that were competent managers but never had alpine resorts as a core interest; however, politically, the ARC's time was up.

It was goodbye ARC and hello resort management boards; the objective was for resorts to be self-sufficient and eliminate the bureaucracy the ARC represented.

As Bentley said, there was an advantage here for Mt Buller – it could retain the fees it raised for its own use, rather than cross-subsidising other resorts through the old ARC model.

WHEN SANDIE JEFFCOAT arrived in 1982, clubs were still strong and 'Mt Buller was just a ski mountain. If you wanted to go skiing you went there and you stayed in a grotty bunk and people were happy with that.

'The place wasn't nearly as professional as it is today. By the time I left in 2005, I think Mt Buller had became a resort, a holiday destination where it's not just skiing, it's good food, luxury accommodation and everything you could want in a holiday destination.

'People's recreation time is so limited now and we are competing, not just against other ski resorts but we're competing against Queensland, against Bali and New Zealand,' Jeffcoat said.

'I think everybody realised we had to become more professional. I recall when I went there, the only road that was sealed was the old Summit Road, what is now the Athletes' Walk.

'Everything was just dirt, people used to queue for a taxi out in the snow, in the rain. John Perks would be on a great big loud hailer telling people that the bus would only be five minutes, when he knew it might be two hours. The toilet block was an absolute disgrace and every street had power lines up it.

'There have been so many changes, there's rock walls everywhere, the streets are all sealed, there's not a power line above ground in the village, it's all street lit and I just think it is a very professional resort,' Jeffcoat said.

'Where the new Summit Road goes out across the old Village run and out toward Shaky Knees and back, I reckon that's one of the best thing to happen to Buller in years, where you stop cars mixing with people on Summit Road – it's just terrific.

'I can remember waking up there in the middle of the day trying to clear snow off the road because we couldn't get cars off and people were all around the snow plough, it was just dangerous,' he said.

'One of the other innovations in my time was concrete roads. Bitumen roads just didn't stand up to it. All the roads on Buller are now concrete, which makes it better to clear.

'I had great staff. Hadyn Purcell, the operations manager, was with me the whole time. Hadyn would get out there and do anything in any weather.'

Jeffcoat also regards the creation of the Mansfield - Mt Buller Regional Tourism Association as a key development for the mountain and the region, bringing together opportunities for marketing, promotion and accommodation bookings under a single umbrella.

The then RMB chief executive Sandie Jeffcoat with World Cup winner Lydia Ierodiaconou in 2003. The RMB was a major supporter of the World Cup aerials events at Mt Buller. MARK ASHKANASY

Just as Mt Buller's businesses have improved their service offering, so has the RMB, leading with the Mountain Host program 'it was primarily to, I guess, give the staff a feeling that they were part of the mountain community and get across the message that the guest was the most important person,' Jeffcoat said.

MT BULLER'S ALPINE Resort Management Board was created in 1997 after the devolution from the ARC. In late 2004, it merged with what was then a separate board running Mt Stirling to create the Mt Buller and Mt Stirling Alpine Resort Management Board.

Phil Nunn took up a position as Sandie Jeffcoat's assistant in 2004, taking over as chief executive in 2005 and taking up the marketing baton.

'I would think that the last 10 years has been more focused on marketing and trying to promote Mt Buller as a destination, whereas maybe in the old days, that was left more to the individuals. Now the collaborative approach that Sandie facilitated is pretty important in terms of marketing and promoting,' Nunn said.

He also reinforces the connection with Mansfield and its region. 'Most of the people who work on Buller are Mansfield residents for at least a part of the year, so a lot of the income that we earn up here is spent in the area … visitors are buying petrol and hiring skis and buying food or accommodating themselves in Mansfield.

'Buller is seen as a key element of the region's tourist infrastructure … increasingly there's a greater cooperation of promotional marketing activities between the Mansfield Shire and ourselves particularly,' Nunn said.

The RMB remains responsible to the Victorian Government and part of its objective is to increase year-round tourism.

'It's a challenge but it's also a great opportunity,' Nunn said, 'to provide things for people to do. So we've been trying to put in place all of the pieces that might make it a good holiday for people and over the last couple of years we've spent money on improving our walking tracks, both physically and in terms of signage and in terms of maps and whatever else.

'We've worked with the lift company to facilitate the introduction of a year-round supermarket which is another component of what people are looking for and we're just about to embark on a significant investment in mountain biking.

'Typically the people who are taking up cycling are of the right demographic; they've got some time and some money and we're trying to complement our extreme downhill mountain bike site with more touring tracks and coupling the mountain biking with some road cycling events,' Nunn said.

The snowmaking dam under construction in 1994. In a cooperative arrangement, the RMB supplies water for the snowmaking system and Buller Ski Lifts operates the system. SANDIE JEFFCOAT

Resort management in 1965. In the back row are an unknown person (left) and Terry Donnell. In the front are Des Maroney (left, of the State Electricity Commission), Hans Steiner and David Kirkham. TREVOR LEMKE

Ron Grose

Gerry Gannan

Sandie Jeffcoat

Michael Coldham

Philip Bentley

Hadyn Purcell

Phil Nunn

Resort management staff in 1990 are Chris Deutscher (sitting at top left), Les Kaye (standing at left in the back row), Peter Hallam, Norm Day and Bill Notley. Sitting below them are Neville Horan (left), Greg Gleich and Trevor Thompson (with the beard). In the front row are Angus Usher (left), Graham Godber, Steve Holland and Sandie Jeffcoat with Alan Alingham and Hadyn Purcell on the oversnow vehicle. MARK ASHKANASY

In control

THE FIRST COMMITTEE of management chairman was Andrew Benallack, from 1948 to 1961, then came:

Dr Frank Moulds   1961 to 1965
Jack Gillespie   1966 to 1968
Dr Ron Grose   1968 to 1982
Dr Fred Craig   1982 to 1985
Michael Coldham   1985 to 1990
John Perks   1990 to 1996
Philip Bentley   1996 to 1998
Michael Coldham   1998 to 2001
Diana Patterson   2001 to 2004
John Dyson   2004 –

In the late 1950s, the committee saw the wisdom in appointing a ranger to help manage the area and it was told that under the new Tourist Bill, the Victorian Government Tourist Committee was empowered to grant funds to Mt Buller for such a purpose. (minutes, January 1958) This took some time, and eventually, in 1962, the committee heard that the FCV had agreed to appoint a full-time warden 'to control activities in the Mt Buller resort.' (minutes, May 1962)

The warden was eventually appointed in May 1963, Douglas Escott, who the committee was told 'had lived on Mt Buller and is aware of the problems which the position poses' but he was a 'single man and therefore accommodation is not difficult at present.' (minutes, May 1963).

In July, the FCV's Mr Harrop told the committee that Escott was up and running and 'the only real difficulty confronting him was to give Mr Escott detailed information as to what to do. However … Mr Escott … has shown initiative and is generally doing a good job.' (minutes, July 1963)

Others to fill the role of warden included David Kirkham. The increasing

Some of the RMB staff in 2007. Jonathan Chivers (left), Cathy Chivers, Mark Evans, Sarah Egan, Susie Klingsporn, Tony Petersen, Anne Walters, Phil Nunn, Julie Dolling, Amanda Reed, Linda Charles, Mandy Nicholls, Chris Deutscher and Maureen Williams. JEFF PLANT/RMB

complexity of managing and developing the resort saw the role expanded to that of area manager with Jack Bayne and Cyril Suggate among the early ones to hold that position. Sandie Jeffcoat was the longest serving, appointed in 1982, becoming chief executive in 1997. He was succeeded by Phil Nunn in 2005. The mountain has had many long-serving staff members, including Gerry Gannan, the FCV's secretary for Mt Buller from 1963 to 1980 and Hadyn Purcell, who first worked for the committee in 1976 and has been the operations manager since 1995.

13

Image

Mt Buller's image has many components. Part of it comes from the identity it is given by its people; part of it comes from the way they tie themselves to the mountain to create their own identity. And then there's the media and the marketing.

IT WAS IMAGE that lured the first skiers – the image of a snow-capped Mt Buller as bait from the Mansfield Progress Association (MPA), nibbled by the Ski Club of Victoria (SCV). Through its magazine, *Schuss*, and other means, the SCV spent decades publicising its chosen sport, asserting its image; the bigger the numbers, the bigger the opportunities.

Resort management's first mention of publicity came early in the piece when the Mt Buller Recreational Reserve Committee, agreed that 'general publicity for the committee and the general attraction of the mount would be advantageous for the development of the mount as a recreation reserve. It was considered that certain information should be furnished to the local papers and perhaps the daily papers.' (minutes, December 1949)

It was another eight years before the committee created a graphic representation of its own existence. In 1955, it first began discussing the idea of a letterhead at its meetings; it sourced pho-

tographs from Edwin Adamson and Eric Burt and at its July 1957 meeting, it finally agreed to 'spend £6-16-0 on 500 letterheads,' that included a 'block' with a distant view of Mt Buller. (minutes, July 1957)

By August 1960, committee chairman Andrew Benallack suggested that 'the time might be approaching when the committee should give consideration to the general question of publicity and it was decided that the matter should be placed on the agenda for discussion at the next meeting.' (minutes, August 1960)

Mt Buller's connection with Melbourne has been deep since the first trips to the snow in the 1920s; it was deepened through marketing in the 1990s, including this tram image. It may be true, it may be an urban myth, but around this time, some international tourists were said to have enquired in Melbourne, 'where is the tram to Mt Buller?'

There was no panic. At the following meeting, October 1960, it was decided to hold the matter over until November. At that meeting, it was decided to place publicity 'on the agenda for discussion at the next meeting' but even then, in February 1961, it was again deferred. Unfortunately, at the following meeting, March 1961, publicity simply fell off the page.

And then, almost out of the blue, in November 1961, the committee moved that 'a sum of £20 be allocated for publicity. The publicity sub-committee to recommend ways and means of spending this sum.'

Where that £20 went isn't entirely clear, but Mt Buller has sought to define and assert its identity in some interesting ways over the decades, and other businesses have attached themselves to the mountain and to snow sports to gain from the association.

Skiwear designers have always been innovative. This outfit, created by Rosalie Kiessling and modelled by Jackie Holmes, is photographed at a Melbourne chemical plant in the 1960s. KIESSLING

June, 1949   *SCHUSS*   207

A 1949 magazine advertisement for Smorgon's 'canned meat delicacies'. Some businesses saw skiing as a means to position their own image, some business people simply expressed support for their chosen sport. *SCHUSS*/NAMA

GIVEN MT BULLER'S proximity to Melbourne and most major Victorian provincial centres, the proposition that guaranteeing the mountain's popularity simply involved keeping the road open when there was snow on the ground once had some validity. But competition for peoples' holiday business has grown, particularly competition from snow destinations in Australia, New Zealand and even Japan and from resorts in the sun and elsewhere.

'It's true, if there's good snow people will come and if there isn't people are less likely to come,' Margarita Gimenez, Buller Ski Lifts' (BSL) marketing manager from 2003 to 2007 said. 'But there are certain strategies and initiatives you can put in place to lessen the volatility.'

That involves grooming, farming and snowmaking infrastructure to guarantee snow cover and also 'marketing initiatives like timely communication about snow depth,' Giminez said.

Here the internet has driven massive change. 'Snow cams are a great tool. It means people don't come into the resort blind; they have realistic expectations about the conditions and they can trust the information. For us, it's all about the credibility of the information.'

The internet has also changed the way people buy holidays. 'Our research reinforces that. Over 50 per cent of people now use the internet as their main information source for finding information about a winter holiday. Five years ago, maybe a booking office would have been the main source,' she said.

Another key factor that builds the identity and redefines the image is the complete resort experience – taking it beyond winter and beyond skiing, where visitors are offered 'spa and wellness, food and wine, adventure activities and shopping – it becomes a leisure precinct, not just skiing, and this buffers the problem of no snow or poor weather.'

MT BULLER IS so many things to so many different people. It is often the site of the first snow experience for people as diverse as migrant families or even outback school children who have never seen a city, let alone the snow.

'The multi-culturalism in Australian society is alive and well at Buller,' Laurie Blampied, BSL general manager said.

'We have an enormous contingent of Asian guests, people from mainland China, Malaysia, Hong Kong, Singapore; we have increasing numbers of people from the Middle East and India and Pakistan.

'That's something you just won't see in any other resort in Australia and I dare say not too many resorts elsewhere in the world.'

Mt Buller is also a magnet for its regulars, a place where family tradition creates such a deep bond, where grandparents ski with their children and grandchildren; 'it's part of that immense loyalty Buller generates,' Margarita Gimenez said.

The lift company plays a joint role with resort management and the wider resort community in managing the mountain's image, in defining it as a brand. This is underpinned by research undertaken at Mt Buller and by Victoria's Board of Alpine Resorts Tourism. That research reveals that people who know Mt Buller regard it

2004 Pocket Guide

Mt Buller

Shai Ashkanasy is the action model for the cover of a 2004 mountain guide. A former Mt Buller patroller and Team Buller member, her image first appeared in a 1987 Mt Buller calendar. This pocket guide was designed by Andrew Hogg. BSL

A magazine advertisement designed by Shane Tasca for the mountain in 1985. NAMA

as being 'all about the community and the history and the heritage of skiing,' Gimenez said. 'Guests see Buller as a resort with a village and atmosphere; a family mountain, a place to go with your family. So what we want to communicate to people that don't know Buller is the reason why the people that do know it love it so much.'

This is reinforced by Gimenez's predecessor, Stephanie Hendrickson (Hamilton) who worked at Mt Buller from 1996 to 2003 and was BSL's marketing manager from 2000 to 2003.

'Because it is a resort that has been operating lifts for more than 50 years … in many respects it was Victoria's iconic ski resort. Once you become a brand that is that powerful – and to many Melburnians and Victorians, skiing is synonymous with Buller – your campaign is still important but overall, the brand is established,' Hendrickson said.

From the outside, the Sydney *Daily Telegraph's* skiing writer, Arthur Stanley, sees Mt Buller as 'an amazing ski resort, right on Melbourne's doorstep with nice, challenging terrain. Strike Buller when the snow and the weather is good and you have a mountain that seriously rocks.

'The village has a touch of Melbourne class about it, and interstate or overseas visitors can get a pretty special holiday by combining a few days in Melbourne with a few days on the mountain.'

Another journalist, Robert Upe, the travel editor of Melbourne's *The Age* newspaper: 'I've grown up with Mt Buller. When I was younger I would visit on day trips with mates. Now, with family, we prefer extended stays. Either way, the fun has never gone out of it. We are lucky to have such a snow asset so close to the city.'

Some of the people who have recorded the mountain's moments. Mark Ashkanasy in 1986 (above left); Mark Borderick in 1994 (above); Mark Woodsford in 2006 (below) and Bill Bachman in 2002 (bottom).
BILL BACHMAN/CHRISTOPH MAIER

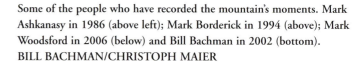

Moving the message

IN 1935, SKIER Mick Hull had a part-time job gathering sports results for Melbourne's *Star* evening newspaper and he recalled discussing with the editor the prospect of publishing the results of the August 1935 championships to be held at Mt Buller. The editor was keen to scoop his rivals at *The Herald* and Hull suggested using carrier pigeons.

'I suggested rolls of 35mm film could be flown out from Boggy Creek (with notes attached), each one taped to the leg of a homing pigeon.'

So Hull took two cages of pigeons with him to stay in the Boggy Creek Hut. The pigeons were released with film and results, but '… as the pigeons had not arrived home, their owners assumed that eagles from the high peaks along the first part of the journey (the Eagle Peaks) must have taken them all.' (Hull, pp239-46)

Things have moved along, with wireless and cable transmission enabling direct feed of television footage from the mountain out into the world.

Snow reports are still provided and remain a vital means of communicating conditions, but they have been usurped by the internet and the development of web cameras.

Particularly for mountain regulars, constantly updated images from web cams in well-known positions give a complete, independent and authentic picture about snow conditions and snow cover.

The 2007 home pages of Mt Buller website in summer and winter.

The internet is used to promote the mountain's image and action (top left), the current conditions and snow grooming status (top right), snowmaking productivity (left) and events like the 2007 Cattleman's Rail Jam (above).

Snow reporting is fed through the internet and to television stations for broadcast. In winter 2007, Dave Clarke (above left) files a report outside the Chalet; and Bethany Lloyd files from a snow-covered balcony at the Whitt as the winter dawn breaks. TIM BYRNE/BSL

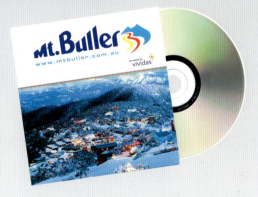

Printed brochures are still produced, as they have been in some form or other since the 1930s, but other media such as compact discs and digital video discs are also used to publicise the mountain.

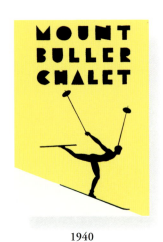

1940

1949

1955

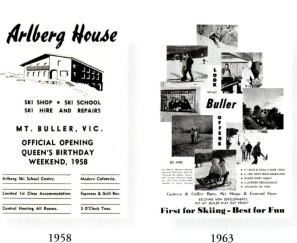

1958

1963

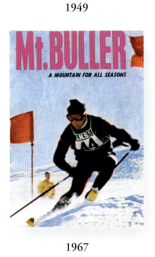

1964

1967

1972

1975

1978

1980

1981

1983

1984

1985

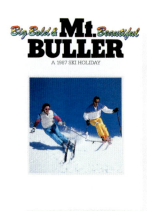

1986

1987

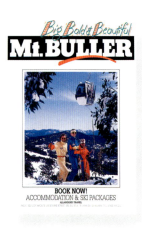

1988

1989

1989

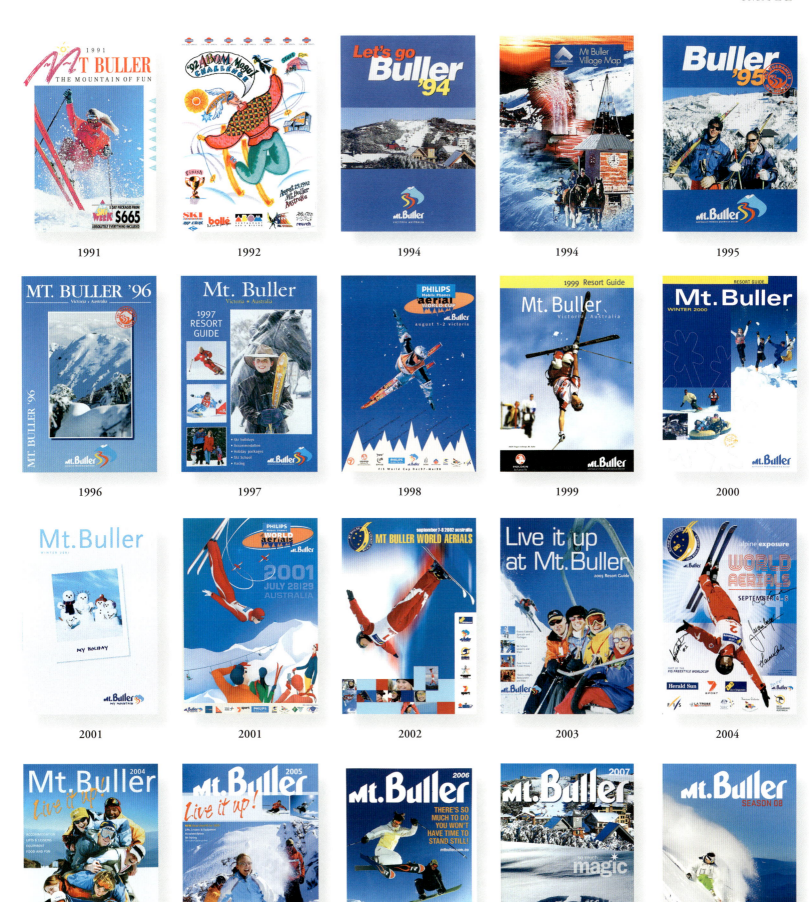

1991	1992	1994	1994	1995
1996	1997	1998	1999	2000
2001	2001	2002	2003	2004
2004	2005	2006	2007	2008

14

Art & architecture

The mountains inspire all their visitors in some way; it's no surprise that they give sustenance to the most creative.

EVERYONE DRAWS INSPIRATION from the mountains. For some the emphasis is on the sport – in some forms, skiing and snowboarding are performance arts – for some, the emphasis is social. For most people, the mountain environment is inspiration in itself. That includes artists who might observe the mountain from afar or might be totally immersed in it.

Jenny Laidlaw (Smith) grew up in Mt Beauty, in the shadow of Mt Bogong and fell for the Bogong High Plains, which she explored as a bushwalker and cross-country skier with her father, the artist Keith Smith.

But then, as fate would have it, she fell for a Mt Buller ski patroller, Andy Laidlaw, and Mt Buller has been her winter mountain home, on and off, since 1996.

Jenny Laidlaw takes to wandering the mountain to absorb ideas for her own works of art, but the wandering seems to give her almost as much satisfaction as the work.

'It took me a little while to appreciate the mountains up there [around Mt Buller] compared to the Bogong High Plains – the accessibility to other mountains is very different at Buller.

'Now I love it, but I love it most between 5.30am and 7.30am, because I have got it to myself. I go out past Corn Hill or past Little Buller and the West Ridge.'

Her favoured form of transport is snowshoe. 'I prefer them for getting around; they're just easier in terms of getting where you want to go, you're really not limited.'

Mt Buller by Jeffrey Makin, 1993, oil on canvas, 182.5cm x 152cm. Makin and his family are Mt Buller skiers. As well as being a full-time artist, he is an art critic and in 2006 judged the Mt Buller Easter Art Prize.
SOTHEBYS/PRIVATE COLLECTION

Easter Arts

The annual Mt Buller Easter Art Show and Exhibition is a drawcard in itself as an event but through its acquisition prizes (in 2008 totalling $32,500 for three paintings and $15,000 for one sculpture) increases the art that is retained on the mountain.

The show provides Australian artists with the opportunity to be part of one of the most significant art events in regional Victoria and in fact in Australia. The Resort Management Board views the exhibition as a way of achieving its aim to increase tourism and visitation, inspire community passion, support participation in arts, culture and heritage-based activities and create a healthier, more prosperous community.

Little Buller Spur After The Fires by Mark Schaller, 2007, oil on canvas, 105cm x 120cm. Schaller's painting was an acquisition prize winner of the 2007 Easter Art Prize and hangs in the Resort Management Board's foyer. He described the painting as 'a view of the Mt Buller region after the devastation of the recent fires. It forms part of a body of work that is dealing with the impact of bushfire on the landscape.' RMB

Apart from her early-morning excursions, when Andy is able to look after their two primary school-aged children, she heads off again at school time.

'I'll drop the kids off at school and go out until it's time to pick them up again – from nine until three, I'm just out there.'

Her style is mixed-media, finely-detailed pen and ink with collage. She takes photographs to draw from, but there are numerous found objects in her work – for both these factors, her mountain wanderings are essential.

'When I went out to Little Buller, after the [2006-07] bushfires, just finding burnt leaves and burnt sticks was inspiring; it's really like putting together a puzzle,' she said.

The mountain environment, she said, also creates a reassured setting for art, works like *The Spirit of the Skier* or *The Mountain Cattleman*.

'When you're looking at those pieces within the different seasons up there, it's almost like looking at a different sculpture every time.'

Chris Skiing the Plughole by Helen Schiller, 2004, watercolour on paper, 53.5cm x 35.5cm. Helen Schiller is a Mt Buller skier; the Plughole is the run in the centre of the Bull Run Bowl. PRIVATE COLLECTION

Mt Buller from Devils River by Robert Russell, 1858, water colour, 24.5cm x 33.9cm. An artist, architect and surveyor, Robert Russell more than likely painted this work at Delatite Station. It is one of the earliest known visual impressions of the area. NGA

Devils Plain Creek Catchment by Eugen von Guerard, 1862, pen and ink on paper. This sketch, from Delatite Station, is one of many by the Viennese-born von Guerard who travelled with expeditions through the Snowy Mountains and the high country of Victoria. PRIVATE COLLECTION

Summit Run – Mt Buller (at left) by Reg Cox, 1978, watercolour on paper, 79cm x 102cm. Reg Cox was invited to Mt Buller by Geoff Henke who commissioned him to create a work to be used to raise funds for the Australian Ski Federation's alpine racing squad. The ASF made a limited-edition run of 50 prints of this painting of the old summit lift hut with Mt Timbertop in the distance. Cox has since produced a huge body of work with a connection to the Australian mountains and Mt Buller in particular. PRIVATE COLLECTION

Craig's Hut by Jenny Laidlaw, 2006, pen and ink on paper with found objects, 30cm x 30cm. Jenny Laidlaw uses a combination of fine drawing, found objects and her own words for this style of work. She has completed numerous commissions based on buildings or features around the Mt Buller village. PRIVATE COLLECTION

Mother and Children. MARK ASHKANASY

The Mountain Cattleman. SHAUN KRATZER

THE TRACES OF sculptor Michael Meszaros aren't hard to find in Melbourne, like the couple of passers-by in bronze, looking from the footpath through the glass of an office building on the central city corner of Exhibition and Lonsdale streets. He made his way to the mountains in three major commissions by Rino and Diana Grollo. In Mt Buller's Village Square, the work called *The Mountain Cattleman* is a tribute to those pioneers of the high country and outside the Alpine Chapel are *Mother and Children* moving through the snow.

The sculpture Meszaros created to represent *The Spirit of the Skier* can be found in many places. It is located at Helicopter Flat on Mt Buller and is dedicated to one of the mountain's great skiers, Bernd Greber (see chapter 8). This sculpture also appears in Mansfield and has also been donated to Nagano in Japan, where it was unveiled at the 1998 Winter Olympics and Vail ski resort in Colorado, marking the 1999 alpine skiing World Championships.

The Spirit of the Skier in finished form at Helicopter Flat (left and right).
MARK ASHKANASY

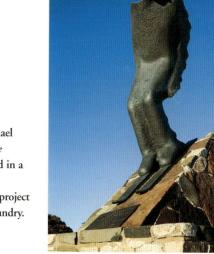

A work in progress - Michael Meszaros' *The Spirit of the Skier* (below) being created in a Collins Street office space he was able to use for the project and finally poured in a foundry.
ANGELO MARCINA

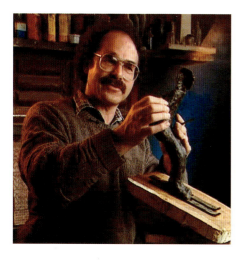

JUST AS THE artists take inspiration from their surrounds, so did the creators of Mt Buller's first structures take whatever was available around them or could feasibly be gathered nearby. Most common was a combination of corrugated iron packed up the mountain on horseback and local timber, first used as whole logs and later milled on site or in the valley.

Caravans and other shanties made for temporary shelter for club lodge-builders, although in Tom Mitchell's observations (see chapter 4) some of the clubs saw the shanties as lodges in themselves. As access improved, building materials started to come from further afield. In 1955, after the Black Tulip ski club lodge was approved, Kevin Ringrose recalled building it from the large wooden box used to import a Volkswagen car.

'It was painted and subsequently carpeted and had heating put in and it was the smartest car box on Mt Buller. 'The frame was made out of railway lines that were auctioned off when the Otway potato railway was pulled up; it was a cheap source of steel for a frame, so it was a steel-framed car box.'

Black Tulip's path was typical of the innovation of the mountain's people. In the early 1960s, the club members decided to knock the old car box down and build a block of 15 units.

The Forests Commission of Victoria (FCV) was opposed to the building of apartments at the time, but Black Tulip got around this. 'We used the Cooperative Act,' Ringrose said. He and his lawyer uncovered a precedent at Glenthompson in the Western District. 'Under the Cooperative Act you had to have a central kitchen and a central lounge room; well that didn't bother us, each member could own the equity in a room and that was negotiable, you could sell it.

'The commission didn't like it at all; we weren't supposed to have kitchens in these rooms but we all had a bit of a bench with an oven. It's still there now. It's a very solid building.'

One to have stood an even longer test of time is the BMW (Brighton Mountain Wanderers) Ski Club lodge.

'We never built something and then had to tear it down,' club veteran Merrick Summers said. 'We've always been on the right side of decision-making and we've always had a mix of pretty sensible people.' That's the nature of architecture; at one extreme it can be sculptural and artistic while at the other end of the spectrum, all that is sometimes sought is practical shelter. But as the village grew its architects began to set some kind of style, even if they were often gems in a desert.

Peter McIntyre is one of Australia's architectural elite with a body of work admired for its innovation, creativity and technical qualities. He pioneered the Mt Buller and Dinner Plain villages.

Despite the intricacies of his architecture, Peter McIntyre has a straightforward understanding of what is required in a mountain home.

'What's really required, beyond all the regulations, is a building which has atmosphere,' he said.

'When people go on a holiday or go skiing for a weekend, what they're actually doing is very similar things to what they would do in their normal life.

Photos by D. Stogdale

TYPICAL CABINS OF THE MT. BULLER SKI VILLAGE

Top left: Ullr Ski Club. Top right: Australian Women's Ski Club. Middle left: Gray Rocks Ski Club. Middle right: Moose Ski Club. Lower left: Buller Ski Club. Lower right: Yurredla Ski Club.

Mt Buller building styles shot in the 1951 or 1952 winter by Derek Stogdale, compiled by the editor of *Schuss*, Stan Flattely and published in the 1952 *Australian Snow Pictorial*. NAMA

'They still go to bed and sleep, they still get up and eat, eat three meals a day, they still sit down in a chair and read a book or read the paper, they do very similar things,' McIntyre said.

So what then is at the essence of the mountain holiday?

'The essence of a holiday in my opinion, is that you're doing the same things you'd normally do, but you're doing them in a different environment, a different place, and because it's a different place, you feel refreshed.'

McIntyre first skied at Mt Buller as a university student in the late 1940s and became a member of the Ski Club of Victoria (SCV) in 1947. In the 1960s, as club architect he designed the two SCV 'family units', the flats known as Bluff and Crosscut that were sold to raise funds for the rebuilding of the SCV's main lodge.

McIntyre built a home of his own slightly above this area, overlooking the Shaky Knees run, an architectural oasis off the Summit Road that hosts signature McIntyre buildings like the bed and breakfast Andre's at Buller (also known as La Grangette) and his own Cuckoo Lodge.

'All my kids skied from the time they were nippers and one [Robert or Robbie] was an Olympian; he did a couple of Olympics.'

In these early years at Mt Buller, McIntyre served on the Committee of Management and also contributed to the overall planning of the village, although not always with the success he hoped for. In the early 1970s, he attempted to assess the mountain's capacity – how many people could ski there and what the population should be.

'It was the first time that sort of work had been done in Australia, trying to work out capacities of ski resorts, but ultimately I got frustrated at Mt Buller … I wasn't able to get Ron Grose [committee chairman] to do the sort of things I wanted.'

McIntyre also sought some kind of overall design control in an effort to achieve some continuity in the mountain village's design and establish a style of Australian alpine architecture.

Peter McIntyre's, La Grangette (above left, also known as Andre's at Buller), above the Shaky Knees run. MARK ASHKANASY

Charles Salter's refurbishment of Howqua Ski Club (above right). MARK ASHKANASY

Mt Buller's loss was a gain further north. In the early 1980s, together with John Castran and Geoff Henke, Peter McIntyre was a founder of the Dinner Plain village development between Mt Hotham and Omeo.

'When I designed Dinner Plain, I set out to make a built environment that was completely different to anything that anyone else had experienced, and the way I did that was to get a sense of unity about the village.

'Because I limited the palette of materials, there was a sense of unity about the whole thing; you knew it was one place … all the buildings were different but because they had the same materials, they all come together … they were experiencing a built environment that they weren't used to.

'You get that in Europe. You go into a 500-year-old-village, a ski village in Europe, it's really a farm village. You'll see that because there was a limit to where they could travel, they all used local materials, the local stone or the local slate. All the buildings were designed individually but because they all used the same materials they all had this sense of unity about them.'

IN THE YEARS McIntyre was absent from Mt Buller, the design of the mountain village moved on nonetheless, particularly in the years Sandie Jeffcoat was the Resort Management Board's chief executive. Rock walling, road sealing and putting wires and other services underground lifted the overall appeal of the village. 'It was

189

The Mt Buller Chalet, designed by Mantesso Architects. MARK ASHKANASY

'a dog's breakfast when I got there but the retro-planning has been very good,' Jeffcoat said.

McIntyre had sold his house at Mt Buller because he simply was not there, but then, after about 25 years at Dinner Plain he sold out of that village and returned to Mt Buller and has even returned to the same location.

'We designed some houses again on the edge of Shaky Knees where my own house was and I built six; there's a seventh one being built at the moment, seven houses in a cluster and I'm in one of those.' Even though McIntyre seems to keep going back to the one loca-

tion – the area on the mountain's northern side above Shaky Knees, looking over that terrain and out towards Mount Stirling – his view is that the mountain environment is so good overall, a built environment of quality can be created in any part of it. You just need the opportunity.

He regards his location as 'the best part of Buller,' but that's not necessarily because of its aspect or outlook, 'it's because I've managed to create a little enclave there of buildings that are really first-class quality.'

Boulders Apartments, designed by Charles Salter Architects and built on the realigned Summit Road looking out towards Mt Stirling and Mt Buffalo. MARK ASHKANASY

The Mt Buller Chalet under construction in 1995; the first time a crane of this size was used on the mountain. MARK ASHKANASY

McIntyre brought some of the principles and some of the style he established at Dinner Plain back to Mt Buller in the design of the Black Forest Lodge on The Avenue and also in his new lodges on the edge of Shaky Knees.

He has worked through an entire era of Australian alpine architecture, a period with an interesting tension between regulation and design.

He doesn't dispute the need for tough regulations so buildings can withstand the unique and quite peculiar Australian alpine environment.

He points to the obvious things that have to be done: sound construction, ample insulation, a northern orientation, double-glazing and ensuring the snow shedding works.

'They're all just fundamental things and they're all required by

A maverick mountain shelter. David McGlashan's design for Koflers – the Helmut Kofler Hutte – has it resting on the snow like a moth. The building and its deck have been extended since their 1959 opening. NAMA/ERIC BURT

regulation anyhow. The regulations are much more profound now than they were 40 years ago; the planning permits are very specific … but that hasn't necessarily produced good architecture or artistic architecture or artistic buildings,' he said.

The challenge in working within the regulations is to retain the quality in the design. On these pages is a small snapshot of Mt Buller's architectural style, numerous other examples are spread throughout the book.

Artist's impression of "Twin Towers" complex, viewed from the Bourke St run.

The mountain environment is harsh, but nowhere is it harsher than at the summit. Aurel Forras, the builder of many Mt Buller lodges, built the Summit Fire Lookout Hut in 1969-70; with the help of some minor refurbishment, it stands strong today. Aurel is pictured above right and in the photo above left is on the roof of the hut. Below him are his children Marika (left), Gina, Peter and his wife Georgina. ERNEST FORRAS

The Twin Towers development designed by Peter McIntyre. NAMA

THE PEOPLE

15 Hospitality

Shelter in the mountains is one thing – a roof and some warmth are all the more welcome in a hostile environment – but hospitality is another thing altogether. Hospitality is the tradition and profession of service wrapped up in the satisfaction of sharing the alpine experience.

HELMUT KOFLER HAD shown some talent for hospitality at the Mt Buller Chalet; it was a profession taken very seriously in his native Austria. Before Kofler, the Lovicks and Klingsporns had offered a bush welcome to adventurous skiers.

After the demise of the first Mt Buller Chalet some local operators took up the slack.

In 1949, Arne Nielsen offered 'bigger, better, brighter' accommodation and meals at Mirimbah – 'Why Be Cold – Crook?' asked the advertisement, 'See The Skiing Cook'. (*Schuss*, Aug 1949, p339)

In 1954, Ma (Mrs EJ) Coombs, proprietor, advertised her Lattice Café in Mansfield, 'on your right when entering town from Melbourne, three course meals supplied, late service Friday Nights when booked, sandwiches always available, cheerful prompt service. Skiers Always Welcome.' (*Schuss*, Jan-Feb 1954, p6)

Mirimbah's timber millers would take skiers in (even if some scratched their heads in wonder at why people would be drawn to the mountains with such passion in the coldest, most inhospitable season).

On the mountain, the Ski Club of Victoria (SCV) maintained standards of hospitality at the Ivor Whittaker Memorial Lodge for members and their guests.

Above the snow line or below it, the welcome was warm but it was the arrival of European-style alpine hospitality to the growing mountain village that made the difference.

The Kooroora dining room in 1954. JOHN HIRAMS

THE NAME KOOROORA was a natural because, in Ernest Forras' recollection, Melbourne ski retailer Andy Broad told him it was 'an Aboriginal word meaning a place of happy gatherings.' (Forras, p96)

Ernest Forras had fled Hungary around the time of World War II and worked in Chamonix as a hotel concierge and tennis and skiing instructor. His brother Aurel later joined him in Chamonix. It was there that Dr Des Hoban, an Australian skier, met Ernest and, impressed with his energy, said to him: 'We need people like you in Australia to help develop our snow resorts.'

Ernest took him up on the offer 'We both had a two year contract – Aurel as a carpenter/builder and me as hotel employee and ski instructor.' (Forras, p50)

They made their way to the mountains and were managing a lodge at Falls Creek in 1951 when some visitors from Mt Buller's Australian Postal Institute Lodge, including Kevin McDonald, invited them to Mt Buller.

The brothers were a good team – Ernest the talker and Aurel the worker – and they quickly hatched plans for a ski school, a canteen and a chalet at Mt Buller – 'apart from a few club lodges,

there was no commercial or private enterprise of any sort.' (Forras, p77) 'We saw potential,' Aurel Forras recalled. 'There were only five or six lodges and we thought, "We can do something here" and we did.

'In 1952, the first year we had been there, we built the Bull Run Canteen – I built it and Ernest helped me with the building – we ran it as a commercial enterprise where you could have a cup of tea and cake and whatever.

'The Forests Commission weren't very helpful; they gave us permission to build the Bull Run Canteen I think at the end of May for that season – we were clearing snow off the ground to put the stumps in.'

With the canteen built Aurel and Ernest drove their supplies as far as road conditions would permit – sometimes only as close as Dump Inn Corner, still a steep climb of six kilometers or more from their destination – and then carried them on their backs past Horse Hill to their new enterprise on the mountain.

'Nine trays [of pies and pasties] was our record. Another record was 35 kilograms of goulash meat, sausages and 20 chickens in one haul.'

Mick Hull recalled passing Ernest Forras early one morning to find him virtually sleeping as he walked.

'What have you got in the pack?' Hull asked.

'Why, meat pies of course, I picked them up from the Dump Inn, where the Mansfield Bakery leaves them for me – he can't get his truck up any further at the moment.' (Hull, pp257-8)

The Forras brothers got the hang of the business and by lunch on the first day, '60 people were crammed into that little canteen.'

Their next step, in 1953, was Kooroora – architect David McGlashan drew up plans for a lodge with 35 commercial and nine staff beds, a 'basic but spacious chalet with a continental atmosphere.' McGlashan's work was exchanged for two weeks' ski lessons and meals from the canteen. (Forras, p87)

Aurel and Ernest called on their mother for help; she came from Europe and cooked first for the building crew and then for the guests.

Ernest Forras wrote of Kooroora's official opening in 1953:

> Mother produced a great meal for more than sixty guests: soup, a Hungarian entrée of pancakes with a filling of veal, pork and sour cream called *hortobagyi placsinta* followed by paprika chicken with salad … we partied on until the wee hours with my wind-up portable record player. The staff did not get to bed at all because we had to prepare breakfast.
>
> We had plenty of good publicity for Kooroora's opening. *Pix* magazine ran a four page picture story … we soon had Melbourne's society booked in with their children for the school holidays.

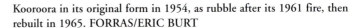

Kooroora in its original form in 1954, as rubble after its 1961 fire, then rebuilt in 1965. FORRAS/ERIC BURT

> Well-known Melbourne establishment families flocked to the mountain including the Wenzels (textiles), Laycocks (blankets), Edgars (real estate), Brockhoffs (biscuits), the Smorgon girls, the devilish entrepreneur Brian Goldsmith, retailer David Bardas, Bruce Matear from the Hotel Australia and Ken Myer … we taught them all to ski. Some, like Peter Brockhoff, Simon Brown and Peter Wenzel became Olympic skiers.
> (Forras, pp96-7)

Ernest and Aurel extended the lodge over the 1953-54 summer, taking forward payments for winter accommodation to fund the extensions. In 1954, Ernest married Judy Dennis at a church in Brighton with a group of skiers forming an archway with ski poles for their exit. Aurel later married Georgina Watson – both Judy and Georgina raced for Australia.

Business was good and the Forras' sister Fay came out from Germany to support the family enterprise.

In 1957 they started on their next venture, a motel at Jamieson, recruiting a team of builders, tradesmen and labourers from the Bonegilla migrant reception centre near Wodonga.

The Kooroora Marina Motel on the shores of Lake Eildon is still there, now known as the Jamieson Brewery and Lakeside Hotel and although substantially rebuilt, some of the original units are in place.

Ernest (left) and Aurel Forras, the hospitality pioneers in the 1950s. FORRAS

Anton Vanhoff (left) and Richard Paine outside Kooroora in 2007. MARK ASHKANASY

Kooroora nightlife in 2007 (above) and in the 1960s (right).
TONY HARRINGTON/BSL/FORRAS

The brothers alternated for a time: 'Ernest was running Buller one year and I ran the motel and the next year he would run the motel and I would run Buller,' Aurel Forras said.

'Then Ernest got jack of that … and I bought his share of Kooroora, so I ran Kooroora on my own for quite a while, for five or six years.

'Then Kooroora burnt down in 1961 – it was an electrical fault – by the time the insurances were ironed out we lost a season and I rebuilt it the next year and it's still there, the same one. The main building is still the same.

'After about five or six years I'd had enough of hotels – I was a builder, not a hotel operator – so Ernest came and he bought it back from me and I went out into building,' Aurel Forras said.

One further development was to add a swimming pool. Richard Paine, who bought Kooroora at auction in 1994, said: 'Ernest saw that European resorts had swimming pools so he decided they'd have one.'

The swimming pool 'wasn't a great success so he stocked it with trout and rented fishing rods in summer; that also had limited effect. Then ski hire became quite a lucrative business so Ernest extended the ski hire over the top of it which was really good – all the wet from the skis drains into the pool.'

Forras sold it to Arthur Tan who in turn sold Kooroora to the Arlberg's then-owner, Adam Adams. A consortium led by John Perks bought it from Adams and Richard Paine bought it in 1994.

The structure built by the Forras brothers was – and is – still sound but in 1996 Richard Paine dramatically changed it internally, removing the ageing carpets, polishing the floorboards and putting in a functional bar.

'Originally they had to have a cabaret licence to sell alcohol after 10pm and that's why they had a guy walking around with a squeeze box making music – that was a requirement of the licence. 'With the changing of liquor licensing two decades ago,

Kooroora needed a shake-up. When I got it I brought it back to life, remodelled it and it came to life quite quickly,' Paine said. 'We were licensed for around 200 people, we're now licensed for 650.'

He also made his focus live entertainment. 'John [Perks] then gave up on live entertainment and the Arlberg became a family hotel, so Kooroora gained or regained its position as a social focal point,' Paine said.

Richard Paine and Anton Vanhoff have come to be identified with Kooroora, Paine managing the operations by day and Vanhoff by night.

Kooroora stayers know the night's over when *That's Amore* plays at 3am. 'I wanted something that was quite different to dance music and everything else so that it was a very clear signal that the night was over.

'People got the hang of it; they hear that and they know it's over, if it was something a bit more current they would probably think they were still partying on.'

Paine sold the building in 2001 and leased back its hotel operations. The current owners, the Grollo Group, plan to eventually redevelop the site.

Until then, and possibly afterwards, *That's Amore* will play at 3am.

The Abom kitchen staff in 1993. Peter Zorzi (left) Mary-Ellen Burnside, Sonia Borich (in front), Jimmy Camarino, Tony Peravich, Paul Camarino and Chris Redmond. BILL BACHMAN

Hans Grimus wears a red suit in 1978 and helps start a tradition – Christmas at Mt Buller. BILL BACHMAN

THE ABOM, OR Abominable Snowman, sprang from a smart café on Victoria's west coast. George Vassilopoulos arrived in Australia from Greece in 1956 and found himself in Lorne working at an avante garde venue called the Arab. Vassilopoulos and Robin Smith worked for the Arab's founder, Robin's brother Alistair Smith.

'I had nothing to do in the winter time and in 1959, Max Otter, in the old Arlberg House, promised me a job at Mt Buller,' Vassilopoulos said.

That fell through but he found work at the Bull Run Lodge. He liked the mountain life and the contrast between a summer on the coast and a winter in the mountains.

In 1962, Vassilopoulos became a partner at the Arab with Robin and Alistair Smith. They saw the opportunity to expand and went to Mt Buller, selecting a site above what was then Bill Duff's ski hire.

In many ways, their site was one of the best on Mt Buller with its central Bourke Street location and proximity to important accommodation centres such as the Ski Club of Victoria.

'In 1968 we split up – Robin Smith kept the Arab and Alistair and I kept the Abom. After three years, in 1972, Alistair left, I bought him out,' Vassilopoulos said.

Like the Arab, the Abom was designed by Robin and Alistair's brother, Graeme Smith, a creative talent who was not an architect but a London-based ballet dancer – he was also the inspiration behind the successful Pancake Parlour chain.

The early Abom was like theatre in the round, with the kitchen in the middle and customers descending into the main room, packed as tight as an audience, even if the nights might sometimes be more Chaucerian than Shakespearean.

After he bought Alistair Smith out in 1972 Vassilopoulos extended the Abom, to a 250-seat restaurant from 150 seats.

'We had good customers. We had a good name and we kept a high standard. If you give value for money you must do well.'

Christmas in the snow became a regular event on the Mt Buller calendar; it started in the Abom. The idea was Graeme Smith's, to give 'the Europeans a Christmas in the winter, as they were used to – turkey fresh-cooked, ham from the bone

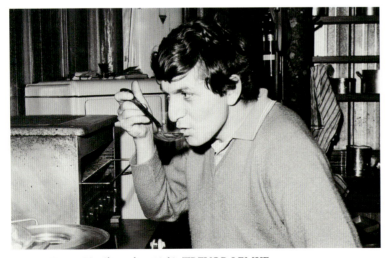

George Vassilopoulos, 1965. TREVOR LEMKE

Robin Smith, 1965. TREVOR LEMKE

and the brandy sauce.' It became an Abom signature, like its whiting, its roast duck and its bolognese sauce. Customers leaving their own signature in the woodwork wasn't unknown at the Abom. The Prince of Wales was one said to have done so during a visit when he was a student at Geelong Grammar School's nearby Timbertop campus in 1966, although the scrutiny he would have been under suggests it was probably another person's handiwork.

On Friday July 22, 1966, *The Age* newspaper reported on a day Prince Charles had skiing the mountain when he 'rode ski tows expertly … [and] tucked his ski poles beneath his arms and, crouching low, schussed at racing pace down the full quarter-mile length of Mt Buller's main Bourke Street run.

'Earlier he lunched on pancakes and orange juice at the Abominable Snowman, the most fashionable of several restaurants at Mt Buller.

to its origins with a unique collection of historic alpine artefacts. It has also played a part in the mountain's summer trade. 'I think that when we first purchased the Abom, we would have been the only one that opened of a weekend [in summer] our little Abom coffee shop,' Diana Grollo said.

'We have seen that increasing … now you can go up anytime and the hotels are open. You couldn't find that in summer time 10 years ago, we were the only one,' she said.

Chris Redmond, the Abom hotel manager in 2007, is a veteran of mountain hospitality.

He started skiing at Mt Buller in the 1960s, sleeping at the bottom of the mountain in his Volkswagen Beetle. 'I was hooked' he said.

After an apprenticeship as a chef at Melbourne's Southern Cross hotel he worked in Switzerland and then, on his return to Australia, became manager of the Thredbo Alpine Hotel.

Melbourne model and publicist Jenny Ham with the great Jean-Claude Killy at the Abom, in 1965. TREVOR LEMKE

Trish and Claude Iezzi were at the Abom year-round from 1994 to 1999. Here they are pictured with their children Kristian (left) and Gemila. IEZZI

Dino Sarpa in 2006. MATT DARBY/BSL

'Prince Charles sat at the rough wooden tables in the restaurant's public section with a party of six adults, including his personal bodyguard,' the newspaper reported.

'There were so many nationalities, it was very cosmopolitan certainly compared with the rest of Australia,' Elena Vassilopoulos said. 'All the Melbourne celebrities would come and visit, arts and business people – Skyhooks played there.'

Mt Buller's Melbourne connections have provided a rich source of entertainment – Ian 'Molly' Meldrum has been a DJ on the mountain, John Farnham, then a guest at Pension Grimus, was enticed into singing the national anthem at the first World Cup aerials event in 1996.

The Abom has evolved and grown. In 1987 it was bought by Rino and Diana Grollo. According to Diana Grollo, the rationale was simple: 'Rino got into skiing and [his brother] Bruno got into skiing and everybody used to ski and there was nobody left to cook.

'We were spending quite a lot on lunches at the Abom so we bought it,' Diana Grollo said.

It has been extended substantially but the Abom still pays tribute

In 1993 he came back to Mt Buller; 'My heart was always at Buller.' He took over management of the Abom and still felt the heritage in the business.

'People would walk in to the restaurant downstairs and knew they would get a good risotto and a good pasta and we had to have the roast duck on the menu because George had established such a tradition with it, same with the spaghetti bolognese and the pancakes.'

The Abom was establishing a new direction however. 'In 1993, we had the first visit by Gabriele Ferron – Ferron rice is famous as a rice for risotto; he set the pace for risotto.

'We had Italian festivals with Gabriele at the Abom in 1993 and 1995; we had Jean Jacques [Lale-Demoz of Jean Jacques by the Sea restaurant in Melbourne] up here and he is Swiss so we had a Swiss festival.'

Although the Bourke Street level is now the Abom's busiest, Redmond said people still have a feeling for the atmosphere and aura of the original downstairs room.

'People still love to have dinners and cocktail parties downstairs at the Abom – the chalet has good function rooms but they don't have the atmosphere of downstairs at the Abom, down by the fire.'

Sunshine always brings the crowd to Koflers; winter 2004.
MARK ASHKANASY.

KOFLERS WAS BUILT as part of the development of skiing in the Summit area. The building was designed by David McGlashan in a style described by David Hume as using 'a parabolic hyperbola' for the roof design. In its original form it sat on the snow like a moth. Despite its innovative appearance it was never intended to be more than basic day shelter, certainly not to be one of the most popular on-mountain restaurants in the nation, as it is now.

The turnaround came with the involvement of its current owner. Bob Fleming had come to Melbourne from Westport on the Buller River in New Zealand's North Island and he decided to pursue the Buller connection.

'Melbourne was too big for me so when [in 1969] I saw a job advertised at Mt Buller I thought I'd give it a try. The job was at Koflers but when I got here it was gone,' Bob Fleming said.

He found some work around the mountain and Hans Grimus offered him work on the lifts. Fleming took him up on it and they became good friends.

Koflers had been in the hands of a variety of operators, then Bob Fleming ran it on behalf of Orange Lifts in 1970 and took out a lease of sorts in 1971.

Over the next few winters he'd work nights at the Abom under George Vassilopoulos and Alistair Smith and during the day run Koflers.

'It was pretty basic, it had no kitchen, it was never made to be a restaurant or anything like that. It had been used by the [Orange] lift company for their managers.'

There was no electricity and the septic system below the restaurant was prone to block and fail although the water from a soak above was reliable and of good quality. Fleming worked on a verbal agreement with the Orange Lifts company: 'Every year I'd go and see Mr [Griff] Morgan and say "Can I run it again Mr Morgan?" and he'd say, "Yes you can mister, but it's $100 more this year".

'We also had to house some of the lift operators as part of the deal but that took beds so we couldn't accommodate more staff. On busy days that made it really hard.'

Fleming was promised a more formal lease but it didn't come through until 1985 – he now owns the building and the business under a lease with the Resort Management Board.

To establish some security Fleming bought the Come and Get It restaurant and associated accommodation at Merimbula in 1980. He'd move his kitchen equipment from one location to the other as the seasons changed, including a large deep freeze, two stoves, all the plates and all the pots. 'It was hard work, very hard on [his family] Christine and the kids.'

Fleming was also something of a packhorse in the early days. Once a week he'd get a delivery from Orange Lifts' Tucker Sno-Cat, but the common means of transporting supplies was to walk them up from the village, two or three times a night.

The original Koflers lunch hut in the 1940s. NAMA

Koflers staff in 1990. In the back row are Gary Haddrell (left), Craig Fink, Shane Fleming, Warren Redman and Stuart Burridge. In the middle row are Nick Barlow (left), Lloyd Brewer, Paula Killoran, Caroline Beach, Gretchen Nadenbousch, Susan Mravlek, Christine Fleming, Kevin Frier and Monica Zaal. At the front are Graham Potter, Ben Fleming, Bob Fleming, Toby Fleming, Mark Vernal and Karen Bigelow. MARK ASHKANASY

If staff wanted to go out at night they'd walk down to the village and then walk home again. 'They still do that, they used to follow the old access Poma line, it went right past the door and you could never get lost,' Fleming said.

'It wasn't an easy place to run, with fluctuating trade and in the early 1970s the lifts closed at lunch time so there was no lunch trade during the week.'

The fluctuations remain although demand is ruled by the weather as much as lift-operating hours.

'When there's a blizzard blowing it can be very, very quiet but sunny days can be scary,' Fleming said.

Bob and Christine Fleming raised their family at Koflers and the

What a difference two days makes. 'Kofler Bob' Fleming shows his frustration on July 14, 1997 and his elation on July 16 after a snowfall. TREVOR PINDER/*HERALD SUN*

couple still live there during winter, accommodation they describe as 'fairly basic, but comfortable'.

Like many in the mountains, residents and regular guests alike, they agree 'it's the people that bring you back,' Bob Fleming, or 'Kofler Bob' as he is now known, said.

'I still look forward to coming up for the winter, to see the people who work here and the customers. There are a lot of people who are very loyal to Mt Buller, that's what makes it such a friendly resort.'

Eating slopeside

The Bull Run Canteen in 1953.
JOHN HIRAMS

Shane Egland in 2007.
MARK ASHKANASY

JIMMY CAMERINO CAME to the mountain after running the renowned L'Aragosta d'Oro or Golden Lobster restaurant in Melbourne's Lygon Street. He agreed to run the Abom for a season and stayed for 16.

He then moved up the hill slightly, to run Tyrol Restaurant, which is used as a venue to feed staff during the evening and during the day is a popular mountain restaurant, perhaps too popular.

The size of the kitchen means meals are made to order at Tyrol, rather than being ready-to-serve in the cafeteria style. Hence the note on the blackboard menu encouraging people who want fast food to find it elsewhere and the sign outside advising that 'you can't make chicken salad out of chicken shit.'

Tyrol is small and intimate in the European style and its slightly remote location makes it all the more appealing.

Camerino: 'I say to people, "Look at the view in my backyard". I get up in the morning and see that view and it keeps me coming back, that and the people. There are some very, very good people at Mt Buller.'

The Bull Run Canteen was the pioneer of slopeside eating, first built and run by the Forras brothers and later becoming the domain of mountain character Vaughan Lucas, better known as Rabbit.

Next came Koflers and this has more recently been complemented by the Wombat Hut, which is supplied by Koflers and former ski instructor Shane Egland's Bull Run Skiosk. At the Skating Rink car park, day visitors, car park staff and other passers-by have made Celia's Mt Buller Kiosk popular, named as it was after its pioneering operator, Celia Brandl.

Vaughan 'Rabbit' Lucas at the Bull Run Canteen, circa 1966.
TREVOR LEMKE

Tyrol's Jimmy Camerino in 2005. MATT DARBY/BSL

Adam Adams (left) with Enzian's Helmut and Lynne Wintergerst in 1988. MARK ASHKANASY/ADAMS

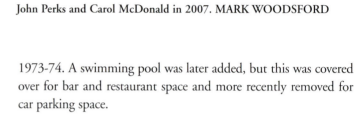

John Perks and Carol McDonald in 2007. MARK WOODSFORD

ARLBERG HOUSE, SITED magnificently at the top of Bourke Street, lent a strong European flavour to the mountain with its Tyrolean-style verandah and eaves. It had been operated by Max Otter, an energetic contributor to Mt Buller as a ski instructor and host who later moved to Mt Baw Baw and then opened a Swiss restaurant in Melbourne. Like the Forras brothers, Otter also had his mother to help with the cooking at Arlberg House.

The name of the Austrian mountains that cross the Tyrol and Vorarlberg regions is applied in tribute in numerous mountain resorts around the world; unfortunately Arlberg House suffered the same fate as many early Mt Buller structures – it burnt to the ground.

Adam Adams, who had been a regular visitor to Mt Buller with his family and friends, first staying at Kooroora – sleeping by the fire if the Forras brothers didn't have a bed – bought Arlberg House site for £2000.

Adams, born Adam Kaminski in Brest-Litowsk, Poland, in 1920, was the son of a Jewish baker. His parents and two sisters were killed by the Nazis but Adams survived using forged identity papers. He was imprisoned by the Russians (who believed he was German) until 1945 and in 1949, landed in Port Melbourne. He met and soon married his wife of 53 years, Gerti. Adam Adams died in 2004, survived by his wife, their four children and 10 grandchildren.

He changed his surname from Kaminski to Adams 'because he wanted to feel like everybody else, without his bitter memories,' his son Mark Adams said.

In a 2003 interview, Adam Adams recalled the mountain was divided over the deal when he bought the Arlberg site, 'some in support, some not. I thought, "I'll deal with the big ones". So I made an appointment to see Peter McIntyre who was the architect at the time … and I started building without a permit.'

In an incredible burst of activity, in 1969-70 Adams built the 34-room Arlberg Hotel, its restaurant and bar and the Twin Towers apartments, ready for occupation for the 1970 winter.

Later additions extended the Arlberg with 14 motel-style units in 1973-74. A swimming pool was later added, but this was covered over for bar and restaurant space and more recently removed for car parking space.

Mark Adams was 13 when the Arlberg opened and started working there when he was 18. The Arlberg had some nights of entertainment that wouldn't necessarily pass 21st century political correctness or responsible serving of alcohol tests.

'We had wet T-shirt nights, we had boat races, Molly Meldrum used to come up and stay in our flat and DJ for us,' Mark Adams said. 'Carnival weekend was a favourite, the three of us boys dressed up as the Marx Brothers one time and another I skied as a toilet, known as the Arlberg shithouse.

'Do you remember the Arlberg taxi? We used to ferry up customers from Kooroora,' Adams recalled.

The Adams family eventually bought Kooroora in 1986, from Arthur Tan who had bought it from Ernest Forras. Adam Adams claimed it was the third time he'd bought it – the first two times Ernest Forras changed his mind and backed out.

The repertoire suggests they delighted in doing business, haggling like market traders. 'Ernest used to invite us for dinner at Kooroora and then he would make us pay!' Mark Adams recalled.

Adam Adams was an energetic builder and developer; he built N'Everest, Snow Gums, Summit Lodge, Beehive, the Arlberg, Twin Towers, Moose, Delatite and Elkhorn. Eventually, in 1988 the family sold its interests on the mountain and their Arlberg Merrijig development.

'We were all getting married and while it's a great environment to be in, it's difficult when you have four family members. We decided we'd had our time,' Adams said.

They never left the mountain as skiers. Mark Adams returned in 1996 to start his real estate business and complete the Elkhorn apartment project with his father.

'I love the mountain, I do business and spend time with my kids, it's great,' he said.

After the Adams family, a consortium led by John Perks took over the Arlberg; it is still run by John Perks and his wife Carol McDonald. However, where once the Arlberg and Kooroora vied to be the nightlife leaders, the Arlberg's realignment as a more family-oriented venue has seen Kooroora become king in that area.

Arlberg is a 'three-star hotel for families and beginners and it works fabulously at the moment. I tell you, it works better than the drugs, sex and rock 'n' roll I did for the first 10 years I was here,' John Perks said.

'It didn't matter what you did, Arlberg was packed in those days; we'd have 1500 people in here every night, Molly Meldrum was a DJ here in Adams' day, we'd have bands like Hunters and Collectors, Painters and Dockers, Joe Camilleri and the Black Sorrows, Relax with Max, Skyhooks and Billy Thorpe.

'One year, in the early 1990s, we had 10 of the best bands in Melbourne all paid for by Bond Brewing. Another year 3MP paid for 10 bands and Shirley Strachan was MC. We had 10 big acts that they paid for and I took a door charge! It was great business.'

Perks, an accountant by training, has a sharp recollection for the numbers and at times they would stretch the Arlberg to its seams. 'I reckon on a couple of occasions we would have had 2000 people here, but you couldn't work; a lot of times we had 1500. From our point of view, I could make as much money with 1200 in the place – any more and you couldn't get a drink.

'In the end it was bad business, people couldn't get a drink and that caused fights. In the mid-1990s, when those numbers started to drop, we went to families mid-week and parties on the weekends. Then we realised we were in no-man's land, so we went all-families.'

Carol McDonald runs the Arlberg with him. 'She hires, fires and interviews; she says I'm a professional coffee drinker. Carol runs the day-to-day side of the business and has done for a long time. She's been here since 1990, I offered her a job then and the rest is history.'

Perks has been active in the wider operations of Mt Buller, serving as Committee of Management chairman from 1990 to 1996.

'I've learnt to take what I can get in this industry, I go into every year with a positive attitude and just work it,' he said.

The late Shirley Strachan, the lead singer of the Skyhooks, during a 1990 photo shoot for the Jukebox in Siberia album cover (right). Strachan was a regular on the Arlberg's list of entertainers.
MARK ASHKANASY

Snowmaking, in particular, has put some stability under the business. 'In 2006, I don't think we would have opened for a day without snowmaking.'

He looks back on the 1980s as a time when he might have made more money, but in bad years might have made far worse losses.

'The quality of life is better for it and at the end of the day, I just love the lifestyle,' Perks said.

Arlberg House in 1960. ERIC BURT

The Arlberg Hotel in 1988. BILL BACHMAN

PENSION GRIMUS WAS created at the same time Hans Grimus was manager of Orange Lifts; he saw the growth in the mountain's popularity and thought of creating a bed and breakfast, a *pension* in the style of his native Austria.

He applied his stunning capacity for work to it, devoting every spare moment to the project, blasting to clear rock from the block, pouring the concrete and organising the contractors. The ground floor was complete by 1970.

Finance was an enduring problem; two blocks of land he had bought following his time working in the Snowy Mountains were sold to finance the project and, thanks to connections he had made on the mountain, he managed to raise a loan with National Mutual. The relationship with his employer, Orange Lifts, was tested dur-

Hotel Pension Grimus and a well-covered winter entrance in 1989. MARK ASHKANASY

ing the process. In 1973, the company's board insisted Grimus accommodate 17 ski instructors and provide them with bed, breakfast, lunch and dinner.

'I was only building a bed and breakfast; I never dreamt I was going to have a restaurant. I had no other choice, I had to do it,' he said.

'My first wife Sylvia worked as a housemaid, she was the cleaner and I had 17 ski instructors staying so I had to get a chef. He was Swiss and his wife was the manageress.

At Herbie's Bar in Pension Grimus in 1989. MARK ASHKANASY

Lotte and Hans Grimus in 2006. MATT DARBY/BSL

See you at the Whitt

THE SKI CLUB of Victoria's (SCV) Ivor Whittaker Lodge was once the beating heart of Mt Buller's social scene.

'Buller was the home mountain for the SCV and the Whitt was a very social place,' former SCV general manager Erich Goetz said.

'We had bands playing every weekend, sometimes we had two bands playing – one in the Dump Inn and one in the main bar; we had two bars going, the dining room was booked out every single day of the week.'

Goetz, originally from Austria, attended hotel school in Vienna, worked at Zurs in the Arlberg and was recruited in 1964 by Dick Dusseldorp to manage the Thredbo Alpine Hotel.

Goetz worked with the SCV from 1969 to 1995, first at Mt Buller and then as its general manager, based in Elizabeth Street, Melbourne, on the third floor of the Molony's building, the ski retailers at the time. It was here that he met his wife Diana, who also worked for the SCV.

Mark Woodsford (left) and Marg Franke-Williams dance the night away at the Whitt in 1988. BILL BACHMAN

Diana and Erich Goetz in 1988. MARK ASHKANASY

'When I started we had only about 260 members and when I left we had 3000 members and a waiting list, it was really a dynamic force on the mountain,' Goetz said.

'It was members-only, you couldn't get in without showing your membership card.' There were exceptions and these helped guarantee the popularity of the Whitt: 'With my Austrian background, we made the Austrian ski instructors honorary members so they could come in.'

Goetz left the SCV in 1995, with his sights set on retirement, but worked for Buller Ski Lifts for a season as its events manager and then for three seasons as assistant manager at the Chalet before retiring completely.

'And I was working on the lifts; 1973 was the worst snow season, people always ask me, "How was the first season, how did you go?" I said, "Amazing, no snow, no people, no problems!"'

'They [the ski instructors] had a lot of women hanging around so I said to the chef, "Look, I need some money, I have to pay the interest on the loan, can't we feed the ski instructors first and get a few guests?" Before I realised it I had a restaurant.'

Grimus left the lift company in the early 1980s to put all his energy into the pension, which has grown to become a 115-bed hotel and apartment complex, with restaurant, bar and ski-hire/shop facilities.

In many ways Hans and Lotte Grimus are the archetypes; she the details person, the standard-setter and he the enduring character, entertainer, friend and counsel in his own way to the mountain's people. They are masters of mountain hospitality in their welcome of new guests and those who return time and again; icons of Australia's ski industry.

Hotel Pension Grimus in 2003. MARK ASHKANASY

BREATHTAKER, WHICH HAS been transformed into an all-suite hotel and spa retreat was conceived as a 'boarding house.'
John McDonald, then chief executive of the South Australian engineering company Macmahon Holdings, first went to the snow on a family holiday, in 1973, to Falls Creek. His professional interest got the better of him – he saw the potential in ski lifting and later became the catalyst for the amalgamation of Mt Buller's lift companies.

Breathtaker was his first venture at Mt Buller however. After Falls Creek, he and some friends went to Mt Buller and then tried to join the South Australian-based Schuss Ski Club.

'Their architect told me that he had put in a bid on a site over near Pension Grimus,' McDonald said. 'They won the bid, but I could see they couldn't perform, so I ended up saying "as a civil engineering firm, we've got a bit of cash behind us, I reckon this could develop into something up there".'

McDonald had his sights set on the mountain's lifting operations and one advantage of this enterprise was to 'get a foot in the door' at Mt Buller. 'What the Forests Commission wanted was a "boarding house" so we put in a proposal for a single-storey boarding house on this site.'

The nature of the site, however, meant the only possible way to develop it was to terrace the building into the mountainside. 'That's why Breathtaker has the shape it has today.

'We started Breathtaker in 1979 and built it over two summers.

Terraced into the mountain with its breathtaking views. Breathtaker in 1989. BILL BACHMAN

Breathtaker has lead the mountain in offering health and beauty treatments. MATT DARBY

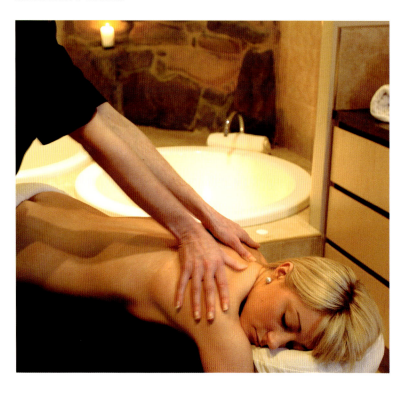

It was a funny opening, we had the press and entertainers and the Victorian government minister and the South Australian premier. 'We had a wonderful breakfast at the gate at Mirimbah and then went up the mountain and the minister, in declaring the place open, said, "John, we recognise this place has been built by South Australian interests and I accept in good spirit that your premier David Tonkin has just been outside and planted the South Australian flag and has usurped the Breathtaker site and declared it part of South Australia!"

McDonald's son, also named John, has a hotel management degree from Switzerland, and is in charge of the expanded Breathtaker, which now includes health spa facilities and services.

THE MT BULLER Chalet Hotel opened in 1995, reviving the name that went with one of the mountain's most ambitious early accommodation developments, the chalet that Helmut Kofler ran at Horse Hill that burnt to the ground in 1942.

At its 1995 launch, the new Chalet was described as 'bringing to Victoria a new era in luxury alpine accommodation and it will be open year round. The magnificent new hotel is situated in the heart of Mt Buller village, so you can ski in/ski out in winter.'

To secure its year-round appeal, from the outset the Chalet's facilities included a fitness centre and indoor swimming pool, two restaurants, two bars and meeting and conference facilities.

Its location – beside Bourke Street and fronting what was once part of the Summit Road but following its realignment is now the

A welcome from Elena Vassilopoulos in 1986. MARK ASHKANASY

Behind every great man

MOUNTAIN HOSTS CAN take on status close to celebrity; they give the mountain's visitors some identities to recognise and, just as importantly, to be recognised by. Guests gain a sense of belonging when they're recognised by the core of the community.

But all that focus on some can unintentionally diminish the contribution of others.

Bob Fleming, Kofler Bob as many know him, points to the contribution of his wife Christine and the difficulty for her in raising a family in such a location.

Lotte Grimus has been instrumental in Hans' operation and before her, his first wife Sylvia. George Vassilopoulos had Elena, the Forras brothers had their mother, Gizell, their sister Fay Forras and their wives – Georgina for Aurel and Judy for Ernest. Carol McDonald as much as John Perks runs the Arlberg.

As Bob Fleming put it: 'Women often get the hard end of the stick on the mountain but they often actually have more dealings with the customers.'

Athlete's Walk – is ideal for the Chalet and with such prominence, improves the village's overall status in hospitality.

'Rino [Grollo] wanted to develop the Chalet to open up new markets; he was offering something to people who would have stayed at the likes of the Thredbo Alpine Hotel; he was offering them something at Buller, accommodation that would suit their style of holiday,' said Chris Redmond, who now runs the Abom but ran the Chalet in its early years.

'There was no other alpine hotel in the country with the facilities of the Chalet, the swimming pool and the sports centre and squash courts, with 24-hour room service – there was no other hotel offering that.'

It may have cut into his trade at the outset but Hans Grimus, whose Pension Grimus was the closest hotel and restaurant business to the level of the Chalet, soon conceded the Chalet was good for his business also.

'He knew that he could send [people like] David Hayes and Wolf Blass and John Farnham down to the Chalet and they would be looked after.

'Conversely, I was able to send the Mel Gibsons, the Schumachers and various others up to Grimus and know they would be looked after,' Redmond said.

The Mt Buller Chalet is now branded Grand Mercure as part of a franchising agreement with the multinational Accor Group, with its fine-dining venue, the Black Cockatoo restaurant remaining a mountain favourite.

OTHER COMMERCIAL VENTURES to endure include Alpine Retreat; the bed and breakfast Andre's, which in its own subtle but powerful way has set a new standard for accommodation on the mountain, and the welcoming Duck Inn, which is a reincarnation of Lantern Lodge.

Enzian was another very European lodge, built in Austrian or Bavarian style. Overlooking Chamois run on the south side of the mountain, it was slightly out of the mainstream, but Ed Adamson recalled its restaurant hosting many a rollicking sing-along with dinner guests from the clubs surrounding.

'Austrian ski instructors, often led by the inimitable Hans Grimus,

gathered there, guaranteeing fun and a good dose of beer drinking songs including the salutory *Tsigi Tsigi*'.

Sometimes for survival and sometimes to expand their facilities, clubs have opened their doors to paying guests.

Michele and Stephen Morrice have run the commercial side of Ajax Ski Club for 20 years. Even for guests on a budget the fundamentals remain the same – 'you just have to make sure everybody has a good time,' Michele Morrice said. 'I like to make sure that everyone remembers the food … and that they've had a great experience at Ajax, then they want to come back.' Even in lean seasons, Ajax is well booked. 'I have a school group every mid-week for the month of July and then the weekends fill themselves.'

With the lodge designed for disabled access, they also cater for disabled skiers and ski racers. Business also comes from the Victorian Interschools and events like the Jewish Interschool. 'Every week there's something. I think generally Buller does a really good job in hospitality,' Morrice, who is also vice-president of the mountain's chamber of commerce, said.

Avalanche started life as a ski club, formed in 1963 by Bill Short and a group of his friends and acquaintances. By June 1964, the lodge had a floor and a roof and a covering of zinc anneal sheet. There was no lining and a few holes here and there, so the place was one big refrigerator – members spent the deep winter of 1964 on the floor in sleeping bags, waking with white eyebrows and a rime of frost.

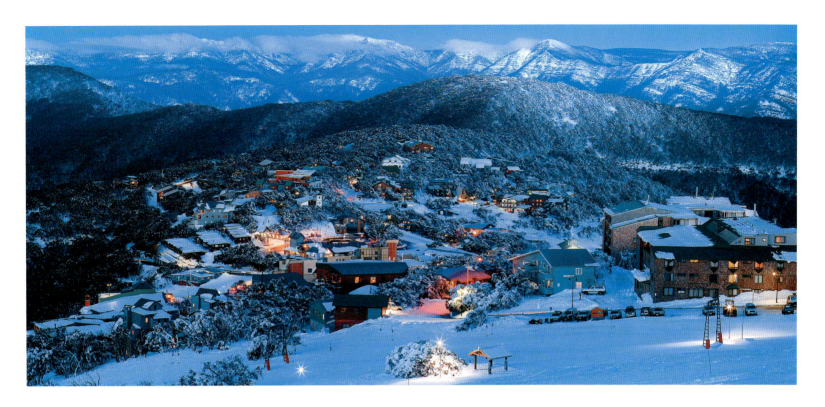

The next few years were spent enlarging, expanding and bricking the lodge and, in the 1980s, adding a four-storey building of apartments. Avalanche became commercial in 1980, with a cook and house staff during the season.

Bill Short was the major shareholder and in 1998 he transferred his shares to his son Shane, who bought out the other shareholders and is now the sole owner.

Night lights and nightlife in the Mt Buller Village, 2003. MARK ASHKANASY

In 2005, Shane started trading year-round as Avalanche Alpine Lodge, with a bar open 363 days of the year and accommodation available at all times. Shane's mother Chella handles accounts and payroll while Mike Short represents the next generation of Shorts at Avalanche.

The hub

THE VILLAGE SQUARE precinct, including Cow Camp Plaza has had a transformation over the years. As a hub for skiers and snowboarders during the day and resort guests in the evenings, it has hosted outposts of Melbourne chains including the Pancake Parlour and La Porchetta. Uncle Pat's is now the pizza and pasta outlet at Cow Camp Plaza.

Cattleman's Café at the base of the Blue Bullet chairlift, 2007. NATHAN RICHTER

The Wok Worx outlet for Asian-style food has been a response to the changing tastes of the mountain's visitors and the Cattleman's Café at the base of the Blue Bullet 1 chairlift has become popular for café-style snacks, for meals and après drinks.

Any venue that draws ski instructors will in turn draw the après crowd.

Cow Camp Plaza in the Village Square, 2003. LIZ GRANT/RMB

16

Clubs

Clubs were Mt Buller's foundation. The first skiing visit in 1924 was organised by the Ski Club of Victoria, which went on to build accommodation on the mountain for its members. As will happen with groups of people, some clubs have endured and some have wilted under the pressure of change.

IN THE LATE 1940s, the Ski Club of Victoria built its Ivor Whittaker Memorial Lodge beside the Bourke Street run, the Council for Scientific and Industrial Research (CSIR) club lodge went up between Horse Hill and One Tree Hill and the Youth Hostel Association (YHA) trucked its Shiver Shanty to the edge of the Skating Rink.

After its formation in 1948, the challenge for the fledgling Mount Buller Recreational Reserve Committee was to allocate sites for club lodges. It initially had only 20 acres (eight hectares) under its control but demand for club sites was substantial. At the committee's inaugural meeting in December 1948, its chairman Andrew Benallack suggested the 'Forests Commission be notified that it may need to extend its area of operation to prevent crowding of Cow Camp site.' (minutes, December 1948)

Cow Camp is the central saddle area of the village, which is a current transport interchange.

At that inaugural meeting, seven sites were allocated. The Australian Women's Ski Club was allocated site 1; Chamois Club of Australia, site 10; Melbourne Walking Club, site 8; Monsanto Ski Club, site 6; University Ski Club, site 5; Youth Hostel Association, site 2; and the Australian Postal Institute, site 13. At the following meeting, in February 1949, the Lazy Eight Ski Club was allocated site 12, Omega Ski Club, site 7 and Ullr Ski Club, site 9. Yurredla Ski Club was allocated site 19 at the committee's October 1949 meeting. (See Appendix 1, page 264 for a full list of clubs and sites)

The creation of a ski club – the Brighton Mountain Wanderers (BMW). BMW/SUMMERS

Among the first to use the SCV Hut were Morry Bardas (above left) and Cec Parkin in June 1933. Humble it may have been, but the Ski Club of Victoria's hut at Boggy Creek (above and on the ridge at bottom right in the photo at right) was Mt Buller's first club lodge.
NAMA/JOHN HIRAMS

Clubs had to have a minimum 25 members and club buildings had to be 'a minimum of 450 square feet [42 square metres] for the accommodation of eight persons.' (minutes, December 1948) Clubs were informed that their buildings had to have stonework above the ground to a minimum height of two feet (61 centimetres).

Although timber was in abundant supply from the mills at the foot of the mountain, some other building materials were limited and club members innovated with bush design and, to an extent, bush construction techniques. The clubs had to supply their own water and their own power, usually from diesel generators.

SCV membership expressed the strength of demand: 'New members' names have been submitted very freely indeed in recent weeks and 117 additions were formally approved at the June General Meeting. They raise the total to no less than 464 for this season, with actual ski-ing only just commencing and the grand total of club members to approximately 2000, as at the June meeting.' (*Schuss*, July 1949, p279).

The SCV also saw itself as the guardian of the sport (a position the growth of other clubs eventually wrested from it). While congratulating itself on its achievements in its twenty-fifth year, an editorial in the SCV magazine in 1949 urged members 'not to rest on our laurels or still less, slacken our interest in developing our chosen sport. Ski-ing is still developing and expanding rapidly and it is the Club's duty to continue to be in the forefront of its progress and give it sound leadership and guidance.' (*Schuss*, January 1949, p12)

Discipline could be a problem in the club however. In an 'important notice to members' the SCV's treasurer, Ted Tyler, sought to reinforce that:

> The Club has tried to enable as many members as possible to get to the snow and has allowed a limited number to sleep on the Canteen floor at the Ivor Whittaker Memorial Lodge at weekends. Several of them have complained of the discomfort, also residents of the lodge have been inconvenienced. The committee have no alternative but to prohibit sleeping in the Canteen after 26th July, 1954. Complaints have also been received that members not residing in the lodge have been making use of the bathrooms, showers, etc. Members not residing in the lodge must not make use of bathrooms. (*Schuss*, July 1954, p156)

THE FORESTS COMMISSION'S Committee of Management had limited capacity to police the building works. It found itself, for example, writing to the Youth Hostel Association (minutes, March 1949) ordering it to cease works on its Cow Camp site until its plans had been approved.

The Committee of Management was again forced to put a handbrake on the enthusiasm of the YHA when it received a letter from the Australian Women's Ski Club regarding the danger caused by blasting operations. 'The chairman said that there was ample evidence that blasting operations which had been carried out by members of the Youth Hostel Association could have been of a very dangerous nature.'

The meeting resolved to inform the YHA that 'more care should be exercised when blasting stone.' (minutes, December 1949)

In a summary of inspection in March 1950, the Committee of Management noted the Gray Rocks Ski Club had erected its building with 'plans not approved and no stonework'.

It was time to take a stand.

The committee moved to ask the Forests Commission (FCV) to hold Gray Rocks' permissive occupancy licence in abeyance until further advised, and it informed Gray Rocks to stop building works and 'submit for approval amended plans' to bring its building into line. Failing this, 'the committee will consider the re-allocation of site no. 5.' (minutes, March 1950).

Demand for club sites continued and in the mid-1950s a further subdivision was approved, expanding the village out from the Cow Camp area.

The three decades of the 1950s, 60s and 70s was the boom era for clubs, but the changing face of society in the 1980s saw the strong endure and others unable to meet the demands placed on them.

'These days,' Sandie Jeffcoat, the resort manager and then chief executive between 1982 and 2005 said, 'a family or a couple want their own room with an ensuite, they don't want to stay in a bunk room with three other people they don't know and share a bathroom. The old clubs were like that. So if you didn't have the money to redevelop your club or upgrade to have those facilities, then your club would fail. 'This happened, and they would sell the site off to someone to build apartments which was exactly what people wanted; they wanted somewhere to have their own personal space or family space. The clubs that have been successful were the ones with a strong membership base; look around the resorts at the good-looking clubs, the successful clubs, and they're the ones that survive.

'I really think that the market will drive what's constructed. One day, we may have an over-supply of apartments on Mt Buller, then people won't build them because there's no profit in them and then it might change again, but right now people want to buy apartments, it's a good investment and is good for the growth and development of Buller,' Jeffcoat said.

The following is a small selection of recollections from Mt Buller's substantial ski club base.

Club life at the Whitt. SCV

Entertainment 1950s-style in the lounge of the SCV's Ivor Whittaker Memorial Lodge. SCV

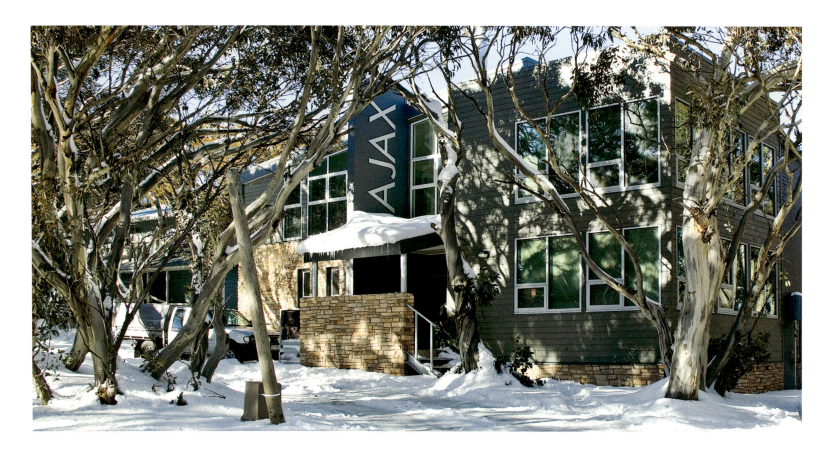

Ajax as it stood in 2007 – extended, renovated and a survivor of the evolutionary challenges that faced Mt Buller's ski clubs.
MARK ASHKANASY

 # Ajax

IN SEPTEMBER 1971, Brian Kino, Ben Burstin and Isi Plack, committee members of the Associated Judean Athletic Clubs (Ajax) were relaxing in the Abom at Mt Buller after a day's skiing.

There they conceived of the idea of Ajax on the mountain. Together with Tom Wodak and David Lipson, they each invested $100 and set about realising the dream.

The inaugural meeting of the Ajax Ski Club took place on February 7, 1972. Ajax purchased the assets of the Matterhorn Ski Club and leased its site with a view to building a new lodge. The first annual meeting of the Ajax Ski Club was held on March 20, 1972 and 120 memberships at $500 each were sold.

A single-storey lodge sleeping 44 people was built and opened by Ajax president Sam Taylor on June 2, 1973. The club prospered, with two additions resulting in a three-level building and a further upgrade in 2002, with the site extended to include the front area to the edge of Stirling Track to allow an addition to the front of the existing lodge.

In 2007, Ajax had 230 members and remained active in inter-club races and in its support of the Jewish Interschools competition.

To support its operations and underpin its upgrades, Ajax has taken guests on a commercial basis since the late 1970s. Club managers, Michele and Stephen Morrice, celebrated their twentieth year with Ajax in 2007.

 # Akla

THE SEEDS FOR Akla were planted when Max Finlason and Geoff Brearley met at the Brighton Yacht Club in January 1956, then recruited friends and family to make up the requisite 25 members. The first Akla lodge was ready for occupation in June 1956, only months after its formation.

There were no lining boards but the lodge was fitted with a pot belly briquette heater; bottled gas provided the lighting and water came from a well or soak. The lodge was one large room with kitchen, bunk area and lounge and beautiful views over Breathtaker Point and across to the Bluff.

Most foundation members have handed their memberships to their sons or daughters. In 2007, three foundation members were still active in the club – Howard Beattie, Geoff Brearley and Barry Cooper. A fiftieth anniversary function in 2006 was attended by these three and other foundation members including Jock Bing, Len Christie, Des Clark, Geoff Goodwin, Joc Hutchinson and Bill Tooth.

The Akla lodge has had a number of refurbishments and overhauls, with a further major redevelopment planned to include 12 new bedrooms with ensuites and new drying room, ski room and children's lounge.

Alkira

THE FIRST SOD for Alkira was turned in October 1964 and the lodge was ready to occupy in June 1965. It had its own generator for electricity, but that became increasingly difficult to start on freezing Friday nights.

Alkira's driving force included doctors, pharmacists, company directors, bankers and their young families, some with technical skills and others with managerial skills. The lynchpin was a civil engineer, John Pendavingh, who designed the lodge and together with his colleague Peter Manger oversaw its construction. The entire lodge was built by club members with a few specialist tradespeople brought in for tasks like plumbing. Sometimes in those early days, the oil for the oil heater froze and when it was really cold, the toilet system could freeze and had to be manually thawed, but the camaraderie that carried members through those trails has endured through the second and third generation.

In the early 1990s, a drive was instigated to completely refurbish the lodge and its facilities. New members were recruited and the membership structure redesigned so offspring of the original members could buy-in at a discount. Original senior members were offered honorary life memberships and some still use Alkira and ski with their grandchildren and their new friends.

The club remains strong in inter- and intra-club racing and has held a club race weekend every year since its inception, with members from the ages of four to 77 years competing.

Alkira is an Aboriginal word meaning 'blue sky', a name put forward by Val Alaway (Val Dent), a founding member.

In the dining room at Alkira with the pennants on the wall and a unique light of many bottles overhead. MARK ASHKANASY

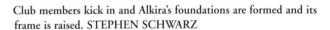

Club members kick in and Alkira's foundations are formed and its frame is raised. STEPHEN SCHWARZ

Apira

IN 1947, A committee including Kevin McDonald and Blanche Dall convinced the Australian Postal Institute's Victorian Division to form a new sports club and on November 19, 1947 the API applied to the Forests Commission, for a site for a club lodge.

On April 12, 1948, a formal, detailed application was made with construction to start in December 1948 for completion in May 1949. The estimated cost of the project was £500 to be funded by a £7.10s levy on the 25 foundation members and a £200 loan from the API. Club membership was to be limited to 80 with bookings open to all 4000 institute members with priority to club members. Under extreme difficulties, they got all materials on site and successfully constructed the first lodge in time for the 1949 season.

The API continued to make small loans and grants and provide meeting rooms. The ski club had full responsibility for operational matters. The first spring mattresses were bought in 1953, the first hot water service in 1954 and the first generator in 1955. The first building extension, to create a lounge room and raise the roof for the sunroom, was undertaken in 1958-59.

In the 1960s, the API opened associate membership to any public servant, leading to an influx of non-Post Master General employees, particularly teachers.

The second re-development increased accommodation to 24-beds in six four-bed bunkrooms and included mains pressure water and electricity. The $14,000 project was completed in 1968-69 and funded entirely from savings, with Aurel Forras the builder and members supplying the labour.

In the 1980s, a major building project negotiated a jungle of red tape for approvals at a cost of more than $200,000. It was in this period that the club broke away from the API and became Apira. In the 1990s, smoking was banned, the main rooms refurbished and modern appliances installed, along with upgraded fire detection and electrical fault protection. Leasing the lodge to La Trobe University for summer student accommodation led to considerable debt reduction.

In 2003-05 exterior upgrades included a new roof, double glazed windows and doors were installed along with better insulation. Rendering, a new fire escape and replacing timber in-fills greatly improved the appearance, safety and energy-saving aspects of the lodge.

Apira currently has 112 members. Two foundation members involved in the building of the first lodge – Doug Akeroyd and Bob Hooppell – remain active members.

John Hollingshead and John Brimage were members of the early ski patrol and John English and Ron Edwards have been resort Committee of Management board members.

Benmore

BENMORE SKI CLUB was founded in 1949 by a group of ice skating friends from St Kilda's St Moritz skating rink with Neville Fletcher the leader of the group. Its first lease cost £10 and each member contributed £20 towards the cost of the building. The lodge was ready for occupation in 1952.

The name Benmore came from 'Ben' meaning mountain in Scotland and 'more' to quite simply make 'more mountain'.

The club started with 25 members and in 2007 had three honorary life members, 19 full members, 14 associate members and six junior members.

Although Benmore is one of the oldest and smallest clubs on the mountain, many of its members are still very actively involved. Bill and Gwenda Bailey, Stan and Helen Ellison, Val and Daryl Gallagher and Jim Simpson are original members still involved in the club.

Gwenda Bailey was the booking officer for the first 30 years and Sally Williams has been the booking officer since 1982.

Benmore has had two major renovations and is in the planning stages of another big upgrade, including the construction of apartments.

Chamois Ski Club was granted its site at the first meeting of the Mt Buller Committee of Management in 1948. MARK ASHKANASY

On the record

Ski clubs were the foundation of the Mt Buller Village. Some club histories are covered in other books, such as the Ski Club of Victoria's *Skiing Into History* by Janice Lloyd and two books by Lynette Sheridan – *University Ski Club 1929-1979* and *Shes* *and Skis: Golden years of the Australian Women's Ski Club, 1932-1982* (see the bibliography for more details). Whatever their level of activity, clubs are encouraged to have their records included in the collection of the National Alpine Museum of Australia.

BMW

THE NUCLEUS of the Brighton Mountain Wanderers (BMW) Ski Club was Jim Nilsson, Jock Robertson, Neil Barter and Merrick Summers who all lived in Brighton and shared an interest in sports cars and motor cycles. The club was granted Site 25 in March 1950 and membership was broadened to include friends at Melbourne Technical College and Melbourne University.

The members took just 23 days to build the lodge to lock-up stage in the summer of 1950-51 and it was functional for the 1951 winter. Due to the pace of construction, the club became known as the 'Bloody Mountain Wonders'. In 1958, the BMW Ski Tow Group was formed to build ski lifts and it obtained the Dopplemayr agency (see chapter 5).

The lodge was extended in 1966 (an extra four beds and ensuite) and in 1985 (10 more beds and ensuites) to cope with the natural increase of members' families. BMW continues as a low-cost, family club of recreational skiers. No ski politics, a little ski rescue in the early days and no club racing. 'With very low energy consumption, the club continues to keep winter cool – we have no heated eaves, no heated patio or sundeck and no heated driveway,' Merrick Summers said.

Chamois

THE FIRST MEETING of what was initially called the Victorian Alpine Ski Club was held on April 29, 1925. The club went through a few names, including the Commonwealth Ski Club and Royal Ski Club before finally settling on the Chamois Club of Australia in July 1926.

The European chamois is a small mountain goat, and Chamois club members saw themselves as having to parallel the efforts of the goat in climbing mountains.

The club had an annual winter sports carnival in the early days at Mt Buffalo. By 1939 this carnival had been moved to Mt St Bernard and Mt Hotham.

Chamois was granted a site at Mt Buller in 1948, the first time it would claim a place of its own.

There were three criteria for choosing its Cow Camp site: protection from the prevailing westerly weather, extensive views and perennial water. In 1949, Chamois and the Cow Camp Hut were the only buildings in the immediate vicinity but water supplies dropped to a trickle as additional clubs and then Kooroora joined the supply line.

Chamois lodge was built by members and officially opened in time for King's Birthday weekend, 1950. The club has seen evenings of parlour games, miniature igloos built with glowing candles inside, a coke-fired Romesse heater glowing red, visits of and to people in other lodges (usually associated with requisite drinking), or going to Kooroora and hob-nobbing with

BMW members dig the club's foundations in December 1950.
BMW/SUMMERS

BMW, the home of the 'Bloody Mountain Wonders'.
MARK ASHKANASY

celebrities. The flip side of the club's proximity to Kooroora is the music resonating through the walls of Chamois until the small hours.

The club has always encouraged skiing at a minimal cost and has guarded its family atmosphere. While not advocating the conditions of that first Cow Camp Hut, the club still avoids such amenities as spas, masseurs or a resident manager. There is still no dishwasher (it is believed that the washing of dishes is a significant social opportunity) nor a television.

Radios were initially banned, although the late Tom Fisher was known to hide away with his ear to his little transistor radio listening to the football. The telephone was never connected but in an age of mobile phones this no longer matters.

Coonamar

BUILDING WORK STARTED on the Coonamar lodge in January 1964 and it was built to lock-up in time for the 1964 winter. Facilities were primitive in that first year but the lodge was built well enough to survive the heavy snowfalls of that year.

Coonamar originally had 32 members. In 2007 it had 25 members, 18 of whom were a part of the original group.

The club originally obtained electricity from Kooroora's generator, then installed its own – a succession of patched-up machines that 'could always be counted on to go bang or fizz once in a weekend – always it seemed to be in the middle of dinner preparation,' in the words of founding member, Monty Russell.

'Over the years the building progressed to a high level of comfort and has always provided homely accommodation for members and their guests.

'Group catering and sitting down to a hearty meal together has always been a feature – by necessity in the early years but now a permanent part of the club's culture.'

Members have competed in inter-club and Victorian Championship events as well as being active in cross-country touring and competition.

Coonamar was built in 1964 with 35 members, many of whom have shown their loyalty and longevity. Of the 25 members in 2007, 18 were in that original group. MARK ASHKANASY

CSIR

IN 1945, A group of employees, mostly scientists and engineers, of the Council for Scientific and Industrial Research (CSIR) became interested in building a hut on Mt Buller – some had lived overseas or had come to Australia from countries where skiing was accessible.

The idea moved closer to reality on October 21, 1945, when 58 people held the inaugural meeting of the CSIR Skiers and Walkers, later to be known as the CSIR Ski Club.

In January 1946, a site for a hut was chosen at Mt Buller, on the saddle between Horse Hill and One Tree Hill. An occupation licence was signed on March 1, 1946 and the main structure of the lodge was habitable for winter 1946, a bumper season as it turned out.

The lodge subsequently went through many modifications and extensions, all with club members' labour.

In 1949, CSIR became CSIRO (the Commonwealth Scientific and Industrial Research Organisation), but the original name of CSIR was retained for the ski club.

In 1955, summer occupancy was granted by the Forests Commission of Victoria and CSIR members took the opportunity to enjoy Mt Buller in warmer months.

CSIR expanded and has two lodges at Falls Creek and one at Mt Hotham, in addition to its Mt Buller lodge.

In 1964, the club engaged the Mt Buller Committee of Management in battle over the illegal rubbish dumping of a commercial lodge that was contaminating CSIR's water supply – a dump at Hell Corner (renamed Tip Corner) had been established, directly over the CSIR water catchment. After much

protest, the dump was moved around the contour, and Tip Corner was renamed Top Corner.

In 1982, the club was formally advised by the Mt Buller Committee of Management that it had to move from the One Tree Hill site to rebuild within the boundaries of the Mt Buller village.

The new CSIR lodge in Delatite Lane was completed in 1985. After the club held an emotional wake at the original site the lodge was bulldozed to make way for what is now known as the CSIR car park.

Gliss

A GROUP OF would-be skiers got together at the Government Aircraft Factory in 1951 with a view to forming a club at Mt Buller. Founding member Ron Friedman recalled a disastrous trial run in July 1951. 'There was heavy snowfall. We got to Dump Inn at 5.30pm, but it took to 11.30pm to walk up to the village through the snow. We decided it was all too hard and not worth the effort.'

They were reinspired when a 1951 issue of *Home Beautiful* magazine featured Mt Buller's lodges, encouraging them to believe it could be done.

'We formed a club and called it Gliss for no other reason than we liked it better than other suggestions. We applied for a site and we were told to take a pick of the newly subdivided Breathtaker Spur,' Ron Friedman said.

They surveyed the area and initially decided to build next to BMW but after admiring photos of the view from block 32 decided to build there, even though there was no road. Stumps were put in on one weekend in December 1951, with members staying at BMW. The lodge was built in 10 days over Christmas, while members camped on the site. 'There were snakes on the site and one went straight into a tent which caused pandemonium. Another one was sunning itself on the site where we were about to start building,' Friedman said.

'We had to cut a track from the bottom of Bourke Street, past what is now Pension Grimus and Breathtaker Lodge, to carry in the materials from Bourke Street.'

'We weren't silly enough to try to drive out to the site, but Reindeer and Benmore were also building their lodges that summer, and one of them broke the transmission in their car,' Friedman said.

A feature of the original hut was a large metal framed window looking out to Little Buller – it is still there. There were two bunk rooms for six people with bunks three-high, separated from the living room by a curtain to keep the rooms warm. The original toilet was a hole in the ground; water came from a tank (when it wasn't frozen) and cooking was on a slow combustion stove along with a four-burner cooker that ran on Shellite. In 1965 an extension was built increasing the bed numbers to 22.

Mawson

MAWSON SKI CLUB was started by members of the 9th St Kilda Mawson Rovers, most of whom were introduced to skiing by the scouting movement, although a founding member, Ern Rothschild, started skiing with his family in 1933.

The office bearers of the original club were Rothschild, Peter Edwards and Dick Foote. They started building their six-bunk lodge in 1951, however it wasn't ready for occupation until 1955. During this drawn-out construction period, an Austin A40 car case provided accommodation, with a corrugated iron roof over the top to catch some water and a wood stove under the snow gums for cooking. The lodge was entirely built by members, their wives and friends.

'It is hard to realise now that at the time there was no power, no water supply and no sewerage and the site rental was 10 shillings a year,' Ern Rothschild said.

In later years, the lodge was extended to accommodate 12 people. In 1974, Ern Rothschild was asked to join the Mt Buller Committee of Management as a ratepayers' representative, a position he held until 1997.

The demand for improved facilities in larger club buildings saw the demise of Mawson. At the end of the 1994 winter, the Mawson lodge site on The Avenue was taken over for a development of what was intended to be known as the Black Stump apartments.

The apartment developers asked for permission to use the name 'Mawson' for the apartments and Mawson's founding club members agreed that they could.

Melbourne Walking Club

ONE OF THE original clubs, the Melbourne Walking Club was granted site 8 at the first meeting of the Mt Buller Recreational Reserve Committee in December 1948. In addition to skiers, walkers were enthusiastic mountain visitors, playing an important part in opening up the mountain and showing the first interest in its year-round use. The club lodge was redeveloped in the 1990s, bringing a new lease of life to its membership.

Merrijig

THE LOCAL NAME suggests a local connection, and there is one, but not as might be imagined.

What became the Merrijig Ski Club started with a phone call from Jeff Moran to Frank Dawson in late 1975 or early 1976, when a notice appeared in *The Age* seeking expressions of interest to lease and develop sites on Mount Buller. One was the Merrijig site, another was the adjoining site now occupied by the Victorian Surf Lifesavers (VSL).

Frank Dawson contacted some people he thought would be interested, including Geoffrey and Heather Rex, Graham Holdsworth, Joseph Zly, Dan Stojanovic, John Yuncken, Alan and Barbara Leary, Graeme Leary, Peter Hopkins, Sue Hopkins, Tony Hampton and Jack and Maggie Ward – all were friends or colleagues at Yuncken Freeman Architects in Melbourne.

Jeff Moran was working at the Catholic Teacher Training College adjacent to Chadstone shopping centre and he recruited colleagues and friends, including David Rayson who was of great assistance to Merrijig in those early years. Another group of early members were recruited from the Oakleigh squash courts, then run by Richard Sanderson. Graham Holdsworth, who was a keen member of the surf lifesaving organisation, decided to recruit his own group, who subsequently made a separate application for the VSL site.

Tenders were sought for Merrijig's construction and the successful builder was Twin City Constructions from Albury – they had just completed the Clyde Cameron College in Albury Wodonga, which is influenced by the concrete 'brutalist' style that was all the go at the time (like Melbourne's Harold Holt Swimming Pool); and there is some of that in the Merrijig Ski Club.

Merrijig's construction crew spent most nights at the Hunt Club Hotel in Merrijig. 'We were very popular in Merrijig,' founding member Frank Dawson recalled and 'our club name was bequeathed to us by the locals in the pub at around two o'clock one morning'.

MUSKI

THE UNIVERSITY SKI Club was established in 1929 by Melbourne University engineering students. In 1934, the members of that club who were students at the University of Melbourne created the Melbourne University Ski Club – MUSKI – so they could compete at the first official intervarsity competition in 1937. MUSKI had prosperous beginnings and played an important part in bringing university students into snow sports. In 1960, the Melbourne University Sports Union purchased a property on Mt Buller, just behind Kooroora. That building was rebuilt in the early 1990s and is now a comfortable lodge with beds for 42 guests.

MUSKI continues to promote snow sports to university students and it has become one of the largest and most successful university sporting clubs in Australia.

The motto – 'we're not arrogant, just damn good' holds true, with the club taking out 11 of the past 14 National University Snowsports titles.

The ability level of members differs greatly, from those who have never seen snow before to international freeride competitors such as Andrew, Christian, Stephanie and Natalie Siriani.

MUSKI aims to develop snow sports within the university community, support members at all levels, from beginner to elite and to provide an enjoyable and social atmosphere.

 # Opal

THE OLD PARADIANS Association Ski Club was formed in 1963 by a group who enjoyed skiing, bushwalking and the alpine environment.

Opal's A-frame lodge was ready for occupation in 1967, built through the commitment of members and a system of compulsory working bees and contributions. The original A-frame is still in place, making Opal one of the older lodges on the mountain.

The A-frame lodge is constructed on a benched-out portion of the site cut into the hill to a depth of approximately 1.5 metres on the building's southern side. In 2005 a new wing was constructed to create a lounge area.

Opal Ski Club currently has 40 full members, including some of its founding members. Its bunkrooms accommodate 22 guests with shared cooking, dining and lounge areas as well as a drying room and members' lockers.

Opal is the last lodge on Goal Post Road in the current village plan – some years ago there were three blocks further north, around the end of the road, but these seem to have been abandoned from the plan. The western side of Goal Post Road from the Delatite Lane intersection heading north has never been proposed for subdivision so Opal Ski Club, Duck Inn and Bayerland are the only three lodges at this end of Goal Post Road.

Views from the lodge are spectacular to the north and east down the Chalet Creek catchment with further distant views across Kings Saddle.

The rebuilt University of Melbourne Lodge. MARK ASHKANASY

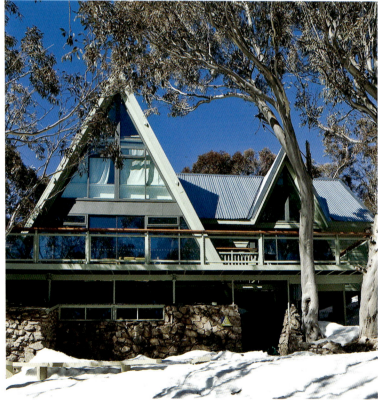

The Opal Ski Club lodge, on the far end of Goal Post Road with views out towards King Saddle. MARK ASHKANASY

OLOS

A MEETING HELD at Cathedral Hall in Melbourne on August 29, 1956 had Des Carroll in the chair and 65 people in attendance. Some discussion took place about the 'problems involved in building a ski lodge,' but the proposal to form a Catholic ski club was put to the vote and carried unanimously.

Despite the anticipated difficulties, in less than a year, the club, under the new name of Our Lady of the Snows Ski Club (OLOS) had its lodge built and the mountain also had its first chapel. The *Catholic Messenger* noted the June 20, 1957 opening of the lodge: 'At Mt Buller last Saturday afternoon, the Most Reverend A. F. Fox blessed the lodge and dedicated the chapel of Our Lady of the Snows Ski Club, erected at a cost of £6000 … "I am privileged and delighted," said Bishop Fox, "to be with you on this historic occasion of the blessing of what I am told is the first Catholic ski club lodge and chapel not only in Victoria, but in the whole of Australia … where Mass will be celebrated each Sunday for you during the skiing season".'

The club expanded its membership base and its building significantly in the late 1960s with a new lounge area and a new wing of bedrooms. In 1982, OLOS was given a new roof and attic area and in 2005 the building was reclad. In 2007, OLOS had 30 beds in 10 bedrooms and around 100 members. The lodge is well used, although the nature of that use changed a little, at least on weekends, after the building of the Mt Buller Chapel in 1993, when Mass was moved from OLOS, where it had been celebrated on winter Sundays since 1957.

Built, beautified and then blessed – the OLOS Ski Club lodge. OLOS

Patscherkofel

NAMED FOR ONE of the host mountains of the 1964 Innsbruck Winter Olympics, Patscherkofel was the offspring of the Australian Alpine Club (AAC), which itself was founded in 1950 and had club lodges in the Snowy Mountains and at Falls Creek.

The AAC's 1963 foundation committee for Patscherkofel included Eric Burt, Malcolm McColl, Geoff Henke, Warren Peck and Peter de Crespigny. The committee started recruiting new members for the project in 1964; part of the benefit of membership was reciprocal booking rights in all existing AAC lodges.

Construction of the lodge started after the 1965 ski season, culminating in an opening on May 26, 1966 by Charles Anton, the AAC's foundation president. The original building had 14 bedrooms, four large bathrooms, foyer, lounge, dining room and kitchen.

Patscherkofel prospered and there were some significant additions, including a manager's flat and, in 1972, a big extension to the living area. There was a major redevelopment in 1987-88 with architectural work performed by Chris Humphries and the building project contracted to Humphries and Cooke. The rebuilt lodge included a spa and sauna, a substantial laundry and large kitchen, dining and living areas. There have been further extensions of the living areas, conversion of all bunk rooms into bedrooms with en suite bathrooms, incorporation of a small number of 'family-style' bedrooms, the addition of a feature fireplace and TV rooms. The lodge now has 20 bedrooms, comfortably accommodating more than 50 people.

Patscherkofel Lodge has 284 members and conducts several special events for members including race weekends and social dinners.

Pol-Ski

POL-SKI CLUB members originally came from Melbourne's Polish community and has expanded to include people from a rich diversity of nationalities.

It emerged from the decision of Yurredla Ski Club to demolish its old club building and develop a single building to accommodate four separate clubs.

Yurredla advertised in the Melbourne daily press and by 1978, resort management had approved plans for Pol-Ski, Eltham, Star Alpine and Yurredla to occupy the site.

Pol-Ski is around 100 metres from Helicopter Flat with easy access to the lifts and spectacular views of the mountains to the south. A comfortable, warm, club building, it sleeps 28 people.

Ullr

ULLR IS THE god of winter in Teutonic mythology; it was believed it was he who spread the white blankets over the fields in winter to protect them from the cold. It was this god, who brought snow to cover the mountains, that the first members of the Ullr Ski Club wished to recognise.

Ullr was established in 1948 by a small group of enthusiasts, including club secretary Mary Wallace. It occupied site 9, on Cow Camp Lane, initially with a small hut and later with a snug, two-bedroom timber building with 12 beds, a bathroom and a small kitchen and dining area.

In 1981, Rino and Diana Grollo bought the site and the club lodge from the only remaining members – Dr T Hudson and his family. The Grollos kept the club and its spirit alive.

As a child, Lara Grollo recalled 'sitting around the tiny table waiting for the older children to come home from skiing, drawing pictures in the fog on the window rising from the steam of the pasta boiling in pots behind me.'

As the club grew from six to 21 members, the building became too small. In 1986 it was demolished but the spirit of the club and the mateship it produced lived on in the new, larger Ullr Ski Club lodge, a building with more beds and more space to support the expanding number of club members.

Each winter, the members of Ullr went out in fog, snow or rain to compete in the Ullr Cup, a giant slalom race to test the prowess of members. On several occasions, lack of snow meant the race was cancelled, but the annual dinner has always gone ahead, with Austrian dancing, music and festivities.

A compact tribute to the god of snow. Ullr as it stood in 1985 on site 9 in Cow Camp Lane. MARK ASHKANASY

University Ski Club

THE UNIVERSITY SKI Club (USC) was formed in 1929; with its earliest bases at Mt Donna Buang and Mt Hotham. Always enthusiastic skiers, USC members were among the first to visit Mt Buller with the early Ski Club of Victoria groups. The club was granted site 5 in the ballot for Mt Buller's first subdivision and charged a fee of five shillings for the first 12 months of its permissive occupancy.

However, the club committee was unhappy with the location and reappplied and in September 1949 was granted site 16 'looking down the Howqua Valley and away to The Bluff' (Sheridan p132). The 'Cabin' – the USC hut relocated from Mt Donna Buang – was ready for occupancy by winter 1950. As demand grew, the Cabin was found wanting, so the USC 'Lodge' was built on the adjacent site 17, with much of the labour in the first summer provided by Keith Webb, Athol Ham, Bill Rennie and Hugh Darby (Sheridan p134).

In the late 1970s, momentum grew for a further USC redevelopment and in 1982, architect Peter Parry-Fielder drew up plans for a new building to replace the Cabin. The Committee of Management responded that USC had to redevelop both sites or relinquish one of them, so it went to work on both. The new Cabin was ready for opening weekend in 1983 and the rebuilt Lodge complete in the 1986 summer, although it was available for the 1985 winter. The two buildings were integrated with a common entrance and now have a total 75 beds. During winter, the tradition of a Saturday night dinner for all members and their guests continues, as does the club's participation in racing.

With a total memberhsip of 750 and accommodation bases at all three of Victoria's major mountain resorts - Mt Buller, Falls Creek and Mt Hotham - USC remains one of Victoria's most active ski clubs.

YHA

HAROLD CUMING WAS a cartage contractor with an interest in the mountains; he was a pioneer at Mt Buller, at Mt Mawson in Tasmania's Mt Field National Park and at Falls Creek until his death in 1968. He made early tracks up Mt Buller with the Youth Hostels Association; the YHA's 50-year history noted that, in August 1945, he offered to 'buy an ex-army hut and take it up to Mt Buller for use by the YHA as a ski hostel, so long as the association could obtain agreement from the Forests Commission.' (Ann Crawford/YHA, p3)

They found their hut in Lancefield, north west of Melbourne, and had it ready for the winter of 1947, thanks to more than 200 members giving at least nine hours each voluntary labour. The hut had 'hot and cold showers, burgundy curtained-off bunks … a large smokeless open fireplace – something to look forward to on blizzard nights … and a certain amount of foodstuffs for sale.' (Ann Crawford/YHA, p7)

The Shiver Shanty, as the hut became known, was improved for the 1948 season when it had Maurice Selle as resident ski instructor. After that season and the establishment of the FCV's Committee of Management, with the encouragement of the FCV, the YHA was offered a site at the new Cow Camp subdivision. They had optimistically hoped to be in it for the 1949 winter, however it wasn't until winter 1952 that the Shiver Shanty was demolished and the YHA completed the move to Cow Camp.

The building was improved over the decades, with heating and power and water connection highlights. It was substantially extended in 1975 and has been continually well-maintained and upgraded.

The quality of the YHA location made it an appealing prospect for developers and it had many approaches to be relocated in major apartment or hotel developments; however in winter 2007, it was still offering budget accommodation at Mt Buller.

The Youth Hostels Association lodge in 2007 – it moved from its site near the Skating Rink to this prime location in 1952. MARK ASHKANASY

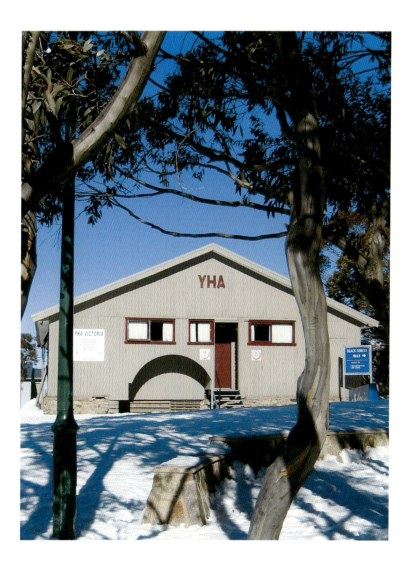

Yurredla

YURREDLA SKI CLUB had its origins in the scouting movement. Two of its founding members, Ernest Goetz and Peter Dyson became Rover Scouts and had their first trip to the snow in 1944, staying overnight at the University Ski Club hut at Mt Donna Buang.

The boys immediately fell in love with skiing and inspired other scouts to join them on trips to the snow, including one to Mt Buller on the 1947 King's Birthday weekend when they camped beside Chalet Creek.

They resolved to build their own ski hut to enjoy increased skiing opportunities. In September 1948, Peter Dyson was staying at the Rover Scouts' chalet on the Bogong High Plains where he met Victorian parliamentarian and skier Tom Mitchell.

Mitchell told Dyson about the Forests Commission's plan to survey 50 sites on Mt Buller and initially offer 25 sites to ski clubs with an interest in building ski huts there.

The 11th Brighton Rover Crew discussed the opportunity and decided that those members who were interested in skiing should form their own ski club and apply for a site; nine of them did, meeting on June 15, 1949 to formalise the ski club with Peter Dyson elected president, Michael Brand the secretary and Bill Roberts treasurer.

Yurredla, an Aboriginal word meaning 'towards the higher place', was chosen as the club's name following some research of Dyson's at the State Library of Victoria.

In October 1949, Yurredla was granted a Permission Occupancy Licence over Site 19, subject to its payment of an annual licence fee of 7/- 6d (seven shillings and sixpence) and conditional upon it building a ski hut by winter 1951.

The club expanded its membership and drew up plans for a two-storey hut to be clad outside with rough sawn local box gum and an iron roof. Bill Roberts, who had electrical, mechanical and woodworking expertise, guided the rest of the club members to complete the hut by winter 1950.

Roberts drew up a budget of £95, which he estimated would cover the purchase of exterior cladding and framing timber from the Delatite Sawmills at Sawmill Settlement, red gum stumps, windows, roofing iron and nails.

The hut was completed to lock-up stage by King's Birthday 1950 when the club held a riotous opening party on the Saturday evening. During the next three summers, under Roberts' guidance, members fitted out the interior of the hut and added an extension to form an L-shaped lodge comprising a 16-bed bunkroom upstairs and a kitchen, lounge/dining area, drying room, pantry and bathroom downstairs. An engine shed was built outside to house a 32-volt electric generator and a pan toilet.

Club voices

THE SKI CLUB of Victoria (SCV) was initially the voice for skiers in Victoria, however, with the emergence of other clubs, some resented the administrative control of skiing in Victoria being handled by another club. In July 1947, seven clubs — CSIR, University, Alpine, the Australian Women's Ski Club, Bull Lodge, Melbourne University Ski Club and Eidelweiss — met to consider the formation of a group to better represent all clubs.

Following that discussion, 17 other clubs, including the SCV, were invited to a meeting in November 1947 at which the Federation of Victorian Ski Clubs (FOVSC) was formed. The SCV resisted, unwilling to lose its control of the sport.

In 1955 a compromise was reached and the SCV and FOVSC settled their differences to create the Victorian Ski Association (first known as the Victorian Amateur Ski Association). (CSIR/Lloyd, p487)

For the resort's first three decades, most of Mt Buller's site holders held their property under a Permissive Occupancy agreement with the Crown through its landlord, the Forests Commission of Victoria.

Permissive Occupancy, although seldom withdrawn arbitrarily, had no formal security – it was a year-by-year arrangement.

The Mt Buller Ratepayers Association (MBRA) was established in 1972, initially to negotiate the transfer of the permissive occupancy status of all ski clubs on Mt Buller to legal leases, with sensible terms (of 25–40 years). Since then, the association has represented site holders in other issues including valuations of sites, leasing policies and tenure, service charges, gate-entry fees, village transport, lease-renewal options, site rental policy and alpine resorts regulations.

The MBRA, with the aim of representing stakeholders' interests has 'established a meaningful dialogue with the Mt Buller Committee of Management, executives of the Forests Commission and most recently the Resort Management Board,' in the words of long-term MBRA member Peter Dyson.

One of the most significant battles was fought in 1989, when the Cain Labor government's Alpine Resorts Commission (ARC) proposed massive increases (on average, from $250 to $4000) in site rentals. The MBRA and Mt Buller Chamber of Commerce developed a strategy to combat the increases, with 125 stakeholders contributing to a fighting fund.

The battle, led by members Peter Dyson and Bill Hazlett, included a strike on rate payments and was eventually resolved through ministerial intervention. Following four public meetings, the ARC/VSA Site Rental Agreement was signed. The site holders (96 from Mt Buller) who agreed to accept the agreement saved as much as 40 per cent on their site rentals.

The MBRA continues to work towards protecting the interests of ski clubs in particular, but at the same time working for the benefit of all alpine resort site holders in Victoria.

In 2007, the committee of the MBRA included John Aird, Ian Blair, Barry Cooper (chairman since 1986) Carole Czermak, Joel Dixon, Peter Dyson, Ron Edwards, Daryl Gallagher, Roger Kemelfield, Kevin Newton, Cliff Restarick and Chris Wilson.

(MBRA/CSIR/Lloyd pp487-450)

plan to build 20 apartments and a new ski lodge for Yurredla. The plan was approved, but the developer pulled out; however the club saw the need to redevelop and provide upgraded facilities for members and the plan was hatched to construct a three-storey building consisting of four ski club lodges, with Yurredla occupying one lodge and the remaining three to be sold to interested ski clubs.

The four clubs – Yurredla, Pol-Ski, Star Alpine and Eltham took possession of the new building in June 1979. The project was recognised as one of the most successful ski-club redevelopments in Australia, with the number of beds increasing from 16 in the old Yurredla lodge to 119 in the four new lodges. With 29 family memberships, Yurredla continues to be family-orientated, with further generations – in some cases the fourth – using the club facilities and taking over its management.

Yurredla in close to original form (above) in a painting by RW 'Bill' Rowed, based on an image of the lodge in the heavy winter of 1964. Oil on canvas. YURREDLA

Yurredla (right) with a fresh cover of snow on a sunny winter morning in 2007. MARK ASHKANASY

In 1958, the club was granted a permit to build a tow on Federation Run. However, during the 1958-59 summer, the club gave its support to and participated in the foundation of Ski Lifts Mt Buller (later known as Orange Lifts) and gave that entitlement to Orange Lifts. Seven club members became Orange Lifts guarantors and Yurredla's Bill Roberts was appointed a company director.

The relationship with Federation endured. When members arrived at Mt Buller for the Queen's Birthday weekend in 1964, a downcast Hans Grimus, then Orange Lifts' manager, informed them that he couldn't operate the Federation T-bar as the early snowfalls had buried part of its cable. Yurredla members and others on the mountain volunteered to help dig out the cable, a job that took two days.

As Bill Roberts was delicately removing the final shovelful of snow, there was an almighty jerk and the shovel was flung five metres in the air as the cable was suddenly released. A loud cheer broke out as it was realised the tow would operate the next day (in 1994, in recognition of Yurredla's initial rights to build a ski tow on the Federation slopes, the Mt Buller Committee of Management agreed to name one of the runs on Federation 'Yurredla').

In 1972 the club was approached by a Sydney developer with a

The club, with 24 beds in five bedrooms with ensuites has a full-time lodge manager during winter and a club liquor licence. All requirements for breakfast and a range of condiments are provided. At the Club's fiftieth anniversary in June 1999, Peter Dyson, who had been president for 40 of the club's 50 years, resigned and John Goetz took over the role. In 2003, Goetz handed the reins to Kaye Dyson, who was still president in 2007.

Peter Dyson was made a life member in 1999 and in 2002, David Ferguson became a life member for his contribution as treasurer and for leading the club's building maintenance activities. In accepting the position as chairman of the Mt Buller and Mt Stirling resort management board in 2004, John Dyson continued the club's involvement in community affairs.

In September 2006, Peter Dyson reached a milestone when he skied on Mt Buller for the sixtieth consecutive year.

17 Community

Mountain communities expand and contract according to the seasons, so the idea of a community itself becomes elusive. Many who regularly work winters on a mountain still feel part of its permanent community, even if they don't have a permanent presence. Long-term visitors often feel the same connection.

DESPITE THE ALTITUDE and the seasonal population shifts, people's needs in a mountain community are not unlike people's needs anywhere else. The problems, collisions and challenges of life don't really change above the snowline, even if the intensity of the season exacerbates them.

Nevertheless, there is a sharper sense of humour. Mt Buller ski patroller Terry 'Speaky' Lyons gave Tony Kerin the nickname and it suited the name tag in a mountain village: 'Father Tony Kerin, Sky Patrol'.

Tony Kerin, a Catholic priest, was working and studying in the Tribunal Office at the Archdiocese in Melbourne in 1992 when the Vicar General, Bishop Hilton Deakin, contacted him to say a Catholic chaplain was required for the new chapel at Mt Buller. The Vicar General mentioned it to Fr Tony because he knew he'd done a lot of skiing in the Italian Alps while he was studying in Rome.

'I volunteered to take the role of Catholic chaplain there. I was there for the opening [of the chapel] and that was where I first met Sandie Jeffcoat, the CEO of the resort at the time, and we started to make plans to develop the life of the chapel within the village. 'Initially it involved a weekend service for the Anglican, Catholic and Uniting church communities during the ski season. I took the opportunity to take a Saturday evening service at the chapel. 'Prior to this, mass had been celebrated from time to time at Our Lady of the Snows [OLOS]. But then, with the opening of the chapel, we started celebrating Saturday night mass at 6.30 on the weekends of the ski season.

Growing up at Koflers Hutte – Ben (left) and Toby Fleming in their front yard in 1986. Ben Fleming died as a result of a car accident in 1998, a memorial snow gauge – Mt Buller's official snow gauge – commemorates the 'place he played as a child and where, on skis and snowboard he developed his love for these mountains.' BILL BACHMAN

'My parents had moved to Mansfield in 1992 so I was able to catch up with them during the visits up there and back each weekend and so it was quite useful for me in those early years of the chaplaincy.' He started to develop a rapport with the resort management, ski school and lift company staff and the various commercial operators. Weddings and baptisms were celebrated and Fr Tony introduced masses for Christmas and Easter 'and we had various other celebrations – whenever there was a long weekend or when there were likely to be lots of people around,' he said.

In his pastoral role, he found the problems of the Mt Buller community were 'the same problems that people have everywhere,' although there was perhaps a release in the remote location.

'People would come and have a chat because they didn't know you and you didn't know them. They were going home so it wasn't like I was going to keep bothering them.

'The staff problems were a little bit different in that, depending on how experienced they were, a lot of them got cabin fever – you know, the first four or five weeks of working at a snow resort is full-on and you're either working, skiing or snowboarding or drinking, and you can only keep that up for so long.

'After a while, the lack of privacy, the cramped conditions, the cold, the drain on their physical health and the partying lifestyle could lead to a bit of depression. Some of the seasons were particularly difficult where staff lived in fear of being laid off because of lack of snow – the 1993 season was particularly distressing – but there were other seasons that were fairly light on. Even a bumper season is very tiring because you're working flat out.

'But as the snowmaking developed on the mountain, the guarantee of there actually being skiing was increased significantly and so was the job security,' Fr Tony said.

Another characteristic peculiar to a mountain community lies in the semi-nomadic nature of its winter inhabitants. Some are from other lands and some Australians are a long way from their home base.

'You know, to have them lose a friend or lose a parent to death, where do they go to? Where's the quiet spot in a ski resort to find some peace and say a prayer? The chapel provided that; it gave the opportunity for these people to find a bit of refuge.'

For 10 years, his role at Mt Buller gave Tony Kerin a delightful routine. 'It kept me sane. I'd get in the car Friday night and the further I got from Melbourne, the more relaxed I became. It was quite

The Grollo family at the 1995 unveiling of a memorial to commemorate 'the 50th anniversary of the end of World War II and the beginning of peace.' Monica (left), Lorenz, Mark, Lara, Diana and Rino Grollo. GROLLO

a refreshing thing to sort of amble up the highway on Friday night and have dinner with my parents and then go up to the mountain.

'Saturday morning was mostly an opportunity to get out and ski and get around and say hello to people and catch the first lifts. On Saturday afternoon, I used to go back after lunch and just catch up, walk around and say hello to various people and catch up with various appointments and people who wanted to see me, have a chat and that sort of thing.

'Then I used to say mass at 6.30 and then pop out for dinner somewhere, often with the staff at the Abom. That continued until 2002 when, after 10 years in the chaplaincy, the Archbishop asked me to take a parish, which meant weekend work in Melbourne instead of Mt Buller.'

It became difficult to find a replacement. 'The few priests who don't work weekends – that is, work in offices and things – didn't have the interest in skiing or driving or the high country,' he said. 'We still have mass from time to time and we try and organise a priest to say mass during the ski season.'

The responsibilities are also spread between denominations. Richard Pennington, the Anglican lay elder, now conducts the Easter service.

'He is the chapel coordinator. He's doing a magnificent job, looking after visiting priests and clergy and showing them around and in their absence, he'll conduct the communion service.' Tony Kerin said. 'So there's still that opportunity and activity there, and Richard liaises with the lift company and the resort staff. If they want to see a chaplain he can contact me or someone else and we'll get someone to see them.'

Maybe it's the holiday atmosphere or the freedom of the outdoor environment or all that fitness and fresh air; it's probably a combination, but there's often a moral challenge in the mountains, reflected in the saying that 'in the mountains there is no sin' or 'above the snowline there is no sin.'

Tony Kerin read it like this: 'I think the origin of the saying is that if there's no one there to tell you you're doing the wrong thing you can't do the wrong thing; so they used to say if there's no chaplain there then there's no one there to admonish you.

'But I prefer the other saying from the twenty-fifth chapter of Isaiah: "On the mountain, the Lord provides".'

Mt Buller's children's ski school manager Sue George and Mansfield school teacher Geoff Walker were married at the chapel in 1997. In the wedding party are Ian McGregor-Dey (left), Cate Sullivan, Geoff Walker, Sue George, John Fry and Cathi Richardson with Jessica Richardson at the front. BRYCE DUNKLEY

Mt Buller Alpine Chapel

The idea of a place of worship had long been discussed at Mt Buller. To some extent, OLOS (Our Lady of the Snows) Ski Club fulfilled the need, offering a venue for Catholic Mass during winter. But a dedicated ecumenical venue was seen as giving the community a tangible foundation for its spiritual needs, a place for soul-searching.

Funding came from a range of sources, including the Grollo family, and the labour was performed by members of the Alpini, former members or associates of the elite corps of Italian mountain troops living in Australia.

It was opened on Saturday, 1 May 1993, in a fetching ceremony that brought together Melbourne's then Catholic Archbishop Frank Little, the Very Reverend DW McMonigle, the Anglican Dean of rural Wangaratta, Father Tony Kerin and the Reverend John Billington, the former Moderator of the Uniting Church of Victoria. The congregation comprised 3000 Alpini, friends and supporters from all over Australia. The first Mass, dedicated to the memory of Emma Grollo and all mothers, was sung in Italian. The Italian feel of the church is evident in its illumination at night; lines of light tracing the outlines of the building provide a striking silhouette visible from all around the township. The bell-tower of a church is a key element of the Italian townscape. (Pascoe, pp132-3)

A newspaper report at the time noted that members of the Alpini Association had spent 'every weekend for 20 months travelling the three hours from their Melbourne homes to build the church.'

The Alpini Association's Gaetano Tomada said: 'Mt Buller did not have a church. Every place needs a church so we decided to build one.' (*The Age*, June 12, 1993)

The building fits the description of a cosy chapel. 'It also has excellent acoustics,' Ed Adamson said, 'something picked up by musical directors in the summer schools of music held annually at Mt Buller. Invitees from the mountain and Mansfield district flock to hear the summer school finale recitals of orchestral and chamber music there. The sound is magical,' he said.

The Crema family donated and built the chapel's bell tower. The bell was donated by the Fleming, Grimus and Vassilopoulos families. Pictured here are Gilberto 'Beppe' Crema (centre), and Father Giuliano Cavarzan. GROLLO

Father Tony Kerin (right) with members of the Alpini at the opening of the chapel. GROLLO

The Mt Buller Alpine Chapel. MARK ASHKANASY

ONE ANCHOR FOR a community is its school; if it at least has a primary school, then a community can claim some permanency. As the Mt Buller village grew, so did the demand for a primary school. It meant the people building the village could remain on the mountain, it would also mean the children of seasonal workers could continue their education during winter.

The first formal school was a private school registered for correspondence, housed in Grey Rocks, adjacent to Kooroora, then the residence of Judy and Ernest Forras.

The first official government school, Mt Buller Primary School

Gina Forras (top left) age 5, gives her brother Peter, 18 months, a lift to pre-school at Grey Rocks in 1965. AUREL FORRAS

School sports in 1968 (above). Marika Forras (left) Susie Forras, Emma Smith, Tracey Duff, Ken Duff, Helen Williams (nee Headen – the teacher) and Niki Duff. FORRAS/SUN

In 1986 (below), Mt Buller and Merrijig primary school students came together to learn snow survival skills and how to build an igloo. BILL BACHMAN

In the snows of Mt. Buller, toboggans and skis have taken the place of the school bus

SCHOOL'S IN!

By DEBORAH GARLAND

In a 1965 photo shoot for *Women's Day* magazine (left), Tracey Duff (at right) gives her sister Niki a tow on a toboggan. Inside the Grey Rocks pre-school, teacher Robyn Williams has Niki Duff on her knee and watches over Sally Steiner and Tracey Duff (at right). The Duff and Steiner families were ski hire and retailing pioneers on the mountain. JACK LAWRENCE/*WOMEN'S DAY*

No 4959, opened on July 19, 1966. Classes were held in a variety of locations, the first of them in a small room at the Forras brothers' Bull Run Canteen. The teacher was Miss J Nelson and there were seven children from beginners to grade five.

In 1967 and 1968, the school opened year-round. In summer, the venue was the Abom Restaurant, downstairs at a big round table. In winter it moved to Bill Duff's Ski Hire, in the lounge room of

At school in 1968 are Emma Smith (front left), Ken Hedin, Marika Forras, Helen Williams, Susie Forras, Niki Duff and Tracey Duff. FORRAS/SUN

The class of 1990 line up with ski heroes Steven Lee (centre left) and Glen Plake. MARK ASHKANASY

the flat attached to the ski hire. The records show Helen Headen was one of the teachers and the students were Niki and Tracey Duff, Susie, Marika, Gina and Peter Forras (Kooroora), Emma and Barney Smith (Abom), Johnny Weichman (Koflers), Kenny Hedin and Tony Aslangul.

Helen Headen recalled the children swimming in summer at the Kooroora outdoor pool. Their favourite movie was *Mary Poppins* and the children held a concert at Kooroora attended by everyone on the mountain, right down to the lift operators.

In 1969, the Victorian Department of Education erected a 20 feet by 20 feet (six metres by six metres) insulated portable school building near the Post Office, behind the old Auski Ski Hire. This was later moved to a site near Enzian on Chamois Close. The primary school moved to the La Trobe University building when it was built and the school building became a police station.

The primary school is now operated as an annexe of the Mansfield Primary School.

Sue Roberts and her partner Andy 'Spook' Kelly put their two children, Emma and Jason through the Mt Buller primary school, giving them the unique experience of attending school above the snowline. Roberts has seen her children go to school 'on skis, on a Polaris (four-wheel motorbike), even on a fire truck. They ski for sport and on sport days they'll do their lessons in the morning and then go skiing,' she said.

The class of 2005. In the back row are Jack Clark (right), Matthew Anthony, Jasper Pluim, Matthew Laidlaw, Angus Pennington, Harrison Coull, Jasper de Campo, Adam Douros, Isabel Hennessy, Pip Sparrow, Grace Woodsford, Brooke Brockhoff, Hope Dyson and Adele Livingston. In the front and middle rows are Ginny McLaren (teacher, at left), Jules Lock, Jason Kelly, Jakara Anthony, Lloyd Miller, Angus Cronin-Guss, Ted Wyles, Bella MacDonald, Louise Pennington, Chandra Temple, Yolanda Fulton-Richmond, Ben Tyler, Ally Laidlaw, Annabel Dyson, Sydney Shearman, Belle Brockhoff, Lily Mattern, Hannah Lock and Janis Jago (teacher, at right). Absent on the day were Chloe Balfe and Eliza and George Honan. FUN PHOTOS

Moving to the university building has transformed the school – it has two rooms within that building and facilities such as the sports hall available to it. The evidence is in the numbers; in 1998, there were 16 children enrolled in the school, in 2007, there were 40.

WHILE WINTER IS still the highlight in terms of population, establishing a significant year-round population has been a long-term quest at Mt Buller.

A strong year-round population generates social and economic momentum. It's a numbers game; people like to be places where other people are to be found.

There is potential for incremental growth, particularly as year-round tourism grows alongside an interest in nature-based tourism and summer activities such as mountain biking, but sometimes there is scope for a bold initiative.

In an informal survey late in 1993, Dr Dino Ruzzene, a pioneer of the Mt Buller La Trobe University project, found there were around 22 people living year-round on the mountain. 'In 2000, we did another survey and it was more like 500 people,' he said.

Although it left the mountain in 2006, the university was crucial in that population growth.

Mt Buller's main businesses, in particular its lift company, had an ongoing requirement for staff training. At various times it ran its

and so there was certainly a climate I think for a lot of things to happen,' Ruzzene said.

The beginnings at Mt Buller were relatively humble, with a small computer centre, office and classroom on the old Summit Road near the Abom.

'There were a number of agendas behind the whole thing; one was obviously to provide training to the lift company and others, and the other was to create a community … if you've got teachers and you've got students, you're moving towards establishing some sort of community,' Ruzzene said.

The AAI started to fulfil the training needs of the lift company and also ran courses in areas as diverse as altitude training for sport, massage and yoga, high country tennis coaching, wine appreciation, alpine photography and ecotourism and a program in Aboriginal culture. (Pascoe, p135)

In late 1994, Ruzzene and the Grollos convinced La Trobe University of the merit in becoming involved with Mt Buller's AAI and this led to an 'affiliation agreement' in April 1995.

own programs and sometimes with others. In the early 1980s, for example, it worked with the Wangaratta College of Technical and Further Education (TAFE).

When they took over total control of the lift company in 1993, Diana and Rino Grollo recognised an opportunity within the challenge of training. They approached Diana's brother, Dino Ruzzene, who at the time specialised in developing TAFE curriculum.

'Initially we looked at three broad fields of study – engineering as it related to the lift company; sport and recreation, including skiing; and hospitality and tourism,' Dino Ruzzene said.

With some seed funding from the Grollos, a research unit was set up within Broadmeadows College of TAFE and Ruzzene and his two staff researched the needs and the opportunities, surveying people on the mountain and scrutinising courses offered by other institutions.

The next step was the registration of the Australian Alpine Institute (AAI) as a private education provider in 1994.

'We had the Kennett government in and it was on about setting up partnerships with the private sector and looking at new ways of doing things … there was a move towards deregulating education

The La Trobe University campus building – a radical experiment in education which, for a time, was an outstanding success. The university has withdrawn but part of its legacy is a facility with many users and much potential. MARK ASHKANASY

'We weren't too sure what it meant, but out of that a very small committee got the task of adding some substance to the affiliation,' Ruzzene said.

That substance grew from a 'wish list' of the kind of facility needed that would include a college block with classrooms, computer centre and auditorium and a sports centre.

'The idea was that the sports centre would satisfy the needs of the lift company and that would include a cinema and the college block would satisfy the needs of the university.'

The connections between La Trobe and Mt Buller strengthened. In 1995, Rino and Diana Grollo endowed a professorial chair in hospitality and tourism at La Trobe University. Its inaugural incumbent was Professor Peter Murphy. (Pascoe, p136)

The Australian Alpine Institute became the Mt Buller campus of

La Trobe University with the opening of its new building on the Summit Road in June 1997. The unique building was designed by architect Peter Parry-Fielder, who has extensive alpine experience. As the founding director of the Australian Alpine Institute, Dino Ruzzene became a director of the new campus, which initially was owned jointly by the Grollos and the university in a 50/50 partnership.

In the late 1990s, Australian universities matched major corporations for their pursuit of mergers and acquisitions, expanding their activities regionally, nationally and internationally.

In this climate, in 1998, La Trobe University took over the AAI; the building that housed it was still owned by one of the Grollos' companies but in 2000, the university bought the Grollos out and took over full control of all programs.

'By then, we had two degree programs running and they were delivered through the school of tourism and hospitality. In 2000, I was transferred down to La Trobe Bundoora, and the idea was that I would go to expand our programs offshore and they appointed a new academic head to run the campus,' Ruzzene said.

Even though the regional campus concept was generally well accepted, the remote mountain location meant the challenges remained.

'In our country we don't establish educational institutions on top of the mountain or away from a population base … it's supposed to have a catchment and you've got to have the demand and respond to that demand. This project covered new ground in as much as we went the other way; the idea was to create a

At the opening of La Trobe University's Mt Buller campus, university vice chancellor Michael Osborne (left) Diana and Rino Grollo. RMB

Mt Buller education pioneer, Dr Dino Ruzzene (above left). RUZZENE

population, put an institution up there to create a population,' Ruzzene said.

Despite the success of the project at many levels, including the development of courses in eco-tourism, hospitality and environmental studies, it proved too great a drain on La Trobe's resources, particularly when the era of academic expansion was followed by a period of constrained spending and new government policy directions.

In 2006, tertiary courses ceased, the university withdrew from the mountain and the Resort Management Board (RMB) agreed to buy the building. How it is used remains to be seen, but it is a remarkable physical asset for the mountain. The RMB will pay in excess of $3 million for the building but Dino Ruzzene estimates the 'cultural loss to Mt Buller and the region will be well over $20 million; it is a great opportunity lost to the local economy,' he said.

Hello possums

ONE BENEFIT OF a university presence is in the fruits of its research. In 1996, Dean Heinze, a post graduate doctoral student at the La Trobe University Campus in Wodonga was sponsored to do some research work through the Australian Alpine Institute (AAI), including crucial discovery work on Mt Buller's mountain pygmy possum (*Burramys parvus*) population.

'His research expanded to include work at Hotham and Falls Creek and I think he also went across to Kosciusko as well … we sponsored him and he was also on our teaching staff for five years up there,' Dino Ruzzene said.

Around the same time, an environmental studies course was established at the AAI, specific to alpine ecosystems. This involved the establishment of a specialist alpine nursery and environmental studies unit at Mirimbah under lecturer and alpine plant specialist, Rob Hall. (See chapter 18 for more on the mountain pygmy possum)

As part of the Australian Alpine Institute program, Dean Heinze was sponsored in some ground-breaking research into the mountain pygmy possum. LA TROBE

IN ADDITION TO the tertiary program, Dino Ruzzene and Diana Grollo were involved in the establishment of secondary schooling on the mountain.

'That created the opportunity for a number of families to actually live up on Buller, certainly for winter, and most of those people ended up buying apartments,' Ruzzene said. 'So that program was instrumental in assisting the property development boom that Buller has experienced since the mid-1990s. From a business perspective in terms of creating something and creating a building boom, it's been very, very good.'

With the university campus building as its base, the Mt Buller Secondary Education Program (MBSEP) runs for 12 weeks, starting in early July, consuming all the normal term three and ending in late September. It takes around 50 students in years six to 10, most of them from Melbourne private schools, with the home school and MBSEP co-operating in the development of an education program for students.

A typical day for students involves training with the Mt Buller Race Club in the morning, usually starting at 8.30am (but some mornings they start at sunrise) and going to around 11.45am. They break for lunch and then school is from 1pm to 5pm. Some may then do dry land training in the gym after school.

As well as an academic staff of 11 teachers, the program co-ordinator Richard Smith uses the mountain's ski school as a source for native-speakers for conversation sessions – 'it's an excellent multi-cultural base,' he said. As much as this environment gives opportunities for children to appreciate their time on snow, the same goes for the teachers. 'There are four contact hours each afternoon, so a lot of the staff ski each morning and ski on their days off,' Smith said.

The gymnasium facilities inside the former university campus building are used by the public, by the various primary and secondary schools housed within the building and by athletes. NATHAN RICHTER/AAI

The search for continuity in primary school programs at Melbourne schools has seen a private primary school program develop alongside the secondary program.

Schools are a significant feeder for the mountain community, with short-stay camps scheduled from schools all over Victoria and throughout Australia and some schools establishing bases on or near the mountain. The Melbourne school Haileybury has established an Alpine Academy at Mt Buller, and nearby, the Princes Hill Secondary College from its base at Mirimbah, Geelong Grammar School from its Timbertop campus and Lauriston Girls' School from its Howqua campus also use the mountain.

National Alpine Museum of Australia

The mountains are rich in history and rich with people who cherish the historic record. A museum or hall of fame at Mt Buller was first discussed by the mountain's Summer Promotions Committee in 1998. There was further momentum following the 1999 50-year celebration of the mountain's original clubs and its first ski lift. A committee of interested people was formed and, with the support of the Mt Buller Ratepayers' Association, it lobbied for funding to begin a museum collection.

The Mt Buller Resort Management Board (RMB) granted the funding and Katie O'Brien was employed to establish the collection. The museum has its own constitution and is owned by its members and donations to it are tax-deductible. It was formally opened by local parliamentarian Graeme Stoney on October 3, 1999.

Margaret Franke-Williams took over from Katie O'Brien as museum manager in February 2001. The extent of the collection led to a name change in 2002 and the museum became the National Alpine Museum of Australia (NAMA).

It is a non-profit, membership-supported museum dedicated to the preservation and exhibition of elements from the broad spectrum of ski history for research, education and entertainment. NAMA has sponsored the publication of this book, with the considerable financial help of donors.

The collection includes historic ski equipment, clothing, film, photography and literature, with an archive used by scholars and historians across the country. Significantly for its status and potential funding, NAMA is recognised by Museum Australia.

Its operations are overseen by a committee that in 2007 had David Hume

Snow sports fashions, photography and other visual records are included in the NAMA collection, along with an extensive collection of magazines and books. MARK ASHKANASY

as its chairman and included representatives from the local area, from other mountain resorts and Genevieve Fahey, the manager of Scienceworks Museum in Melbourne and Patricia Stokes, the collection manager at the Australian Centre for the Moving Image.

'We were very fortunate to enlist Genevieve Fahey and Trish Stokes,' David Hume said. 'With them, we have had our hand held well, and were educated in the art of running a museum.'

With the transition of the university campus to the RMB and the potential expansion of that building, NAMA may get a more prominent home within it, enhancing its gallery space and enabling the establishment of an Australian Alpine Hall of Fame.

DESPITE THE UNIVERSITY'S departure, the year-round momentum remains and there are numerous examples of the community's good health. Michele Morrice, the vice-president of Mt Buller's Chamber of Commerce, runs the commercial operations of Ajax Lodge with her husband Stephen.

What they do with this club lodge shows what can be achieved. During winter, the Morrices host guests on a commercial basis with dinner, bed and breakfast packages.

As soon as the lifts shut and the snow season ends 'we have a big container in Mansfield with all our equipment in it and that comes up and we turn Ajax into a factory,' Michele Morrice said.

In that 'factory', from October to December they employ 10 local people and make 60,000 Christmas puddings under the 'Stephen's Fine Foods' label. These are not second-rate or amateur puddings; they have been voted best-on-test by metropolitan newspapers in Sydney and Melbourne and have been seen in specialist supermar-

kets as far afield as Hong Kong. Once the pudding season has passed, they take a short break and then the lodge becomes a base for the mountain's builders.

'We've opened in the last five years for the builders and we've got a huge trade, we might have 25 builders living-in and we're feeding 40 a day. We've created a really good summer business,' Michele Morrice said.

THERE ARE SOME unique gatherings for mountain staff and regular visitors outside winter, exemplified in the establishment of a curious body for a ridge-top mountain resort, the Mt Buller Yacht Club (MBYC).

According to Mark 'Woody' Woodsford, who runs real estate and photography businesses on the mountain, 'it all started when Mark Buckley, chief executive of the Vantage video conferencing business and a Mt Buller regular, visited Auckland when the America's Cup was

At a 1980 Carnival Weekend, Mark (left), Alan and Roger Adams make a fair imitation of the Marx Brothers. ADAMS

A pre-regatta meeting of the Mt Buller Yacht Club in 2007 on the banks of their cruising waters, the snowmaking dam (also known as Lake Hume). MARGOT BUCKLEY

Tim Donaldson, ski hire hand and corporate high flyer. Carnival Weekend 1985. BILL BACHMAN

In 1995, Rino Grollo made a bet that Mt Buller wouldn't get over a metre of natural snow. The mountain got more than two metres. Grollo was true to his wager and on July 30 1995, a busy Sunday, he snow-shoed across Bourke Street wearing a pair of boxer shorts donated to him by Ernest Forras. GROLLO

John Zelcer and Pam Raymond of the ski patrol make the cover of Fall Line magazine in 1977, described as a 'couple of rare birds'. NAMA/BILL BACHMAN

Roman (left) and Ivan Pacak photographed in the mid 1980s. They both skied at World Cup level for the former Czechoslovakia, coming to Mt Buller in 1985 and maintaining an unbroken connection with the mountain ever since. PACAK

Stephen and Michele Morrice in 2007. MARK ASHKANASY

Hans and Lotte Grimus with their sons Anton and Hannes at the 1992 Merrijig Rodeo. GRIMUS

Mt Buller stalwarts, Vivienne and Robert Green. IVAN PACAK

Manola Grollo, Kirstie Marshall and Lorenz Grollo at the World Cup aerials in 1999. MARK ASHKANASY

Rudy Liebzeit from Sawmill Settlement. GROLLO

Mt Buller business pioneers Joan and Bill Duff outside their ski rental shop in 1984. BILL BACHMAN

Old Mt Buller hands gather to celebrate a return visit of former ski school director Brian Maguire and his wife Elizabeth. Brian is third from left in the back and Elizabeth is directly below him. FUN PHOTOS

Ernest Forras, Sam Climi and Adam Adams on Bourke Street in 1983. ADAMS

Fireworks over Bourke Street (right) in 1995 to celebrate the start of the Interschools events. MARK ASHKANASY

John Perks, Reg Martin and Mei-Larn Whan in the late 1980s. MARK ASHKANASY

Derek Smith (left), Celia Brandl and Dr Peter Braun in 1988. MARK ASHKANASY

Jacqui Cooper serving in the supermarket in the early 1990s. Its owners, Dick and Loretta Armitage were key supporters of local athletes. TREVOR PINDER/*HERALD SUN*

being held in the city. He noticed some match racing in miniature.' The yachts were Wind Warriors, radio-controlled craft designed and built in Auckland. Buckley brought two back and it just started from there. There are about 25 of them now in the MBYC, which has one major regatta each year, at Easter, in the snowmaking dam. 'We leave the buoys in the dam all summer so people can have a sail whenever they like; sometimes Spook [Andy Kelly] and I whip up there and have a sail,' Woodsford said. Because most MBYC members are sailors, they tend to understand the rules of engagement, but Woodsford says it's 'very, very hard to get a protest over the line.'

One event that gained strength in the 1970s and 80s but has since waned was Carnival Weekend. For mountain staff, spring is a release in many ways. Longer days and brighter weather make a welcome break from the depths of a cold winter. As business eases off on the mountain, so does the workload. In the 1970s and 1980s, the spring Carnival Weekend was a highlight, for visitors as much as residents.

Its demise probably came about through a run of lean snow years in the 1990s and also the emphasis placed on the World Cup aerials and the festival atmosphere created around that event.

FIRE GALVANISES AUSTRALIAN communities, especially those that neighbour forests or farmland. A mountain village is even more exposed; in summer because of its location (fire has a distinct preference for uphill travel) but also in winter, because of the use of fire for heating and, in earlier days, for cooking.

Proof of its impact came in the demise of so many structures – Kooroora, the Arlberg House, Moose Lodge, the original Chalet at Horse Hill and the Lovicks' and Klingsporns' huts before that.

Following a fire in the YHA Lodge in 1978, which was fortunately contained, Mt Buller's Committee of Management raised the issue of fire suppression:

> Discussion was centred on the need for an improved fire fighting organisation including fire picquet membership … it was resolved that Mr [district forester, Hugh] Brown contact the Commission's Fire Protection officer to discuss the matter and again report to the Committee. (minutes, September 13, 1978, p5)

The Mt Buller Fire Picquet (picket is now the more common spelling, meaning a group of people, its origins are military: 'a small detached body of troops' according to the *Oxford Dictionary*) was formed in 1979 and until 1996, it remained under the Committee of Management/Forests Commission (FCV), although training was conducted by the Country Fire Authority (CFA). In Victoria, the basic split is that the Department of Sustainability and Environment (DSE) (and its predecessors like the FCV) is responsible for firefighting on public land and the CFA is responsible for private property.

In 1996, the brigade's status changed when the CFA took over responsibility for fire protection in the mountain village, building a fire station in the central village area.

From a community perspective the fire station is a vital emergency facility – it can be used as a command centre for firefighting or for search and rescue emergencies. But fire stations and firefighting

appliances are nothing without people to work them. Fire brigades are about people. Like most in Victoria, Mt Buller's CFA brigade has no permanent staff, all members are volunteers.

The brigade is made up of receptionists, cleaners, bar staff, teachers, ski instructors, lift operators, lodge managers – people from virtually every walk of mountain life.

A volunteer fire brigade is a reflection of the community it supports – it comprises people from the community and the community tends to rise and support it when confronted.

In terms of confrontation, wildfire is nothing new; the mountains have been burning as long as there has been lightning to strike them, even if there is debate about the intensity of those fires.

> Members of working parties to Mt Buller over [the 1949] Australia Day weekend had a warning of bushfire risks when lightning started a fire in the Howqua Valley on the Saturday afternoon. In a very short time it burnt to the top of Mt McDonald and covered a wide area. Fortunately rain extinguished it on Sunday evening before it assumed dangerous proportions. (*Schuss*, March 1949, p86)

In 1973, a Melbourne newspaper report noted:

> A huge bushfire was still raging out of control near Mt Buller late last night. The fire, burning on a two mile [3.2 kilometre] front, was less than three miles from the Mt Buller skiing resort near Mansfield … Another flank of the fire was also threatening the small township of Mirimbah, eight miles west of Mt Buller. The Mansfield district's chief forester, Mr Hugh Brown, [said] 'If we can't hold this, then we stand to lose a ski resort and 200 million super-feet of prime mountain ash.' (*Sun*, January 4, 1973)

They did hold it in 1973 and they have held fire back again since. Depending on the wind direction, people in the Mt Buller village had a phenomenal view of the 2003 fires that swept over the Snowy Mountains and Bogong High Plains and into Gippsland. It was an indicator of what would come.

When lightning struck the Australian Alps on December 1, 2006, it touched down on flint-dry, drought-baked mountains, igniting the first in a series of fires that were not declared contained until February 7, 2007.

After 69 days, the fires had burned 1,116,408 hectares of mainly public land. For many of those days, Mt Buller and surrounding towns were under threat. The King Valley was hit hard and on December 10, a fire at Tawonga Gap put the Ovens and Kiewa Valleys at risk and threatened the Falls Creek and Mt Hotham resorts. Mt Buffalo also burned.

Old hands were planning early. In light of the drought conditions, Mt Buller CFA captain, Andy 'Spook' Kelly was well into the planning process before the fires came.

He worked with David Wells from the DSE . 'He came up and we walked out the boundary and put a plan of attack together,' Kelly said. 'We went around all the places like Arlberg and said, "Are you willing to take strike teams?"'

The Mt Buller Fire Picquet in 1980. In the back row are Rob Macgregor (left), Hans Grimus, Hans Thulke, an unknown person, Hugh Brown (at back), Angus Usher, Cyril Suggate, Andy 'Spook' Kelly and Wally Morrell. In the front row are an unknown person (left), David Kirkham, John Wildschutt and Graham Potter. NAMA

The 1995 Mt Buller fire crew – shortly before it came under the Country Fire Authority. On top of the vehicle are Greg Gleich (left), Ozzie Ramp, an unknown person and Paul Richmond. Below them, holding on to the vehicle at its rear are Terry Smedley (left) and Leeroy Johnson.
At the front are Andy Stringer (left), Gabby Crehan, Paul Kelly (kneeling with axe) and Hamish Thornton.
In the middle are Steve Holland (left, standing with moustache), Rob Sparrow (obscured), John Bellchamber, an unknown person, Tim Byrne (with axe), Herb Chrystagurgl (with beard), John Bischof, Mick Werle, Les Fraser and the person at extreme right is Wayne Peters.
At the left of the snowmobile is Mick Ford and on it are Kim Henderson, Andy 'Spook' Kelly, Carolyn Renwick and Megan Knapp.
MARK ASHKANASY/NAMA

Ironically, resort management had scheduled a fire ready weekend for the village for early December 'in the wake of unseasonably dry weather'.
Spook Kelly has been Buller's CFA captain since 1980 – it is a volunteer position, but one that fits in well with his paid work on the mountain running the transport operations for Buller Ski Lifts.
The 2006 fires were anticipated but they arrived earlier than they traditionally should, even in a severe fire season.
'That lighting storm came [on December 1] so I was up spotting lightning strikes for DSE,' Kelly said.
The threat to Buller was soon apparent. By December 5, the Resort Management Board (RMB) advised that 'Fires are now approaching … people located on-mountain are advised to leave in advance of any immediate danger.
'There will be a community meeting … today [December 5] to brief residents, operators and visitors about the impending fires.'
The RMB also advised that, 'As a result of the fire situation, we have had to cancel our fire ready weekend that was to take place on the ninth and tenth of December.'
The fires first approached Mt Buller from the area around Mt Stirling.
Kelly: 'Then it came up McLaughlins Shoulder, around to the summit [and it worked its way around the mountain] to South Buller Creek, up Little Buller Spur.'

January 11, 2007 and Little Buller is ablaze with the Wombat chairlift in the foreground. The lift was run at slow speed to avoid the cable stretching in the heat, snow guns were used to wet the slopes and protect lifts and buildings. BOB BATEUP

Helicopters and crop dusters were among the appliances used to fight the 2006-07 fires. Here a helicopter fills a belly tank from the snow-making dam. MARK WOODSFORD

Some members of the Mt Buller CFA brigade in 2007. At the front is the captain, Andy 'Spook' Kelly, in the Polaris behind him are an unknown person and Drew Wilson. Standing between the appliances are Carly Reudavey (left), the brigade secretary and Katie Head, the second lieutenant. On the pumper at the back is Steve Kaiser, the first lieutenant and in the cabin are Keren Freeman and Hannes Grimus (at front). KEREN FREEMAN

Local residents Sue McDonald and Ed Adamson reconnoitred around Mirimbah on December 28 in the evening, noting the bushfires had burnt out the Mirimbah area, even burning the store signs, though the store still stood intact. The fire was still burning up the ridge along the Klingsporn track above Mirimbah.

'On the night of January 5, the west face of Buller was a pattern of fire working across the face and over the ridges towards the top of Buller,' Adamson said. 'You could see the lights of the firefighter's vehicles near the summit and around the Koflers area. Concerned Mansfield people kept a night vigil at the top of the Buttercup Road hill near Merrijig almost nightly during the weeks that the fires continued.'

Then, according to Andy Kelly, it hit Family Run. 'That was the first place it popped its head was Family Run – that's as close as it got to a ski run.' The firefighters were able to hold that fire front at that point.

'We held it back there and switched down to Little Buller, around to Federation, Bull Run and Chamois,' Kelly said.

Then two separate fires met – the one from the southern slopes and another coming in from Howqua Gap to the east of the village. 'It came in from Howqua Gap, around the back of the lodges there and we back-burned into the main front, round by the lodges, so it lessened the impact; we could control it a lot better and that worked,' Kelly said.

The combined force of CFA and DSE firefighters, Buller Ski Lifts, RMB and other staff fought the fires. Their fire prevention work was to become vital.

Back-burning took place on the northern side of the mountain and, with aerial assistance, fire retardant foam was dropped above the perimeter of the fires to create another barrier.

In alpine areas, cooler temperatures should theoretically dampen fire behaviour, but this advantage can be countered by wind and the angle of the slope on which the fires are burning.

Even so, 'the fire was doing stuff that it shouldn't have been doing,' Kelly said. 'At 10 o'clock at night she's raging where it shouldn't be. There was no actually dormant period.'

In a bizarre twist, a white Christmas marked a temporary truce in the 2006 firefight. The front page of Melbourne's *Age* newspaper marked the surprising turn in the weather with a photo of Mt Buller CFA captain Andy 'Spook' Kelly (left), firefighter Carly Reudavey and Luke Corbett from CFA headquarters. *THE AGE*/KEREN FREEMAN

The vegetation was another factor – 'Kerosene bush takes off pretty quick. It was just so unpredictable. We didn't know where it was going to come from, so we had fire plans in place so no matter where it came from, we still had something in place for it,' Kelly said.

That involved using ski field infrastructure like snowmaking equipment. Buller Ski Lifts had 40 personnel available to assist in the firefight and that included operating the snowmaking system.

In the 30 years he'd been manning Mt Buller's fire watch hut, Chris Deutscher was quoted in the CFA magazine *Brigade* as saying 'nothing came near these ones'. During his watch, the fire came perilously close to the hut as can be seen in this photo. Deutscher had a unique view of the event. 'Some of the trees are pretty enormous. Big, tall eucalypts. I was looking out at the fire one day and I saw one of them just explode high into the sky. It was like a rocket taking off'. KEREN FREEMAN

Fire crews working in the Wombat Bowl, at Thulke's Run on January 11, 2007. BOB BATEUP

'So no matter where the fire came from, we had snowmakers in that area ready to go, we just had to hit the button and that was it, she was up and running,' Kelly said.

'Personnel were also on spotting duty, on all our restaurant buildings.' At one point the fires went over the top of the Wombat quad chairlift which had been kept running to avoid heat damage to the cable. 'We had snow guns on the bottom station so it didn't burn anything there; we didn't lose any infrastructure at all. She came close to a hell of a lot of lifts but we didn't lose anything,' Kelly said.

During the firefighting campaign, the RMB became a point of contact and source of information and, along with CFA and DSE, issued regular briefings to residents and visitors and others with an interest in the mountain.

Mt Buller's CFA was supported by two CFA strike teams (up to 28 personnel in five appliances and a leader's vehicle). The CFA strike teams come and go – appliances might stay and be re-crewed every three or four days, depending on the shifts, but the local crews tend to simply keep on working. Kelly went for 55 days straight, but he ensured the Mt Buller CFA brigade swapped roles around.

'One day they might be on logistics or something like that and the next day they might be out on the fire front. We tried to split them up a bit, give as much time off as we could,' Kelly said.

As much as they receive support from nearby brigades or, in a campaign like this, those further afield, interstate or even overseas, that support is reciprocated.

Once rainfall eliminated the risk at Mt Buller in February 2007, its brigade was working on other fire problems in the Mansfield, Merrijig and Goughs Bay areas.

A SUSTAINABLE
FUTURE

Skier Nicole Lewis (above) weaves her way
through the trees under the Howqua chairlift
in 2007. MARK ASHKANASY

Mountain biker Petri Miniotas (left) takes on
the summer trails along Burnt Hut Spur in
2004. MATT DARBY

18

Environment

The quality of the environment underpins the appeal of the mountains for almost all visitors. The understanding and management of that environment have changed dramatically over the decades.

THE GREAT DIVIDING Range is the mountain chain that runs all the way up the east coast of Australia. It is home to all the continent's alpine and sub-alpine terrain, the grasslands, herbfields and heathland above the tree line; the contorted, camouflage-coloured snow gum forests and the huge, ruler-straight stands of alpine ash and mountain ash.

Charlie Lovick is one of the seven generations of his family of horse and cattle people who have made the high country around Mt Buller their home. 'The Victorian part of the Great Divide is the most spectacular, the most savage. It's what's called the true divide,' he said. 'The area of Mt Howitt and Mt King Billy [King Billy No.1 and King Billy No. 2] sheds more rivers north and south than any other part of the Great Divide, it's Victoria's main watershed.

'It can be the most beautiful place on earth and, as Tom Burlinson said in that movie [*The Man From Snowy River*], the next day it's trying to kill you. It lulls you into a false sense of security. It's magnificent, beautiful, sun's out and if you look behind you, coming up

another way there's a big black cloud and there'll be snow on your back within an hour,' Lovick said. (Kenihan)

Mt Buller is a divide in itself, with Boggy Creek, Buller Creek and Chalet Creek bubbling their way into the Delatite River from one side of the ridge and on the other, Black Dog, Cow Camp, Gin, Whisky, Little Buller and South Buller creeks fall into the Howqua River. It takes its time and has some adventures in snowmaking, irrigation and town water supplies along the way, but run-off, snow melt and seepage from springs and bogs that rise from Mt Buller work its way into the Delatite and Howqua rivers, then into Lake Eildon and along the Goulburn River to meet the Murray River around about

The snow gum, *Eucalyptus pauciflora*, the gnarly, rugged survivor that grows at the highest altitudes of any Australian tree. JOHN NORRIS

Echuca. It eventually makes its way into the Southern Ocean near Goolwa, in South Australia.

On the mountain, water is pumped from Boggy Creek to reservoirs on Burnt Hut Spur and Baldy Spur, while a waste water treatment plant treats sewage (see chapter 12) and after that, treatment is discharged into Black Dog Creek.

According to independent water monitoring commissioned by the Resort Management Board (RMB), effluent has a negligible effect on the catchment (Environmental Management Plan, EMP, 2007, pp15-16). A recycling scheme has been implemented to better use Mt Buller's waste water, including supplementing supplies for snowmaking.

STANDING TALL AS it does on the western edge of the Australian Alps, with the rolling farmland of Mansfield and district to the east, and the rising or rugged peaks of the Great Divide surrounding it in virtually every other direction, Mt Buller and its massive ridgeback are a magnet for the weather.

It can sparkle in the sun one day and on another it can be a shroud of cloud. It can see snow fall gently in dry, quiet, soft flakes or it can take a wild buffeting with snow and sleet and rain flying like needles along the wind. It's an Australian mountain.

Most of the winds that bring precipitation come from the west and south-west; the average annual precipitation, including snowfall and rainfall, is 1580mm, but this varies from 1600mm in its higher

Mountain mist settles over the Klingsporn Bridle Path (left) and settles like a veil over the ranges (below) looking north from Mt Buller towards Mt Buffalo. RMB/BOB BATEUP

reaches to 1000mm at Mirimbah. The mean daily summer temperature is 11.1°C and the mean daily winter temperature is -0.6 °C. For those who know it, however, its shape is its virtue, for in virtually any weather, in any season, there is always some place for shelter. On the tail of a winter snowfall, the best skiing or boarding will unfold according to the direction of delivery, which way the wind is blowing and which way it has blown the snow in.

Much of the mountain is granite, 'formed during the Devonian period about 370 million to 400 million years ago… before about 200 to 65 million years ago, a series of massive earth movements uplifted the region to form a high plateau.

'About 30 million years ago, lava flows formed a layer of basalt, seen today as a basalt cap upon which the Mt Buller village is built.

'A long period of erosion has left the present-day landscape characterised by a high open plateau and some sharp peaks, bounded by sharp ridges and deep, sheltered valleys.' (EMP 2007, p7)

The highest point serviced by a lift is 1780 metres at the top of the Grimus chairlift, and the lowest lifted point is 1375 metres at the Chalet Creek load station on the Horse Hill chairlift. The summit, the peak known as Mt Buller, is at 1804 metres and the entry gate at Mirimbah is at 630 metres. The mountain is home to a diverse range of plants and animals – 319 indigenous plants have been identified in the forests, woodlands and shrublands of the mountain, about 196 of them above 1200 metres.

The late-flowering Mueller's snow-gentian *Chionogentias muelleriana* (above right) was named after the outstanding botanist of the 19th century, Baron von Mueller and is found in bogs in alpine grassland. *Grevillea victoriae* (right), a sub-species of the alpine grevillea is a large shrub with spectacular clusters of red flowers. RMB

AMONG ITS FAUNA are some creatures with a very delicate status in life. Probably the best known of them – despite its relatively recent discovery – is the endangered marsupial, the mountain pygmy possum *Burramys parvus*. The mountain pygmy possum is one of five species of pygmy possums to be found in Australia and the only one to live at altitude, typically between 1400 and 1780 metres in the terrain above the snow line in certain parts of Victoria and New South Wales.

About the size of a child's fist, an adult pygmy possum weighs in at around 45 grams. It lives for up to 12 years – a long life for a small mammal – and spends its winters hibernating under the snow. It eats the seeds and fruit of alpine and sub-alpine heathland, plants such as the mountain plum-pine, as well as the seasonally abundant bogong moths. The preferred habitat is that alpine and sub-alpine terrain that includes boulders and heathland, the boulders offering shelter from extreme temperatures and predators. Studies have shown that the male to female ratio of pygmy possums at Mt Buller ranges from 1:3 to 1:22. Some of them are busy boys.

'After mating has occurred, males and females use different habitat areas, with most males being found in lower elevation and less resource-rich areas than the females and young.' (Biosis, p9)

They need to move around however and make the connection between habitat areas. Man-made structures such as roads can critically inhibit that movement. One of the first attempts to rectify this was the successful 'Tunnel of Love', a tunnel that runs under the Great Alpine Road at Mt Hotham, created for the pygmy possum in the mid-1980s and upgraded in 2001. Similar connections have now been made between habitat areas at Mt Buller.

Ski patroller Andy Laidlaw (above) takes some early-morning turns in 1984, through fresh powder snow among the Village run's stands of alpine ash, *Eucalyptus delegatensis*. BILL BACHMAN

The pygmy possum was thought to be extinct, having first been recognised from fossilised remains in the late 19th century. It was probably seen since, but was never formally recognised until it was identified at the University Ski Club lodge at Mt Hotham in 1966. It wasn't recorded at Mt Buller until 1996. Its habitat at Mt Buller is now known to be in the areas on the north side of the Grimus chairlift; north, south and west of the summit in areas including Fanny's Finish and the Fast One; east of the Wombat chairlift; in the Federation and Bull Run bowls and around Chamois.

To determine the health of the species, scientists monitor the population by undertaking an annual trapping program.

In 1996, the population at Mt Buller was estimated at 300 adult females. Surveys since then have estimated a decline in the pygmy possum population to 150 in 2002 and less than 100 in 2003 and 2004. (Biosis, p10) Threats to the species include feral pests such as foxes and cats, and the impact on habitat from ski field development, although as noted in Mt Buller's Recovery Plan for the mountain pygmy possum, 'most of these impacts occurred before the presence of the species was known, and some began many decades ago.' The response has been to create a recovery program that brings

Boggy Creek (right) makes its way towards White Bridge with a healthy spring flow in 2007. MARK ASHKANASY

A curious look from the bush bulldozer (left), the common wombat *Vombatus ursinus*. TREVOR PINDER/*HERALD SUN*

together the entire mountain community, even its visitors through interpretation and awareness, and is led by the Resort Management Board, the Victorian Government's Department of Sustainability and Environment (DSE) and Buller Ski Lifts. Predator control programs are in place – such as fox baiting and feral cat eradication – and rehabilitation of vegetation and boulder habitat on Robin's Run and Outer Edge has been undertaken.

About 4000 square metres of rock have been carefully placed to create boulder connections between habitat areas, particularly in the Wombat Bowl and across Whisky Creek Trail and the Southside access track. Sediment control works have been undertaken on tracks and a vegetation management plan has been implemented. Revegetation work includes planting of species grown from seed and cuttings collected at Mt Buller and nurtured at plant nurseries off the mountain. 'We planted 9000 in 2007, we've been aiming to plant 10,000 each year since 2005,' Louise Perrin, the RMB's environmental manager, said. The restriction is in supply, because alpine plants are so difficult to propagate.

The 30-year objective of the recovery program is to ensure a self-sustaining population of the mountain pygmy possum of approximately 500 adult females. That involves ensuring habitats are connected, vegetation remains intact or is restored and human movement or impact is minimised or eliminated in fragile areas.

Further understanding is also being sought of the impact of movement over the snow above hibernating pygmy possums and the potential impact of traces of arsenic carried in from farmland by the migrating bogong moths.

FIRE IS A serious threat to the mountain pygmy possum, par-

The threatened mountain pygmy possum *Burramys parvus* (below right). Boulder fields with connecting tunnels (below) have been recreated to increase the animal's habitat and a breeding and study program has been established off-mountain at Healesville Sanctuary. RMB

ticularly given its limited habitat across the Australian Alps. The potential impact of fire was most seriously felt in 2006-07, when the Great Divide fires that burnt more than 1 million hectares of land across Victoria encircled Mt Buller.

As specified in the Recovery Plan, the mountain's Country Fire Authority brigade captain, Andy 'Spook' Kelly, along with government conservation representatives, accounted for the pygmy possum habitat in their fire pre-planning.

On the one hand, this involved affording the habitat the same level of fire protection as the mountain's structures – lodges, buildings and lifts – but on the other hand ensuring fire appliances and firefighting activities didn't in themselves have an impact. However, the scale of the fires meant some of that habitat was burnt. 'We spent three or four days walking around with DSE and the local people up here, doing our pre-planning. Some of it [the habitat] got burnt but we pretty well kept the fires off those areas,' Kelly said.

Louise Perrin said they considered themselves 'quite lucky – the fire burnt the entire south side of the hill but only about 10 per cent of the boulder field habitat.' She said the DSE had described it as 'one of the first times they've had such success in protecting the built [environment] and habitat areas.'

The reality of climate change is generally accepted but there is no consensus regarding its impact on snow cover. Any change in the quantity of snowfall and particularly the altitude of the snow line could have a critical impact on pygmy possum populations.

Off the mountain, a captive breeding population of mountain pygmy possums has been established at the Healesville Sanctuary near Melbourne with the aim of breeding additional animals to supplement the Mt Buller population.

19

Mt Stirling

Mt Stirling is well regarded for its natural attributes, its cross-country skiing, bushwalking and inspiring mountain views. It is also often thought of in the context of the development debate that surrounded it from 1977 to 1997.

THE DEVELOPMENT PROPOSALS for Mt Stirling as an alpine ski resort are sitting on the shelf – and it's a crowded shelf given the amount spent on related consultants' reports and environmental impact statements – but its popularity as a winter destination among cross-country skiers and people looking for a first-time snow experience on a toboggan has steadily grown.

Mt Stirling was named after a Victorian government geologist, James Stirling, and its early history mirrors Mt Buller's – aboriginal people visiting for food and ceremony, followed by various waves of stockmen, miners, foresters and eventually tourists.

The first structures on the mountain were the Razorback Hut near King Saddle, built by the Purcell family as a base to manage the cattle grazing on their lease, and the Geelong Grammar School Hut, built in 1965 below the summit as a base for the school's outdoor activities.

The Bluff Spur Memorial Hut was built in 1986 as a further shelter – its construction followed the death of two young tourers – Xavier Clemann and Robert Harris – who became lost on the mountain in August 1985 and died of hypothermia.

In the tradition of the mountains, these huts remain open as shelters for bushwalkers and ski tourers.

Craig's Hut, at nearby Clear Hills, was first built as part of the film set for *The Man From Snowy River* movies. It became a major draw card for horseback and 4WD excursions, bringing people up the Stirling Road and through King Saddle. It was destroyed in the 2006 fires, but has been rebuilt.

AMONG THE FIRST skiers on Mt Stirling were adventurers from Mt Buller – a 1940 brochure from the Mt Buller Chalet described the 'excursion to Mount Stirling' as a 'strenuous but interesting day-trip for the cross-country ski-ers or those who wish to go further afield.' (NAMA)

Significant growth in its popularity as a destination for cross-country skiers and ski tourers came in the late 1970s.

A landmark was the 1977 formation of the Mansfield Nordic Ski Club, which turned logging trails into cross-country ski trails and blazed some new ones of their own.

Telephone Box Junction became the focal point or launching point for skiers, but without snow-clearing on the road, the reality was that they would simply drive to the snow line and ski away from that point.

A ranger was appointed to help manage the area in 1982 and also collect stream flow and snow depth data to better understand the mountain and its potential.

Like the mountain itself, Mt Stirling's ski patrol has been variously independent of and aligned with Mt Buller.

It currently operates with one permanent patroller and back-up 'from a very enthusiastic group of volunteers, locals and people from Shepparton and Melbourne,' Barb Jones said.

Barb and Craig Jones are Mt Stirling's enduring commercial operators. In 1985, they took over the mountain's small ski hire and have built Stirling Experience into a ski hire, ski school and bistro business for winter, along with year-round outdoor education and corporate team-leading programs.

'The way Stirling is at the moment is that it's a great complement to the hustle and bustle of Mt Buller … it's a good contrast,' Jones said.

'The mountain probably has enough [cross-country] trails now to satisfy the people who are coming there.'

The expense of downhill skiing also works in Stirling's favour: 'Downhill skiing is a seriously expensive weekend excursion for a family,' Jones said, 'but at Mt Stirling [in 2007] you can still have hire and lessons and transport up the mountain for under $200 for a family.

A school group has its introduction to the snow, and to cross-country skiing, on Mt Stirling in 2004. ANDREW DEAL

Looking east over Mt Stirling, 1747 metres, with Stanleys Bowl to the left, in winter 2003. Mt Buller, 1804 metres, and its northern slopes are in the background. MARK ASHKANASY

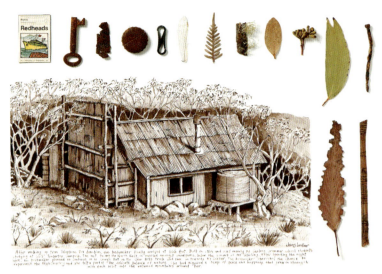

Michael Stapleton telemarking on Mt Stirling's western slopes in spring 2007. The mountain's extensive cross-country trail network winds through the trees on old logging tracks and up above the treeline towards the summit. JEFF PLANT

The Geelong Grammar School Hut as seen by Jenny Laidlaw (see chapter 14). The hut is about 500m below the summit of Mt Stirling. This is a 2006 mixed media drawing of pen and ink on paper, with found objects, 27.7cm x 39.7cm. PRIVATE COLLECTION

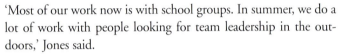

'Most of our work now is with school groups. In summer, we do a lot of work with people looking for team leadership in the outdoors,' Jones said.

Mt Stirling has been formally linked with the Mt Buller Resort Management Board since 2004.

'There's a lot of potential for Stirling,' Jones said, 'as a year-round resort for hiking and with huts for people to stay in and improved facilities higher up.

'The view from the top of Mt Stirling is absolutely fantastic; one of the few summits with 360-degree views. It's a matter of being open-minded about where Stirling can go, it could be a leader in green tourism.'

A related issue is what happens to the road – the physical connection with Mt Buller.

A link road with Mt Buller, probably going past Corn Hill to Howqua Gap, could benefit both mountains.

'One of the problems Buller faces is that, under risk management, they don't have an exit road. When the landslide closed the road in 1986 [see chapter 11], there was no traffic in or out of the mountain. They need to find a way to have an exit should an emergency occur,' Jones said.

MT BULLER'S NEAREST neighbour has a slightly lower summit – 1747 metres for Mt Stirling compared with 1804 metres for Mt Buller. Stirling has less skiable terrain overall, but some of its best runs, in Stanleys Bowl, have the same southerly aspect that enhances snow retention in bowls like Federation and Bull Run at Mt Buller.

The formation of the Mansfield Nordic Ski Club in 1977 was a landmark in terms of opportunities for cross-country skiers on Mt Stirling. Another significant event in that year was the release of the report of the State Government's Land Conservation Council (LCC) into the use of Victoria's alpine areas.

One of the LCC's recommendations was that Mt Stirling be developed as a resort for downhill and cross-country skiing. The LCC's review also led to Mt Stirling's inclusion as an alpine resort when the Alpine Resorts Commission (ARC) was formed.

In 1982, the Forests Commission of Victoria (FCV), which still controlled Mt Stirling, commissioned consultants to prepare a development proposal for the mountain.

The rationale for development was the growth in snow sports at the time. The battle for Mt Stirling has been waged passionately by conservationists against developers, but the reality of the struggle is that momentum for development has directly followed growth in snow sports participation. Growth has equalled pressure to develop; a plateau or decline in growth has seen proposals shelved.

That contention aside, in 1982 the FCV's consultants came up with five development scenarios with a cross-country ski area with no accommodation at one end of the scale and a full-service alpine resort with village and lifts at the other. (Loder & Bayly Mt Stirling study, 1982, NAMA collection)

The intention was to release the proposal for public comment but the objective was to have the mountain operating as a destination for alpine skiing by winter 1985.

The establishment of the ARC did nothing to accelerate Mt Stirling's development – it engaged North American consultants Ecosign and the NSW-based MSJ Group who in 1988 released a report proposing the integrated development of Mt Buller and Mt Stirling.

The ARC said, 'Once developed, the Mt Buller/Stirling resort has the potential to be as large as the NSW resorts of Thredbo and Perisher combined.'

The options for access included a six-passenger gondola from the Delatite Valley (near Mirimbah) along with improved roads.

'After due consideration, a village on Mt Stirling is seen as having considerable merit since it would help offset infrastructure costs and assist in mid-week utilisation,' the ARC said. (Mt Buller/Stirling Development Plan Study, ARC 1988, NAMA collection).

In 1989, the then tourism minister, Steve Crabb, announced plans for a 5000-bed alpine village at River Spur, below Mt Stirling, and the development of the twin Mt Buller/Mt Stirling resorts. The proposal would have involved enormous infrastructure costs.

It coincided with the Grollo family's growing involvement in the area. 'Steve Crabb came to me and offered us Mt Stirling. He said we could have it for nothing if we would take it over and develop it. 'I said; "No it was too hard, we couldn't afford to do it",' Rino Grollo said.

The review and debate continued, along with the government's pursuit of Rino and Diana Grollo as the prospective developers.

In 1993, a locally based group, the Mt Stirling Development Taskforce (MSDT) was formed with the aim of 'developing a viable tourism model for the mountain which could satisfy all existing users of the mountain.'

As the chief executive of the ARC, Philip Bentley recalled 'negotiating with Rino Grollo over Stirling for some time. I saw Stirling as an opportunity to get a twin-resort going, the Beaver Creek of Australia with top quality accommodation. It only needed four lifts if you put them all in the right spot.

'I went overseas early in 1994 and on my return nothing much had happened about Stirling. The minister's [Geoff Coleman, minister

A media release (right) from the Victorian tourism minister in 1989. NAMA

Summer near the summit (below); the development debate was settled with Mt Stirling's future decided as an all-season, natural destination. MATT DARBY

Bentley's reply was that the developer would be required to 'spend $20 million on roads … and other infrastructure.' (both quoted in the *Mansfield Courier*, April 6, 1994)

The Kennett government responded to the public outcry by putting the mountain's future back in the hands of consultants, this time commissioning an environmental effects statement.

After considering the EES and the public input to that process, the debate effectively ended in February 1997 when the Kennett government announced that it had 'rejected downhill skiing for Mt Stirling,' ruling it out for 'at least the next 15 years.'

MINISTER FOR TOURISM

27 April, 1989

CRABB UNVEILS CONCEPT PLANS FOR SNOW FIELDS

The Minister for Tourism, Mr. Steve Crabb today unveiled concept development plans for major Victorian ski resorts worth $650 million in 1989 dollar terms.

Under the plans, the capacity of Victorian skifields will be more than doubled over the next 10 to 15 years.

A team of Australian and world renowned North American consultants have developed the plans over the past 12 months. They cover the expansion of Mt. Buller/Mt. Stirling, Falls Creek and Mt. Hotham Alpine resorts.

"The Mt. Buller/Mt. Stirling twin resort has the potential to be as large as the New South Wales resorts of Thredbo and Perisher combined," Mr. Crabb said.

"Implementation of the plan, which comprises a new ski lifts system and a new Alpine village at River Spur accommodating 5,000 at Mt. Stirling, will require an investment of about $250 million.

for natural resources in the newly elected Kennett government] chief of staff contacted me and asked me to write out what we were going to do, what we wanted to do with Mt Stirling and it came back signed by the minister as a press release, it was word-for-word what I had written.

'He asked me to go and read it to a public meeting in Mansfield, which I did and all hell broke loose,' Bentley said.

That proposal essentially involved the ARC appointing Buller Ski Lifts to develop Mt Stirling for alpine skiing.

The response from Alan Kerr, chairman of the MSDT, was to denounce the handover of 'a whole mountain to a monopoly without any capital payment to Victoria.'

The conservation minister at the time, the late Marie Tehan, said 'Mt Stirling, as an all-season, nature-based tourism destination, would complement neighbouring Mt Buller's downhill ski fields and village attractions.' (media release, February 1997)

Although at one stage ambitious for the mountain's development, Rino Grollo has no regrets about the way it turned out.

'There is only one area [Stanleys Bowl] that would work for downhill skiing, but for cross-country skiing and for sightseeing and for snowplay and enjoying the mountain environment in summer or winter, it can work. But it needs a circuit road connecting it with Mt Buller,' Grollo said.

The future

The clues for Mt Buller's future lie in its past. Since the first skiers' visits in 1924 there has been constant evolution – interrupted by the occasional revolution – in the way the mountain has been used and understood. Bush huts and car packing cases have given way to luxury lodges; skiers who struggled with rope tows now speed up slopes in chairlifts.

MT BULLER'S VILLAGE is unique. Part of its appeal comes from the way it has grown – not always planned, not always perfect, not always perfectly planned. That kind of growth might create some problems, but it also creates depth.

'It means it's genuine, not contrived – you have to work a lot harder to create a village than a resort,' Nick Whitby said, 'a village has a community at its heart.' Whitby is the Grollo Group's chief executive for Mt Buller. He and his partner, Monica Grollo, are the new generation on the mountain, those who will guide the next phase of Mt Buller's development.

The mountain remains central, but they foresee a far broader range of facilities and services to enhance people's experience. 'Snow is critical, hence the continued development of the snowmaking system, however skiing is only a part of it, it's about the overall visitor experience, in winter and in other seasons,' Whitby said.

Within the structure of an expanded village will be more choice, more variety in cafés and bars and retailing, and leisure services such as massage and spas and health therapies. But this will come with a particular style, with an emphasis on character over quantity. 'What we're looking for is that combination of intimacy and vibrancy – more like the European mountain villages that have grown over the centuries than purpose-built resorts,' Whitby said.

Character also comes down to individuals. If a mountain village can be a masterpiece, then its brush strokes come from its characters, but how do you find the Hans Grimus or 'Kofler Bob' Fleming of the next generation? This is increasingly difficult when the pattern, in Australian mountains and around the world, is for a major enterprise – usually the lift company – to dominate, to buy-up and operate more and more of the mountain's businesses.

'You can't find these characters using a corporate model. By definition, characters are individuals or eccentrics who don't run with the pack,' Whitby said. 'We need to create opportunities for more independent operators, develop the village in such a way that it can be bite-sized for smaller operators to encourage that kind of diversity.' Coming from the head of Mt Buller's largest commercial enterprise, this comment has all the more significance.

The Village Square is one area where this opportunity arises, to enhance the character of the village and add to its range of characters. In the redevelopment of Kooroora and Cow Camp Plaza within the Village Square, the buildings themselves could include smaller tenancies and encourage new operators.

There is also a need for a signature architectural style. The Cattleman's Café area on the eastern side of the Village Square gives a sense of what might come. 'Those principles will remain, using stone and timber in an interesting way. Our quest is for an Australian alpine identity, a modern architectural style that has some traditional themes that won't date and can be applied elsewhere in the village,' Whitby said.

'The village needs to serve many different groups, we need to ensure that everyone is welcome – those who live here, those who stay for a week or those who come for the day.' That means ensuring the right facilities are available. For day visitors that includes areas for tobogganing and snowball throwing, right through to covered areas for shelter.

'These people are our future skiers and snowboarders,' Whitby said. 'The challenge with all of this is to ensure we achieve it, but at the same time make the mountain affordable for all its visitors.'

THE UNIVERSITY CAMPUS building also offers potential to broaden Mt Buller's appeal, with the building extended at street level to provide a year-round cultural centre housing the museum, a hall of fame, an art gallery and café and the shop fronts for the Resort Management Board (RMB) and Post Office.

'You have to build the momentum piece-by-piece. For us, the purchase of the La Trobe building was a bold and long-term decision that was all about increasing the appeal of Buller in winter and non-winter periods,' RMB chairman John Dyson said.

Beyond this central area, even though, with 7819 beds (as at October 2007) Mt Buller is Australia's largest mountain village, there is still potential to expand – down the Stirling Track to areas like One Tree Hill, or on the upper reaches of Bourke Street on the Fawlty Towers site with its spectacular views.

It would even be possible to revisit the site of the original Mt Buller

Looking east from the summit past Baldy in winter 2007, over Tyrol to a winter sunrise behind Mt Stirling, Mt Buller's closest neighbour and a vital component of its future. MARK WOODSFORD

Chalet around Horse Hill, building a podium over the car park as the base for an alpine village-style development.

One challenge is to contain costs, not simply to maintain the accessibility of the village, but also to encourage staff to invest, in this way underpinning a year-round population. Elsewhere in the alpine world, structures are put in place to make this possible. In some French villages, local people can buy property at affordable prices, but if they want to sell within a certain time they can only sell it back into that pool; after about 18 years their property can be sold at market rates.

In some areas of Colorado, like Aspen's Roaring Fork Valley, staff and others who meet the criteria can enter a land lottery to purchase property at affordable rates. Given its size and given the strength and diversity a permanent population gives to the character and nature of a mountain village, these could be options for Mt Buller.

THE MOUNTAIN'S FUTURE also lies in its year-round appeal. Chris Redmond, the Abom hotel manager in 2007 has been a Mt Buller visitor since the early 1960s and has worked full-time on the mountain since 1993. He knows its seasons. 'Summer is fantastic, totally under-utilised and totally under-rated. You've got a mountain with 360-degree views, a summit from which you can see probably a third of Victoria on a clear day and the most spectacular views in the Australian Alps.

'We've got four-wheel driving at our doorstep, we've got some of the best fly fishing and river fishing in the country in the Delatite and Howqua rivers, we've got bushwalking which is unsurpassed. We've got it all,' Redmond said.

Part of the stimulation for growth in summer will come from the growth of tourism in the region. When former RMB chief executive, Sandie Jeffcoat, who became the Shire of Mansfield mayor, came to the area in the early 1980s, the economy was based on timber and agriculture.

Looking into the future. Monica Grollo (left) and Nick Whitby, photographed in 2006 at the Torino Olympics. GROLLO

Riding the mountain bike trails (top), with Mt Cobbler in the distance. MARK W ASHBY

'Now the economic base is tourism. Anywhere that's within 200 kilometres of Melbourne is going to be a good tourist destination and we've got the geographical features here to attract people, it's just a magnificent outlook. The employment is in tourism now,' Jeffcoat said.

Mt Buller's relationship with the region will strengthen – the Mansfield area will continue to draw visitors who will incorporate a trip to Mt Buller in their holiday, just as Mt Buller will draw visitors through the Mansfield region. This will come through the addition of facilities and the extension of events like the Easter Art

Show or competitive road cycling and mountain biking. 'We'll have more trails for walking and mountain biking, horse riding extending over Stirling and a stronger connection between Stirling and Buller,' RMB chief executive Phil Nunn said. 'We're embarking on a significant investment in mountain biking. Along with road cycling, they're growing leisure activities. We're complementing our extreme downhill mountain bike site with touring tracks for families and other riders.'

Mountain bikers can ride virtually anywhere. The appeal of Mt Buller is in the mountain environment and the availability of the Horse Hill chairlift for summer use by mountain bikers. This is an example of keeping a facility open so the visitors come, but how do you justify staying open in the pioneering stages of this process? Who wants to be the chicken before the eggs arrive?

It's a gradual process. The RMB and Buller Ski Lifts (BSL) have worked together to establish a supermarket on the mountain that remains open year-round; this in itself was an important breakthrough. Commercial lodges like the Arlberg remain open, although John Perks says it's more to ensure the continuity of his staff than a money-making exercise.

All those empty summer beds in club and other lodges frustrate Rino Grollo, not for his own ends so much as the missed opportunity for others. Rino and Diana Grollo nurtured the Interschools program and saw it bring new skiers into the sport. Why can't the mountain offer similar scope in summer?

'We need to get these school groups up here outside winter, the accommodation is there, they should be able to use it and learn what it's like in the mountains like they do at Timbertop. Why can't we use 20 of our lodges to do that?' Rino Grollo said.

SUPPLYING FACILITIES LIKE walking and mountain biking trails enhances the experience outside winter, as do health and beauty services like Breathtaker's.

Other recreational facilities proposed over the years include a golf course, overlayed on some of the existing ski runs. In 1962, the Committee of Management was approached by a WC Lucas with a proposal for the 'construction of a golf course on the snowfield'. They agreed 'that the applicant be advised that the Committee is not unsympathetic to the construction of a golf course on Mt Buller but is not in favour of the erection of a club house in this area.' (minutes, June 1962)

There was some further research into the idea, including advice on suitable grasses from the Soil Conservation Authority, but the proposal seemed to lapse. Other facilities could include a luge run adjacent to one of the existing ski lifts, a sports oval at Tyrol Flat and a 25-metre training pool adjacent to the university campus building.

'Mt Buller, I've been told, is the perfect altitude for training. We have been allocated the status of "official Olympic training

A plan for summer recreation, including a luge course below the Horse Hill chairlift, a 25-metre swimming pool in the village and a sports oval at Tyrol Flat. ERM/BSL

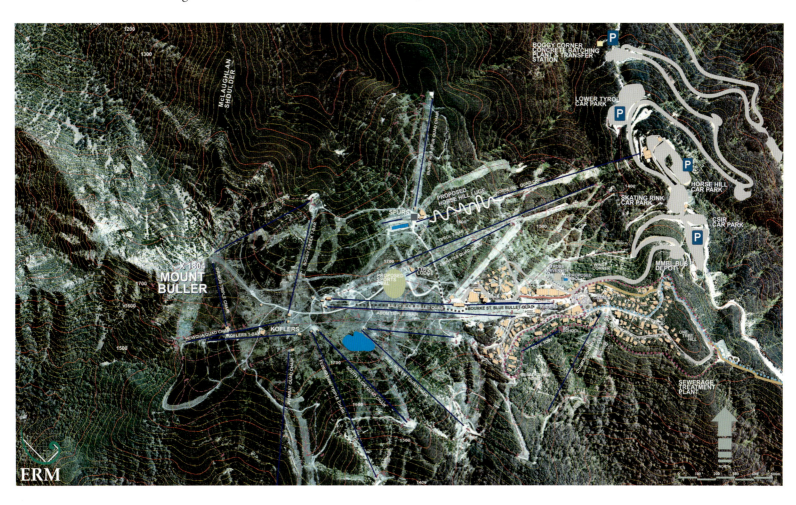

A 1954 *Schuss* magazine cartoon imagined snowmaking. Five decades on and it's a reality, even if the machine has been turned on its tail.
SCHUSS/EGON HIERZEGGER

venue" but we need to do more work on it; we need more facilities, like the swimming pool – the plans are done – you could have levels of car parking above it and the car parking could almost pay for the pool,' Rino Grollo said.

Another link in the chain would be the upgrading and sealing of the link road between Mt Stirling and Mt Buller, via Corn Hill, eventually creating a loop road connecting the two mountains. With the rebuilding of the popular Craig's Hut after it was destroyed in the 2006-07 bushfires this could be a very well used touring route.

Overall access could also change. 'I think we'll have a much more sophisticated way of getting people onto the mountain,' Phil Nunn said. One idea first contemplated in the 1970s and still on the agenda is gondola access from the Delatite Valley, possibly Pinnacle Valley or the entry gate at Mirimbah, direct to the village.

WHILE SUMMER USE will grow, winter will remain the main drawcard and Mt Buller will maintain its dominant position among Victorian mountain resorts. It is this popularity that has made it the engine room for snow sports in Victoria.

The health of all the other mountains involved with the snow sports industry and the related retail and service businesses relies on the health of Mt Buller. If Mt Buller has a good season Victoria has a good season, it's that simple. Securing the reliability of snow cover therefore has significance beyond this mountain. Snow cover is traditionally unreliable and unpredictable, characteristics brought into a sharper focus in the face of climate change.

'There's no doubt snowmaking and with that, the provision of water is going to be increasingly important,' RMB chairman John Dyson said. In Mt Buller's approach to snowmaking (see chapter 6), the RMB covers water supply and BSL operates the system. The RMB has a licence to take 700 megalitres of water from the catchment and a further 100 megalitres is available through the recycling program.

'The catch is, despite the licence, we can't always take that much from the catchment, because we have an obligation to maintain flow rates within the catchment,' BSL general manager Laurie Blampied said.

'What we're looking at is putting another 100-megalitre dam in the Boggy Creek area. You see, you want to be able to catch the water over a six-month period, store it, pump it and use it in a short period of time.

'For example, if we get a day in early July when it's -8ºC, we want to be able to produce as much snow as we possibly can, so we need the infrastructure in place to make the best use of those conditions when they occur,' Blampied said.

While it may seem a major consumer of water, snowmaking actually returns 97 per cent of water used to the catchment; there is minimal loss in evaporation. Snowmaking can help secure winter cover for committed winter sports enthusiasts, but the thousands of visitors who come to Mt Buller to throw a snowball or try tobogganing – to experience snow for the first time – also need improved facilities.

Demand in this area is already high but could accelerate if climate change impacts on lower-altitude destinations such as Mt Baw Baw and Lake Mountain with reduced snow cover. With snowmaking, a snow play and dedicated beginner skier/boarder area could be created at Horse Hill. Closer to the village centre, other sites earmarked for expanded snow play facilities are the areas either side of the university campus building.

WITH SKI LIFTS, the pattern has been established. 'It's all about consolidation,' Blampied said. 'Our current lifting capacity is about 40,000 skiers an hour and that was designed for a time when there was a substantial peak on weekends.

'Over the years, we've flattened the trends. We don't have the huge peaks on the weekends that we used to have and that's good for our lifting system and our customers.

'There are isolated issues, during periods of bad weather or in a season where poor snow cover confines skiers to particular areas, but overall, when the mountain's fully open, you have sufficient capacity, there are no capacity issues.'

An example of that consolidation is in the 2008 removal of the Abom triple chairlift and Blue Bullet 2 quad detachable chairlift and their replacement with a six-seat detachable chairlift, the first of its kind in Australia, with no sacrifice in capacity. This improves the visual amenity of Baldy, and the removal of the Blue Bullet 2 lift towers also increases the skiable terrain on what is an extremely popular beginner run, another virtue of consolidation.

'When we took out the Shaky Knees T-bar and replaced it with the Emirates Chair, it worked a treat. Basically, a third of the run was taken up by the old T-bar. It wasn't until we pulled it out that we realised how much skiing we were missing out on,' Blampied said.

'You need to start looking at replacing lifts as they get older and you can't put in drag lifts any longer; no one wants to ride them. You have a market expectation to put in chairlifts, but they cost a lot of money compared with drag lifts.'

Timing and location are in the hands of the seasons and the rev-

Photo:

"Grosse Oesterreichische Illustrierte."

The Ski-jet is reported to give a wonderful effortless trip up a steep slope. Gear can be dismantled into several pieces and stored in a rucksac for the downhill run.

Uphill by jet was a concept spruiked in *Schuss* magazine in 1953. The lack of movement in the skiers' hair or at their feet gives the game away, but lifting has been transformed nevertheless, with chairlifts providing a faster, more comfortable ride in summer or winter. *SCHUSS*/FUN PHOTOS

enue that flows from them, but BSL intends to continue with the consolidation. A lift near the front of the queue is the Grimus triple chair. 'It's too noisy at the bottom and it doesn't really have the capacity we need,' Blampied said. 'We're planning to upgrade that to a quad along the same line, potentially with a mid-station.'

Other ideas are to replace the Koflers T-bar and upgrade the Howqua chair from a fixed grip (current) to a higher capacity quad detachable chairlift. The mountain's oldest lift, the Skyline T-bar, with its expansive U-shaped towers could also be replaced by a chairlift, improving capacity and opening up more terrain.

BEYOND THE FACILITIES that have been put in place to enhance it, the quality of the mountain environment, the natural appeal of a snow-covered mountain, is the key for all the mountain's visitors. Conserving that environment is a fundamental charter for the RMB and it is increasingly influencing the mountain's business operators. As well as being an ethical imperative, it is a commercial necessity.

This is sharpened in an era of acute awareness about climate change but limited understanding of its precise impact on snow cover. There comes a need to get your own house, or mountain, in order to help in a quest that is global.

Here's the key: 'The future of tourism is in a guilt-free experience,' Nick Whitby said. 'It's critical; people don't want to feel guilty on holiday. Tourism is discretionary. You need to provide an experience that is environmentally sustainable, rather than have people feeling they're going away polluting.'

With that in mind, BSL is minimising its own impact and continually improving its environmental management systems, adopting the international sustainability standard of ISO 14,000. 'We'll be one of only about 10 ski resorts in the world and the only one in Australia to achieve that. We have to work on continually improving our environmental sustainability and reducing our carbon footprint,' Laurie Blampied said.

Looking west from Tyrol across to Baldy at left and the sunset behind the summit in 2007. MARK ASHKANASY

IN THE END, it all comes back to two things – the mountain and its people. There are those who have met there and married, whose children or grandchildren now carry the thread, who still shriek at the sight of snow or long for a summer expedition with the scent of snow gums sharp in the air, amazed at the ease of access outside winter. There are those who slip out of Melbourne on a Friday afternoon in August and cruise into their Mt Buller garage a few hours later, never having felt the sharp breath of winter air. There are those who have struggled up Mt Buller on a school trip, thrilled to silence as they spy the big, ridge-backed mountain looming larger and larger out of the distance as they close in on Mansfield.

There are those who have a social network at Mt Buller that makes a walk through the village something like an old hand's Saturday morning stroll in a country town. There are those who have uncovered the mountain for the first time and might have been soaked through for the experience but are still seduced by the environment and its sports. Mt Buller embraces all equally, provided they are willing to embrace it right back.

Others work there, some stay for a season that stays in their hearts forever, some have stuck at it for decades simply because they have found what they're looking for. All have contributed to that uncanny application of Australian ingenuity that stretches a snowflake as far as a farmer might stretch a shower of rain.

The future these people will bring to the mountain will include a more sophisticated but accessible village, rich with mountain character and mountain characters. The population profile of the village will change; as communications and work patterns evolve, and as the heat of summer inspires people to look away from the beach in that season, the mountain's more permanent population is likely to increase.

The future will see a more secure snow cover on slopes covered by a more efficient lift system. The people at the core of the mountain's operations – those who run the lifts, prepare the slopes, clear the roads, park the cars, patrol the mountain and teach the sports – will continue to innovate, to find new and better ways of applying their skills and improving the way visitors experience the mountain.

Where environmental principles permit, the mountain's winter trails will be used for other forms of recreation outside winter –

such as mountain biking, walking or altitude training for a range of sports. The mountain's year-round appeal will be enhanced by signature Mt Buller events and new facilities and people more inclined to use them. The connection between Mt Buller and Mt Stirling will strengthen through a better road link and more people exploring the two summits and the trails and rivers that run off them, in summer and in winter.

Wrapped around all of this will be an improved appreciation of the mountain environment and because that is central to people's experience at Mt Buller, it will flow through to a heightened regard for the global environment. If a consequence of climate change is reduced snow cover at lower altitude mountain resorts, this will more than likely lead to an increase in first-timers and day visitors coming to Mt Buller and these people will need more facilities on the mountain.

The comet McNaught leaves a trail over the summit in January 2007. The small tank beside the hut contains water for firefighting.
CHRIS HILTON-WOOD

But how will all this emerge? How will this future be shaped? There is a generous spirit in the mountains. It comes in part from people's need to collaborate to survive the conditions. It comes in part because the mountain environment and the sport and social contact it encourages are so enriching, people want to share it and its ways.

Mt Buller is not unique in having this spirit, but if passion for a place could be measured, then its devotees would mount a fair case that their passion runs deeper. It is this passion that will shape the future and drive all the arguments around it. And Mt Buller, as always, will be all the better for the argument.

Village timeline

This list, produced by the National Alpine Museum of Australia, is based on the records of the Mt Buller Committee of Management/Resort Management Board. The year refers to the year of approval (not construction) for the building. At right is a map of the village in 2007. The number of sites has expanded but the numbering system is unchanged from December 1948.

Year	Name	Site No	Year	Name	Site No	Year	Name	Site No
1964	ABV	55	1954	Cedar	34	1962	Heathcote Bus	116
1988	Ace of Clubs	31	1969	Cedar	92	1957	Hima	37
1982	AE Co-op/Aeski	93	N/A	Celia's Skating rink	209	1963	Holland	181
1973	Ajax	54	1994	Chalet Apts	206	1962	Hoppers	82
1956	Akla	36	1995	Chalet Hotel	207	1961	Howqua	81
1965	Alaska	63	1929	Chalet Kofler	Horse Hill	1966	Hu'ski	128
1961	Aleko	99	1949	Chamois	10	1960	ICI/Icicles	66
1965	Alkira	82	1993	Chapel	217	1957	Igloo	52
1961	Alpha	103	1955	Chetwynd	20	1963	Iltis	89
1951	Alpine Club of Victoria	17	1996	Christiana Apartments	31	1959	Inca	70
1982	Alpine Retreat	48	1961	Cobbler	185	1947	Ivor Whittaker Lodge	195
2002	Alto Villas		1964	Collegians	147	1967	Jungfrau	127
1962	Amber	102	1964	Coonamar	90	1950	Junior	Horse Hill
1963	Anjarra	82	1965	Corio	139	1953	Kandahar	199
1988	Apres	113	1959	Cortina	64	1961	Kida Hara	84
1958	Arlberg House	189	N/A	Corviglia	8	1959	Koflers Hutte	205
1966	Arlberg Lodge	190	1985	Cresta Apartments	9	1957	Koomerang	180
1965	Army	100	1966	Cristal	112	1953	Kooroora	3
1988	Army Alpine 3MD	100	1969	Crosscut	194	1965	Kooroora Flats	76
1963	Auski	117	1946	CSIR	One Tree Hill	2000	La Grangette	181
1949	Aust Postal Institute	13	1985	CSIR	138	1997	La Trobe Uni	225
1950	Aust Women's Ski Club	1	1964	Currawong	80	1964	Lantern	97
1966	Australian Alpine Club	30	1950	Dandenong	22	1950	Lazy 8	12
1965	Avalanche	141	1962	Delatite	88	1961	Macura	101
1979	Avenue 17 The	19	1964	Discobolus	104	1963	Maganni	59
1961	Bayerland	98	1956	Double B	39	2002	Malamute	129
1973	Beehive Apartments	198	1961	Down Hill Only	100	1964	Mansfield	145
1951	Belmore	24	1964	Downhill	137	1961	Mark II	78
1961	Benalla	74	1989	Downhill	262	1996	Mark II Apts	78
1952	Benmore	29	1992	Duck Inn	97	1957	Matterhorn	54
1993	Black Forest Lodge	219	1961	Duff's Ski Hire	108	1953	Mawson	18
1955	Black Tulip	40	1956	Edelweiss	33	1984	Medical Centre	196
1962	Blitz	89	1955	Elk	27	1964	Meki	144
1961	Blizzard	93	1997	Elkhorn Apts	71	1951	Melb Walking Club	8
1961	Blue Eyes	95	1979	Eltham	19	1978	Merrijig	131
1969	Bluff Lodge	197	1961	Enzian	69	1971	Mitre	148
1998	Bluff View Apartments	60	1961	Etna	87	1982	Molony's	115
1951	BMW	25	1996	Fire Station	223	1964	Monash Uni	84
1956	Bombora	38	1964	Firmow	50	1951	Monsanto	6
2000	Bombora Apartments	38	1952	Firn	23	1949	Moose	14
1961	Bracken	85	1961	Four Winds	91	1950	Morgan Pattern	21
2000	Brackenwood	85	1962	Geebung	119	1994	Mt Buller Chalet Hotel	207
1982	Breathtaker	152	1954	Geelong	26.1	1963	Mt Buller	
1961	Brighton	102	1964	Glacier	142		Home Units	111 + 112
1952	Bull Run Canteen		1952	Gliss	32	1960	Mt Buller Lodge	67
1982	Burwood	87	1965	Gonzaga	162	1988	Mt Buller Ski Lodge	132
1961	Candoux	79	1950	Gray Rocks	5	1958	Mulligatawny	57
1956	Caribou	62	2000	Grimus Apts	224	1960	N'Everest	65
1961	Cawarra	86	1949	Harding/ MUSKI	11	1964	Neringa	120

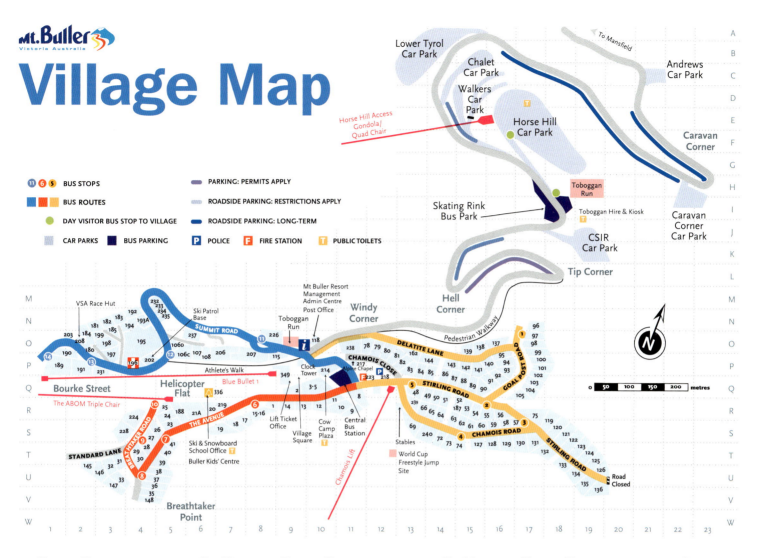

Mt.Buller
Village Map

Year	Name	Site No
1956	New Buller Lodge	67
1961	Nicholas	92
1965	Nomad	33
1988	Noorinya	113
1988	Number 96	188
1965	Nutcracker	103
1959	OGG	49
1964	Old Paradians/Opal	96
1956	OLOS	51
1949	Omega	7
1982	Omski	137
1955	Patscherkofel	30
1973	Pension Grimus	149
1961	Perpetual Snow	113
1966	Piringa	129
1961	Planica	80
1979	Polski	19
1960	Pontresina/Engadin	184
1961	Port Phillip	73
1977	Preston	133
c1972	Primary School	218
1952	Reindeer	28
1961	Ringwood	83
1961	Roos	94
1956	Royal Aust Navy	35
1961	Royal Children's Hospital	75

Year	Name	Site No
1965	Schuss	121
1982	Shaky Knees Flats	192
1965	Ski Lib	105
1983	Ski Patrol Base	202
1964	Ski View	146
1962	Smith Bros/ Abominable	106
1964	Snow Gums Flats	109
1965	Snow Gums Flats	110
1965	Snowdown	140
1973	Snowflake Apts	56
2000	Snowmass Apartments	21
1959	Sorrento	56
1952	Southern Cross	12
1959	Spark	58
1963	St Bernards	61
1961	St Christina	183
1959	St. Albans	60
1979	Star Alpine	19
1982	State School	163
1982	Summit Lodge	190
1962	Sundowner	132
1961	Tatry	72
c1962	Telemark	94
1965	Terama	101
1971	The Avenue	20
2000	The Drifters	61

Year	Name	Site No
1954	Timberline	41
1986	Timberline	41
1971	Tower Octagons	107
1954	Twenty Five	31
1971	Twin Towers	191
1949	Ullr	9
1957	Uni of Melb	15
1950	Uni of Melb Cabin	16
2000	Valley View Apts	108
1978	VSL	130
1959	Wapiti	71
1968	Wardens Office ARC	118
1996	Whistler	73
1964	White Star	143
1961	Windy Corner	114
1961	Windy Corner Store	115
1992	Winterbrook	27 .2
N/A	Winterhaven	63
1961	Wombats/Cuckoo	182
c1995	Woolybutt Apts	193
1947	YHA Skating Rink	
1964	Yokahama	148
1952	Youth Hostel Association	2
1950	Yurredla	19

Index

Bibliography & acknowledgements

Interviews/oral histories

Unless specified in the text or below, all people quoted in this book were interviewed by the author in 2005, 2006 or 2007. Adam Adams was interviewed by Janice Lloyd in 2003 (NAMA collection).

Books

Australian Alps Liaison Committee, *Cultural Heritage of the Australian Alps*, self-published, 1992.

FGA Barnard, 'Some early explorations in Victoria.' *The Victorian Naturalist*, Vol XXI-No.3, July 7, 1904.

Barbara Cameron-Smith, *Wildguide Plants & Animals of the Australian Alps*, Envirobook, 1999.

DB Caldere and DJ Goff, *Aboriginal Reserves and Missions in Victoria,* 1991, Aboriginal Lands Group, Department of Conservation and Environment.

CMH Clark, *Select Documents in Australian History, 1788-1850*, Angus and Robertson, 1950.

Alec Costin, Max Gray, Colin Totterdell, Dane Wimbush, *Kosciuszko Alpine Flora*, CSIRO/Collins, 1979 (reprinted in 2000).

Ann Crawford (compiler), *A Proud Achievement, 50 Years of YHA on Mount Buller 1947-1997*, YHA.

RM Darcy, *Beolite's Country*, Warrior Press (Mansfield), 1998.

Jim Darby, *Thredbo 50*, tSm Publishing, 2007.

Ian Dillon, *Tracks of the Morning, A Timbertop History Text*, published by Geelong Grammar School, 1989.

Ernest Forras with Jan Henderson, *Earnest Escapades*, published by Ernest Forras, 1994.

Tom Griffiths, *Forests of Ash*, Cambridge University Press, 2001.

Tim Hall with photography by Trisha Dixon, Cornstalk Publishing, *Banjo Paterson's High Country*, 1992.

RW Home, AM Lucas, Sara Maroske, DM Sinkora, JH Voigt (eds), *Regardfully Yours, Selected correspondence of Ferdinand von Mueller, Vol 1: 1840-1858*, published by Peter Lang, 1998.

Klaus Hueneke, *Kiandra to Kosciusko*, Tabletop Press, 1987.

Klaus Hueneke, *People of the Australian High Country*, Tabletop Press, 1994.

Mick Hull, *Mountain Memories*, self-published, 1990.

David Hume, *A Short History of the Orange Ski Lifting Companies*, self-published, June 2004, NAMA collection.

David Joss, *Mt Buller, a history*, published by the Alpine Resorts Commission, undated.

Peter Kabaila, *High Country Footprints,* Pirion Publishing, 2005.

John Landy, *Close to Nature*, Currey O'Neill Ross, 1985.

Janice Lloyd, *Skiing into History, 1924-1984*, Ski Club of Victoria, 1986.

Craig McGregor, photographs by Helmut Gritscher, *The High Country*, Angus & Robertson, 1967.

Ian Mansergh and Linda Broom, *The Mountain Pygmy Possum*, UNSW Press, 1994.

Mansfield Historical Society, *The Mansfield Valley, 150 Years of History*, published by the Mansfield Historical Society, 1993.

Momoko Oshita (photography), *Bernd Greber, A Legendary Snowman*, Bijutsu Shuppan-Sha, 2002.

Mudrooroo, *Aboriginal Mythology*, Thorsons Harper Collins, 1994.

Lynette Sheridan, *Shes and skis: Golden years of the Australian Women's Ski Club, 1932-1982*, 1983, SLV.

Lynette Sheridan, *University Ski Club, 1929-1979*, 1988, SLV.

Tony Sponar, *Snow in Australia? That's News To Me*, Tabletop Press, 1995.

Ian Stapleton, *From Drovers to Daisy-Pickers, Colourful Characters of the Bogongs*, self-published, 2006.

Harry Stephenson, *Skiing the High Plains*, self-published, 1982.

James Tehan, *For the Land and its People*, self-published, 1991.

Robert Upe and Jim Darby, *The Snow Guide to Australia and New Zealand*, Explore Australia, 2005.

Garnet Walch, *Victoria in 1880, with illustrations on stone and wood*. George Robertson, 1880, SLV.

Alan Wylie, *Gold in the Shire of Mansfield*, Mansfield Historical Society, 1987.

Michael Young, *The Aboriginal People of the Monaro*, NSW Department of Environment and Conservation, 2000.

Plans and reports

Mt Buller Resort Plan Final Report, Interplan, 1973.

Mt Buller Village Centre Redevelopment Plan, Alpine Resorts Commission, 1987.

Mt Buller/Stirling Alpine Resort Development Strategy, prepared by Ecosign, MSJ Group, Sinclair Knight & Partners for the Alpine Resorts Commission, 1989.

Ski Lifts Mt Buller Limited Prospectus, April 1959, Gadsden family collection.

Mt Buller Environmental Management Plan, Resort Management Board, 2007.

Andrea Murphy, Final Report, Mt Buller Ski Resort – A Preliminary Cultural Heritage Survey, (Aboriginal Affairs Victoria, Project No 1841) Tardis Enterprises, 2001.

Robert Russell, Map of Mount Buller and Surrounding District, 1846, Latrobe Library map collection, SLV.

Club histories

Akla, Geoff Brearley; Alkira, Steph Schwarz; BMW, Merrick Summers; Gliss, Ron Friedman's recollections by Karol Connors; Chamois, Sue McDonald; Coonamar, Monty Russell; Mawson, Ern Rothschild; MUSKI, Lara Grollo; OLOS, Alex Bunting; Ullr, Lara Grollo; YHA, *A Proud Achievement, 50 Years of YHA on Mount Buller 1947-1997*, compiled by Ann Crawford/YHA; Yurredla, Peter Dawson.

Internet

adbonline.anu.edu.au Australian Dictionary of Biography (ADB), entries for Hamilton Hume and Thomas Mitchell.
americanheritage.com Tom le Compte, 'Snow Biz'.
biographi.ca Dictionary of Canadian Biography Online, entry for Charles Buller.
mtbuller.com.au
skiclub.co.uk The Ski Club of Great Britain, snow sports equipment timeline.
oldsnowboards.com

Minutes

Mount Buller Alpine Resort Committee of Management (1948 to 1984), archived in the NAMA collection (referred to in the text as 'minutes').

Magazines

Australian Ski Yearbook, various editions held in the NAMA (Mt Buller) collection.
Brigade, Autumn 2007, Country Fire Authority Victoria.
Newsrail, September 1991 Mansfield Railway centennial edition, NAMA.
Schuss, various editions, NAMA.
Ski Australia, various editions, NAMA.
Ski Club of Victoria *Year Book* (which later became *Schuss* magazine), various editions, NAMA.
Ski Extra/ExtraVert magazines, 1984-2000, various editions, author's collection.
theSKImag, 2001-2007, various editions, author's collection.

Visual & audio

Barry Humphries, 'Snow Complications', *Moonee Ponds Muse*, Vol 1, Raven, 1998 (first recorded 1959).
Melissa Kenihan, *High Country Life* (five generations of the Lovick family), Front of House Studios, 2005.
The Merrijig District Bush Fires 2006/2007, Appaloosa Films, 2007.
Parks Victoria, *Dancing and the Devil Fire* (the cultural heritage of the high country), Outsider Films, 2005.

Abbreviations

ARC, Alpine Resorts Commission
BSL, Buller Ski Lifts.
EMP, Environmental Management Plan.
FCV, Forests Commission Victoria.
MHS, Mansfield Historical Society.
NAMA, National Alpine Museum of Australia.
NGA, National Gallery of Australia.
NGV, National Gallery of Victoria.
OWIA, Olympic Winter Institute of Australia.
RMB, Mt Buller Alpine Resort Management Board.
SCV, Ski Club of Victoria.
VSA, Victorian Ski Association

Abbreviations for archives and photographic collections

Adamson, Edwin Adamson collection.
Bardas, Bardas family collection.
Brockhoff, Brockhoff family collection.
Court, Court family collection.
Grollo, Grollo family collection.
Kiessling, Kiessling family collection.
Moore/Tinsley, Kit Moore and Walter Tinsley family collection.

NAMA, National Alpine Museum of Australia collection.
SLV, State Library of Victoria.
SSDF, School Snowsports Development Foundation collection.
STL, Sport The Library.
Summers, Summers family collection.

Acknowledgements

The author and photo editor express their gratitude to the following people for their assistance and cooperation:
Mark Adams, Ed Adamson, Martin Ansell, Ben Ashkanasy, Max Ashkanasy, Shai Ashkanasy, Bill Bachman, Mike Balfe, David Bardas, Sandra Bardas, Bob Bateup, Debbie Bennett, Philip Bentley, Laurie Blampied, Helen Bohren, Marnie Brennan, Andrea Broad, Alex Bunting, Eric Burt, Jimmy Camerino, Heath Chidgey, Michael Coldham, Wendy Cross, Cosmo Darby, Joanna Darby, Matt Darby, Olivia Darby, Patrick Darby, Michael David, Rolf Denler, Bruce Dowding, Chris Dunlop, John Dyson, Peter Dyson, Bob Fleming, Christine Fleming, Aurel Forras, Ernest Forras, Peter Forras, Margaret Franke-Williams, Andrew Freeman, Amber Gardner, Sue George, Margarita Gimenez, Robert Green, Ben Griffiths, Hans Grimus, Lotte Grimus, Andrew Grimwade, Erich Goetz, Diana Grollo, Lara Grollo, Lorenz Grollo, Mark Grollo, Monica Grollo, Rino Grollo, Ron Grose, Lee Healey, Stephanie Hendrickson, Geoff Henke, Egon Hierzegger, Chris Hilton-Wood, John Hilton-Wood, David Hume, John Hutchins, Trish Iezzi, Sandie Jeffcoat, Barb Jones, Andy 'Spook' Kelly, Roger Kemelfield, Tony Kerin, Jenny Laidlaw, Jean-Marc Laroque, Nicole Lewis, Geoff Lipshut, Janis Lloyd, Terry 'Speaky' Lyons, John McDonald, Sue McDonald, Sam McDougall, Peter McIntyre, Brian Maguire, Ed Mahon, Alan Marshall, Kirstie Marshall, Judy Monk, Michael Monester, Wally Morrell, Michele Morrice, Phil Nunn, Rob Osborne, Ian Parfitt, Richard Paine, Andrew Pattison, Dave Pavlich, Louise Perrin, John Perks, Rebecca Pickett-Heaps, Thor Prohaska, Lou Pullar, Bob Pullin, Hadyn Purcell, Sharon Rainsbury, Chris Redmond, Kevin Ringrose, Simon Ritchie, Sue Roberts, Sally Rodd, Paul Romagna, Dino Ruzzene, Eliana Schoulal, Stephen Schwarz, Noga Shub, Sam Shub, Brian Singer, Michael Stapleton, Cait Steiner, Graeme Stoney, Merrick Summers, Steve Thompson, Laura Waters, Eleanor Vassilopoulos, George Vassilopoulos, Anne Walters, Randy Wieman, Mei-Larn Whan, Jacqui Whitby, Nick Whitby, Mark Woodsford.

Financial support

The generosity of the following people and organisations made the publication of this book possible: Mark Adams Real Estate, Doug Akeroyd, Bruce Brockhoff, the Boag family, Louise David, Michael David, the Dyson Bequest, Peter and Cath Dyson, Ron Edwards, Alan and Barb Green, the Grollo Ruzzene Foundation, Dean Gosper, David Hume, John Law, Nathan Lyons, Terry Lyons, McCormack Timbers, Andrew Miller.

Printed in Australia by Highlight Printing, Crnr Howes Street and Rodd Road, Airport West, Victoria, 3042, Australia.

tSm Publishing
Mt Buller, The story of a mountain, was produced for the publisher, the National Alpine Museum of Australia, by tSm Publishing.
Publishers: Jim Darby, Lou Pullar
Photo editor: Mark Ashkanasy
Design and creative: Anthony Pearsall, Typographics
Copy editor: Mary Kerley
Proof reader: Marcelle Munro
tSm Publishing Pty Ltd, PO Box 631, Bright, Victoria, 3741, Australia.
Go to: www.theskimag.com

Jim Darby, author

Jim Darby's first season skiing was the legendary winter of 1964, with snow so deep it broke the lodge roof. He was hooked. His parents, Geoff and Heather Darby, kept him going to the mountains every winter and sometimes in summer. His first trip to Mt Buller to ski was in 1968, when he recalls being bewildered while riding a Poma one way (the Summit Access) only to see skiers emerge from the fog and pass him on the same lift riding the other way (Howqua). In 1972, he spent a year at Geelong Grammar School's Timbertop campus when he explored the mountains around Mt Buller and walked and skied over Mt Buller itself. After school, Jim started an arts degree at the Australian National University in Canberra. He got about halfway through and, despite invitations to study honours in history and philosophy, decided to escape the nation's capital and head for the hills. He spent five years working as a lift operator, ski patroller, mountain guide, ski instructor and summer maintenance worker, eventually returning to study and completing the arts degree but in recreation, with mountain resorts his specialisation. Jim has been editing skiing, snow sports, lifestyle and travel magazines since 1981 and currently edits *theSKImag* and *Alpine Style* magazine. He has co-authored three guide books to the Australian and New Zealand snowfields and is the author of *Thredbo 50*, a history of the Snowy Mountains resort. He also writes about skiing, travel and the mountains for Australian and international magazines and newspapers. Jim was the winner of Skiing Australia's print media awards in 1989 and 1997.

Jim is a volunteer firefighter with Victoria's Country Fire Authority and had an active part in the campaigns to fight the fires that swept through Australia's alpine regions in 2003 and 2006-07. He skis whenever he can, in Australia and elsewhere, and takes all the greater pleasure in it when joined by his family, Marnie Brennan and Olivia, Patrick, Cosmo and Joanna Darby.

Jim Darby (top), on location at the keyboard, 2007. MARK ASHKANASY

Mark Ashkanasy (left) and Jim Darby on location in the shadow of New Zealand's highest mountain, Aoraki/Mt Cook in August 1995. DARBY

Mark Ashkanasy, photo editor

Mark's first encounter with Mt Buller was early in 1975, ascending via the West Ridge accompanied by fellow students from Geelong Grammar School. His father taught him to ski, with his first turns at Mt Buffalo in 1964, so he was already proficient when he first skied Mt Buller during the winter of that 1975 Timbertop year. Every Friday, teachers and students would make their way up the road in the school's Land Rovers for skiing and sport. Mark took a camera even then to record the day's activities.

By 1979 he was shooting the ski racing at Mt Buller and developing the film in an old laundry in between shifts behind the bar at Kooroora or in the kitchen at Pension Grimus. While completing his photography degree in 1982, he moved in with the Forras family, photographing the sport, working at Koflers and producing a final year folio based on his time on the mountain. His photography really got going during the seasons of 1984 and 85, when friend and freestyle skier Geoff Lipshut asked him to shoot some sponsorship images for Tribe Gonzo. In 1986 Team Buller exploded on the scene and Mark started commercial photography full time, working as official photographer for the lift company.

He met his wife Shai through Team Buller and she has since appeared in many images promoting the team and Mt Buller. As members of Alkira Ski Club, they enjoy the winter experience skiing with their two boys Ben and Max. Within the framework of Team Buller, Mark, Geoff Lipshut and Alan Marshall developed and ran the Abom Mogul Challenge from 1987 to 1997; it is still going and remains one of the world's longest continually running mogul events. Mark was also a member of the organising committee for the World Cup aerials events at Mt Buller.

Mark's photography has led him to New Zealand, Europe and the United States and also as the Australian Olympic Committee's team photographer in Lillehammer, Nagano and Salt Lake City.

On his home mountain, Mark emphasises 'the importance of being able to ski well and understand the terrain of Mt Buller. Being in the right place at the right time is the constant challenge, but Buller is always beckoning me back.'

Mark Ashkanasy, on location at the 2002 Salt Lake City Winter Olympics. BARRY WHITE/ASHKANASY

Mark, Max, Shai and Ben Ashkanasy ride the Wombat chair, 2007. ASHKANASY

Nicole Lewis (left) and Peter McNiel disappearing into Wombat Bowl, July 2007. MARK ASHKANASY

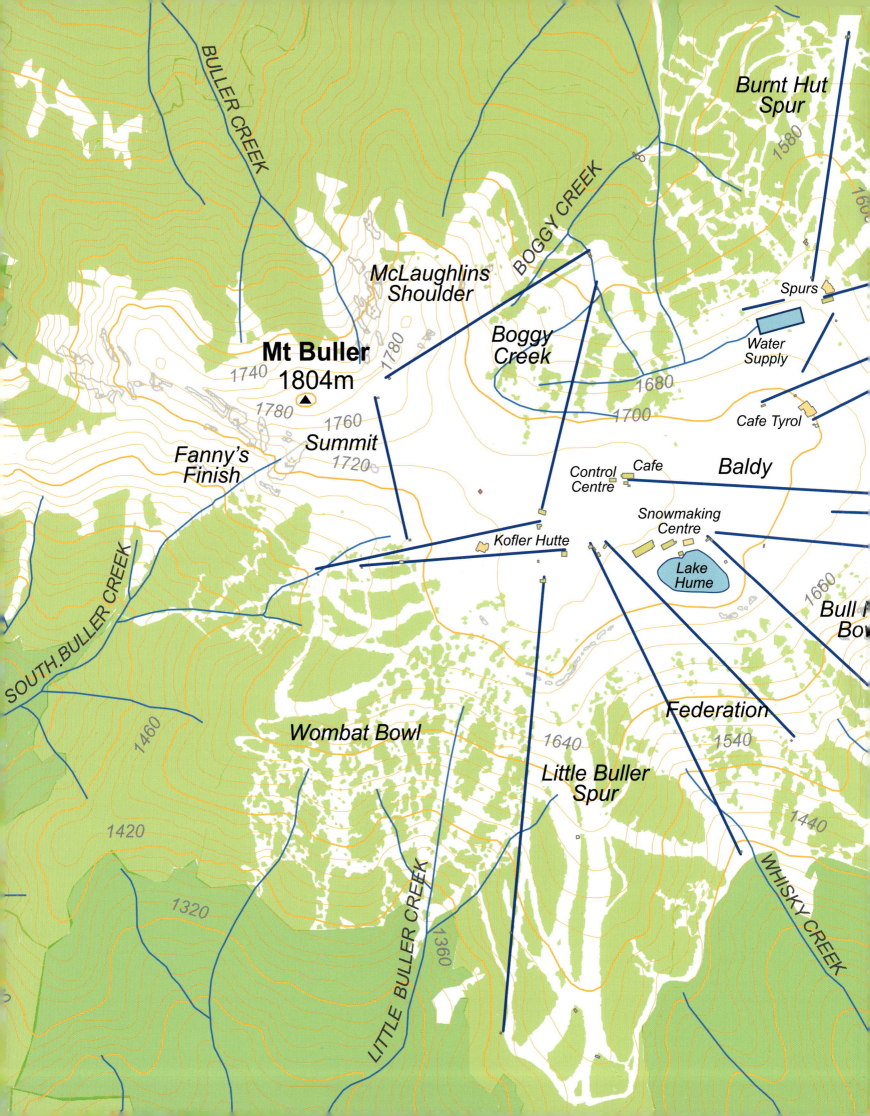